Tourism and Animal Welfare

Tourism and Animal Welfare

Neil Carr
Department of Tourism
University of Otago
Clyde Street
Dunedin 9016
New Zealand

Donald M. Broom
St Catharine's College and
Department of Veterinary Medicine
University of Cambridge
Madingley Road
Cambridge CB3 0ES
UK

With 14 guest contributions

CABI

CABI is a trading name of CAB International

CABI
Nosworthy Way
Wallingford
Oxfordshire OX10 8DE
UK

Tel: +44 (0)1491 832111
Fax: +44 (0)1491 833508
E-mail: info@cabi.org
Website: www.cabi.org

CABI
745 Atlantic Avenue
8th Floor
Boston, MA 02111
USA

Tel: +1 (617)682-9015
E-mail: cabi-nao@cabi.org

A catalogue record for this book is available from the British Library, London, UK.

Library of Congress Cataloging-in-Publication Data

Names: Carr, Neil, 1972- author. | Broom, Donald M., author.
Title: Tourism and animal welfare / By Neil Carr & Donald M. Broom.
Description: Wallingford, Oxfordshire, UK ; Boston, MA : CABI, 2018. | Includes bibliographical references and index.
Identifiers: LCCN 2017060810 (print) | LCCN 2018006694 (ebook) | ISBN 9781786391872 (pdf) | ISBN 9781786391889 (ePub) | ISBN 9781786391858 (hardback : alk. paper) | ISBN 9781786391865 (pbk. : alk. paper)
Subjects: LCSH: Tourism--Moral and ethical aspects. | Animal welfare. | Animals--Effect of human beings on.
Classification: LCC G155.A1 (ebook) | LCC G155.A1 T589335 2018 (print) | DDC 179/.3--dc23
LC record available at https://lccn.loc.gov/2017060810

ISBN-13: 9781786391858 (hbk)
9781786391865 (pbk)
9781786391872 (PDF)
9781786391889 (ePub)

Commissioning editor: Claire Parfitt
Editorial assistant: Alexandra Lainsbury
Production editor: Marta Patiño

Typeset by SPi, Pondicherry, India.
Printed and bound in the UK by CPI Group (UK) Ltd, Croydon, CR0 4YY

Contents

To access an online video of the *Tourism and Animal Welfare Symposium* presentations hosted by CABI in 2018, please visit https://www.cabi.org/openresources/91865/ or scan the QR code below.

List of figures

List of tables

List of boxes

Acknowledgements

The idea for this book was Claire Parfitt's, as was the idea to bring together Neil Carr and Don Broom to work on it. The result, which threw together a social scientist and a scientist, has been an interesting and educational journey. Neil (the social scientist) and Don (the scientist) share a passion for animal welfare but, not surprisingly given their academic backgrounds, come at the issue from slightly different perspectives. The strength of the book, we hope, is the existence and blending of these differences, which on reflection is something Claire was probably hoping for. So thanks, Claire, for your subtle driving of us and the book onwards.

A central part of this book are the opinion pieces from a range of academics, tourism industry operators and employees, and animal welfare proponents. A debt of thanks is due to all these people who have volunteered their time and energies to contribute to this book and in doing so have provided it with a degree of richness that would have otherwise been unobtainable.

At a more personal though no less significant level, thanks are as ever due to the families of the authors. These people have aided in the completion of the book by helping to keep the authors fit and healthy and they have never complained when the book has dragged the attention of the authors away from them. For this, Neil offers his thanks and love to his wife Sarah and children Ben, Tat and Gus. Don offers love and thanks to Sally for support and ideas. Neil would also offer thanks to his dogs (first and foremost, Snuffie, but most assuredly also Gyspy and now Ebony, who have followed in Snuffie's footsteps). They are the whole reason Neil became interested in animal welfare, changing his entire mindset in the process, and are now often his sounding board for his ideas. As the Head of the Department of Tourism at the University of Otago, Neil also recognizes that thanks are due to all the staff in the Department, but most especially Trudi and Pip, for helping to allow him the time and space in which to write.

1 Introduction

Most of us are tourists at times and many of us would like to think that we are responsible tourists. Animals are among the most sought-after tourist attractions, so the impact of tourism on them is a frequent matter of concern to tourists and to those who seek to conserve animals or to ensure that their welfare is good. Sustainable practices are sought by national and local government agencies, commercial organizations with a reputation to preserve and those who live in areas frequented by tourists. This book provides answers to some of the questions posed as a result of the impacts of tourism.

While a large proportion of the text in the book is based on carefully evaluated information, this is not a traditional academic book. The references in the chapters have been kept to a minimum to prevent them getting in the way of the reading of and engagement with the text. For anyone who wishes to find the sources of the ideas in this book and how they have evolved, a bibliography is provided at the end of the book. This list is not comprehensive and we apologize in advance to anyone who feels we have erroneously missed a particular reference. We hope that the book will appeal to academics who are either researching in the field or undertaking related courses as part of their degree. However, we expect that it will appeal to the wider community because animal welfare in tourism should be of concern to all of us.

Throughout this book, we emphasize the responsibility of everyone to do all they can to ensure that the welfare of animals in relation to tourism is as good as possible. As a step in this direction, the book incorporates a series of opinion pieces from tourism operators, industry bodies and animal welfare organizations, as well as academics working at the coalface of concerns regarding animal welfare in the tourism experience. These pieces are designed to add context and weight to the earlier chapters of the book, as well as the final one, and to enliven debate on issues of animal welfare. They are an integral part of the book but can also be read as stand-alone pieces if the reader prefers. In this way the book is designed to be what academics have in recent years been told they must be: relevant to the 'real' world, and capable of aiding change and innovation outside the education environment.

The main authors of the book are dyed-in-the-wool academics. Neil is ostensibly a tourism studies or leisure studies academic, while Don is an animal welfare specialist. Our collaboration in producing this book is a reflection of the diverse issues at play in relation to animal welfare and tourism and the benefits for all of bringing together those who have worked in these separate though interconnected areas.

This chapter provides an introduction to the key concepts dealt with in the book, namely tourism and animal welfare, offering a brief overview of the foundations of each field without going into detail. Some readers may be knowledgeable about one of these fields and may prefer to spend more time on the sections with which they are not already well-versed.

The State of Tourism and Animal-Related Tourism

The first question needing addressing is: What is tourism? This is a question that is asked in every first-year undergraduate course on tourism and in every associated introductory textbook (see Lickorish and Jenkins (1997) and Hall (2003)). It is also a question that many academics working in tourism seem to love to debate. Resultant definitions tend to focus on tourism being composed of people travelling, temporarily, outside their home environment to engage in leisure-oriented activities. This is the dry academic terminology utilized to define a holiday. Those who take part in this activity are said to be tourists and the industry that facilitates this experience is the tourism industry. Within this context we must recognize that tourism is both a social phenomenon that people seek and desire and an industry that caters to these desires and also creates new ones and helps to drive demand. The result is a continual feedback loop that is a wonderful example of societal and industrial interrelationships in a neo-liberal capitalist reality.

Problems begin to creep into definitions of tourism that talk of the points noted here when we attempt to quantify what exactly 'temporarily' means. How long do you have to be away before you become a migrant? Can you be a tourist for an hour? If so, what minimum time must be surpassed before you become a tourist? In addition, there is the issue of whether it is only those people who travel solely for leisure purposes who can be defined as tourists or whether those travelling primarily for other purposes but engaging in some touristic activities during their time away from home can also be defined as tourists. There is also, of course, the problem of what actually constitutes 'leisure'. If discussions about the precise definition of tourism have a long and tortuous history, they are as nothing compared to debates about what leisure is. Is leisure a measure of time free from outside obligations; is it related to the nature of the activity undertaken; or is it about the search for self or the freedom to be what you wish to be away from external restrictions and impositions? (See Carr, 2017a,b; Godbey, 2003; Bramham and Wagg, 2014 for a discussion of the meaning of leisure.)

There is also the problem that when we begin to examine the so-called tourism industry, we can see that it actually overlaps and borrows from a variety of other distinct industries. This can be seen to occur to such an extent that it has been asked, somewhat mischievously, whether there really is such a thing as the tourism industry. To travel to a tourism destination requires access to the travel and transportation industry. This is distinct from the tourism industry in that the infrastructure associated with it is often used for distinctly non-tourism purposes. Furthermore, roads, railway networks and ports are generally constructed primarily for reasons other than tourism. Even airports and airlines are not only used for tourism purposes. Once a tourist is at a destination, they will engage with the hospitality industry. Again, there is an overlap between this and the tourism industry but the former is a distinct industry in its own right that caters to more than just tourists. For example, restaurants will cater to local people as well as tourists and even hotels do not cater solely to tourists. Indeed, in some locations that are not dominated by tourism, hotels may cater primarily to business people, sometimes with an under-the-counter side where prostitutes rent rooms on an hourly basis either without the knowledge of management or as a result of management turning a blind eye. Finally, even so-called tourist attractions are not really accurately named, as they are generally open to all those leisured people who wish to and can afford to visit them irrespective of whether they are still within their home environment or are visiting from elsewhere. As such, these attractions may be more accurately defined as leisure attractions than tourism attractions. Thus, it may be suggested that tourism is merely a component of leisure.

While we may quibble over definitions of tourism, the tourist, and the tourism industry, it is clear that tourists do exist and that there is a tourism industry, even if components are borrowed from other industries. If we employ our definition of tourism and tourists, it is clear that tourism today is a global phenomenon of considerable size. The concept of tourism is nothing new, but since the end of the Second World War and the associated economic boom it has grown significantly into something that touches all parts of the planet. The growth of international tourist numbers at the global level is depicted in Fig. 1.1.

While the definitional issues, noted earlier in this section, and a plethora of concerns regarding the difficulties associated with collecting data affect calculations of the number of tourists the world sees each year it is clear that tourism is a huge phenomenon. In 2016 it is estimated by the United Nations World Tourism Organization that there were 1235 million international tourist arrivals in the world (UNWTO, 2017). Purchases by these tourists are said to have generated US$1.5 trillion in exports and generated one in every ten jobs on the planet. Furthermore, it is important to note that these figures only take into account international tourism. They do not consider domestic tourism, mainly because it is much harder to obtain accurate figures for this as tourists do not need to be processed through international gateways, such as airports. Yet, all the indications are that domestic tourism is, in terms of tourist numbers and spending, far larger than its international counterpart. For example, in New Zealand in the year ending March 2016 it was estimated that while international tourism expenditure in the country amounted to NZ$14.5 billion, domestic tourism generated NZ$20.2 billion (Ministry of Business, Innovation and Employment, 2017).

The tourism industry, and the tourists it attracts and serves, is not spread evenly over the planet and consequently its impact (both positive and negative) is likewise not evenly distributed. Furthermore, tourism tends to be highly seasonal, with the result that these impacts are not consistent even over a single year. It is also clear that tourism comes in a great variety of flavours, though arguably all have the same foundations. These foundations, as noted earlier, revolve around the idea of leisure. This can be distilled slightly further to note that all tourists are, to varying degrees, interested in escaping from the mundane reality of their day-to-day existence and exploring the 'other' (i.e. something exotic that cannot be found in their home

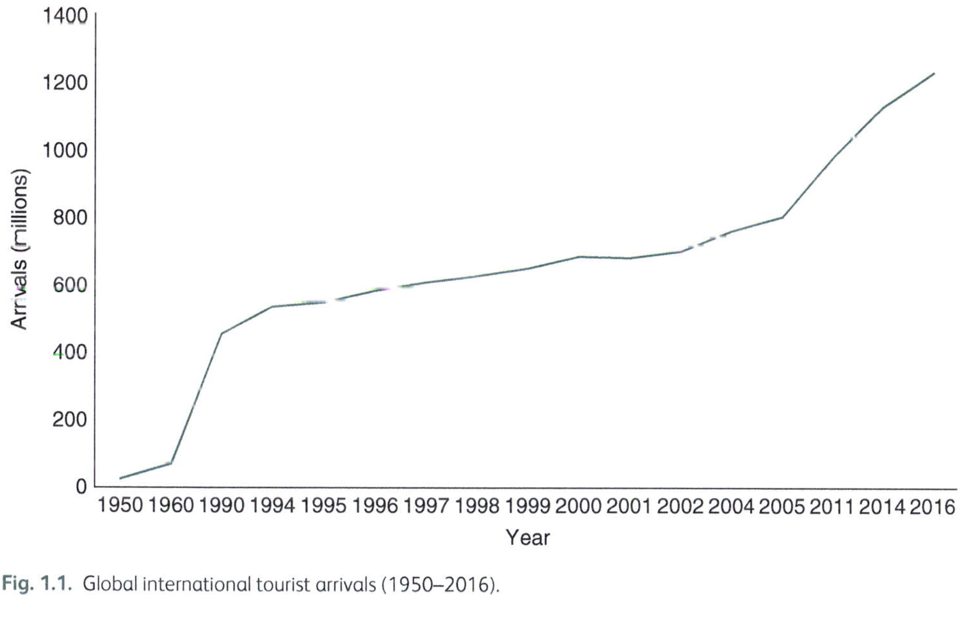

Fig. 1.1. Global international tourist arrivals (1950–2016).

environment). Doing so offers the potential for satisfaction of desires, enjoyment and pleasure. Among the varieties of tourism on offer to anyone seeking to take a holiday there is of course the sun, sand and sea experience. This is potentially the quintessential mass tourism experience; think of the beaches of the Spanish and Greek Mediterranean islands for example. Yet to this we can add rural tourism, adventure tourism, urban tourism, cruise tourism, sex tourism, winter sports tourism, ecotourism and, potentially, space tourism. These encompass types of tourism defined by the nature of the destination and the primary activity. As such, there is clearly scope for overlap between them.

Some destinations and activities associated with tourism are chosen because of interest in, or exploitation of, animals. This book is concerned, not just with tourism focused on animals but also how all types of tourism have potential implications for animals and hence animal welfare. The position and experiences of animals in tourism will be discussed in detail later in the book. Suffice for now to say that animals of all types are influenced by and impacted upon by tourism in a wide variety of ways. One distinction that it is important to make now though is the difference between animal tourism and animals indirectly impacted on by and through tourism. The former is focused on animal experiences that tourists deliberately seek while on holiday and that the tourism industry provides. This encompasses everything from zoos to horse riding, bird and whale watching, and big game hunting. The latter is concerned with instances where animals are impacted by tourism and tourists, both directly and indirectly, but are not a focus of the tourist gaze. Examples include everything from pest control operations in hotels and restaurants to the controlling of birds in and around airports, the destruction of wild animals' natural habitat and the international spread of invasive species.

Animal Welfare

The evolution of thinking around animal welfare is discussed in detail in the following chapter, so it is sufficient here to give just a brief description of welfare and how it applies to animals. In essence, the concept of welfare is no different for humans and for non-human animals. Human welfare, or well-being, encompasses mental and physical health. In this way it is related to practices aimed at proactive health management. The fundamental issue that scientists, social scientists and, increasingly, society in general have been dealing with is whether animals have needs that extend beyond their conceptualization as objects owned by humans. This leads us to the question of animal sentience and whether or not it exists. If it does, then there are implications for how we view and treat animals and their welfare. It is becoming increasingly clear that a large number of kinds of animals are sentient. These debates about animal sentience and welfare are paralleled by discussions about animal rights. The divide between those who concern themselves with animal rights and those who talk of animal welfare is in some ways blurred but in some instances very distinct. At their most extreme, animal rights proponents think that animals should not be used in any way by humans, to the extent that they view pets and animal companions as inappropriate. Those concerned with animal welfare, on the other hand, may not have any problem with the reality of animals' lives being intertwined with those of humans as long as sufficient consideration is given to the welfare of the animals.

As noted later in this book, while we may be able to scientifically assess sentience it is always done using human metrics. Furthermore, the very notion of sentience is a human construct. Following on from this, animal welfare and animal rights must be recognized as human constructs that, as a result, are situated in human societies and cultures. These in turn are spatially and temporally specific. As will be seen, this all has implications for how animal welfare is seen and presented within tourism; especially as tourism inherently involves the meeting of different cultures as tourists move across space. It also has implications for our ability to enhance animal welfare within tourism around the world.

The position adopted in this book is clearly a welfarist one. It is based on a clear belief that animals are sentient beings, capable of feeling and thinking for themselves. Based on this sentience we stand with those who believe that animals have needs that it is beholden on humans, as the creatures in the position of power relative to animals, to meet and deal with. In other words, as discussed in detail in Chapter 2, the book is based on the notion that humans have obligations to *all* animals. The emphasis placed on 'all' is important, as it acknowledges the obligations we have to animals irrespective of whether we like them or not. This builds on the notion that humans tend to divide animals up between those we love, those we hate, those we eat, and those we simply ignore. A true animal welfare perspective must cover all of these animals, as it adopts an animal-centric rather than a human-centric perspective.

As will be discussed later in the book, there is also a need to recognize the differences and overlaps between animal welfare and conservation. The primary focus of the former is on the individual while the latter has traditionally been focused on the species level, largely ignoring the welfare of the individual. As discussed later, these perspectives arguably need to shift and recognize that species survival without individual welfare is insufficient as is individual welfare without attention to long-term species survival. This speaks to the issue of sustainability, something that will also be discussed later in the book.

Why Is This Book Needed?

As has already been noted in this chapter and will be discussed in more detail in the following chapters, animals play a central role in much of tourism and are influenced by tourism in a multitude of ways. If we only saw them as automated objects devoid of sentience, then the only welfare concerns about animals would be focused on ensuring their maintenance for the benefit of their owners and tourists. However, if we reject such a position and recognize the sentience of animals then looking at the welfare of these creatures becomes significantly more important and nuanced. The book and any work associated with it also almost automatically becomes a part of an activist agenda to raise awareness of the welfare of animals, in this case among tourists and the tourism industry specifically, as well as in governmental organizations and society in general. In other words, this book is all about positioning animals and their welfare at the centre of animal-related debates within tourism. This is necessary given the number of animals influenced by tourism, but numbers alone are not the reason for the book. Even if only one animal was influenced by tourism its value would demand we give it and its welfare our attention.

The sentience of animals, as will be noted in Chapter 2, is a reality that is increasingly driving social concerns regarding both animal welfare and the ethics of animal treatment. These changes are being overlaid on pre-existing tourism experiences that have been created prior to the emergence of any appreciation of the welfare of sentient animals. Consequently, it is probably true to say that there is now no way in which animals are influenced by tourism that is without controversy. This controversy provides sufficient rationale in its own right for a book focused on animal welfare and tourism as a means of highlighting and beginning to address such controversies.

Despite the centrality of animals to the tourism experience and the impact of tourism on the lives of many animals, there has, until recently, been relatively little published on animals in relation to tourism. Such publications have tended to focus primarily on wild animals and those we like the most, as noted later in this book. Furthermore, while the relatively small number of books published to date on animals and tourism have dealt with issues surrounding animal welfare they have not focused on this issue. Consequently, the need for this book is grounded on the lack of previous books focused on animal welfare in tourism, increasing recognition in the scientific community and society in general of the necessity to consider the welfare of animals, and the central position of animals in tourism.

Content and Structure

When reading this book it is important to recognize that it is not possible to deal in detail with all animals and their situations in relation to and experiences of tourism. Put simply, there is not the space in any book to do justice to all the myriad animals that are in one way or another impacted, directly or indirectly, by the tourism experience and its associated industry. Rather, the book is designed to cover the relevant concepts that are arguably core to beginning to understand the relation between animal welfare and tourism and the animals and tourism experiences discussed within the book are utilized as examples on which to develop understandings. Following on from this introductory chapter, Part I of the book provides a conceptual and historical foundation upon which to analyse animal welfare and the position of animals in tourism, and how these two issues intersect. Within this part of the book, Chapter 2 focuses on the issue of animal welfare, examining the evidence for animal sentience and moving from there to the needs of animals and how to scientifically assess their welfare. The chapter then shifts to the concept of obligations, recognizing that it is not sufficient for humans to simply say animals have needs, but that we, as the ones in the position of power, have obligations to ensure that those needs are met and that individual animals are properly valued.

In Chapter 3 the book explores the nature of the position and experience of animals within tourism and why people seek out animal attractions while in the holiday environment. The chapter also explores the rise of animals as guests and employees within the tourism experience. It also examines how the tourism industry has sanitized the holiday environment, removing from it animals and animal behaviour that offends or scares us. Chapter 4 builds on the previous two chapters to explore whether animal welfare and tourism are mutually exclusive or can be inclusive of one another. The chapter explores who is responsible for ensuring that tourism and animal welfare can be considered together, building on concepts of sustainability. Chapters 3 and 4 draw links to the opinion pieces presented in the book after Chapter 4.

Part II of the book consists of 14 opinion pieces that discuss various issues associated with animal welfare and tourism. These pieces, presented as individual chapters, are written by tourism operators, tourism organizations, animal welfare and conservation organizations and advocates, or academics with particular expertise in the area of animal welfare and tourism and links to the industry. Any references specific to these opinion pieces are situated with them rather than integrated into the reference list at the end of the book that has been constructed by the authors of the rest of the book.

Part III of the book talks about the future of tourism and animal welfare and charts a potential path for the future of the welfare of animals in tourism and a related research agenda.

References

Bramham, P. and Wagg, S. (2014) *An Introduction to Leisure Studies: Principles and Practice*. Sage Publications, London.

Carr, N. (2017a) Meaning of leisure. In: Henderson, K. and Sivan, A. (eds) *Leisure from International Voices*. Sagamore Publishing, Urbana, IL.

Carr, N. (2017b) Re-thinking the relation between leisure and freedom. *Annals of Leisure Research* 20(2), 137–151.

Godbey, G. (2003) *Leisure in Your Life: An Exploration*, 6th edn. Venture Publishing, State College, PA.

Hall, C.M. (2003) *Introduction to Tourism: Dimensions and Issues*, 4th edn. Pearson Education, South Melbourne.

Lickorish, L. and Jenkins, C. (1997) *Introduction to Tourism*. Butterworth-Heinemann, Oxford, UK.

Ministry of Business, Innovation and Employment (2017) *Key Tourism Statistics*. Available at: http://www.mbie.govt.nz/info-services/sectors-industries/tourism/documents-image-library/key-tourism-statistics.pdf (accessed 10 July 2017).

UNWTO (2017) *Tourism Highlights. 2017 Edition*. UNWTO, Madrid, Spain.

Part

I

A Conceptual and Historical Foundation

2 Animal Sentience, Ethics and Welfare

Introduction

This chapter provides a discussion of the concept of animal welfare and the development of our understanding of this. This discussion is set within the wider discussion of animal sentience, recognizing that an awareness of the sentience of animals is related to concerns about and our definition of their welfare. While recognizing that our understanding of animal sentience and welfare and operationalization of the latter are situated within the reality of a human-centric world, the chapter argues that analysis of the welfare of animals must be led from a scientific perspective, which identifies how animal behaviour and welfare can be objectively assessed. However, to close the loop on the relation between animals as independent entities and their position within a human-dominated world where their welfare, directly and indirectly, is almost always influenced by humans, it is necessary to think about evaluation of happiness and human perception of animal welfare. The balancing act required by this is both controversial and potentially problematic, as it may bring into conflict the epistemological and ontological beliefs of those concerned with animal welfare. Yet within a postmodernist world that seeks to understand the complexity of the world rather than engage in reductionist rhetoric, there is arguably no reason why all methodological perspectives should not be able to come together to gain a better understanding of animal welfare for the benefit of animals. Following on from a discussion of the measurement of animal welfare, the chapter ends with a brief examination of the position of animal welfare in law.

It is important to recognize that this chapter is meant as an overview of wider discussions of animal welfare that have a significant history and weight behind them, both in and outside an academic context. The chapter provides, as does the Bibliography at the end of this book, direction to material for those wishing to read more about the topic. In this way, the chapter provides a foundation upon which to examine and think about the position and welfare of animals in tourism.

Animals

When we speak of the welfare of animals, we refer to all animals, including humans. What biologists mean by the term 'animal' is a living being with a nervous system and other complex mechanisms for obtaining energy, using energy and reproducing. Other living beings also have some of these mechanisms but not a true nervous system. Animals survive by consuming and hence utilizing the energy of plants, other animals and bacteria. Most animals have an effective means of locomotion and a range of sense organs. They range in size from microscopic protozoans, worms and insects to squid, sharks and whales that are very much bigger than humans. Humans have always had great interest in other species of animals; first because of their diverse, brain-controlled behaviour and second because humans are also animals.

Despite this biological meaning of the term 'animal' to include insects, fish, snails, spiders, monkeys etc., people have sometimes limited the meaning to farmed animals, owned animals, mammals, or warm-blooded animals. People may also, mistakenly and pejoratively, use the word to describe a being with the implication that it is more aggressive, less controlled, or more subject to lust than the average human. The idea that humans control their emotions but non-humans never do is now known to be quite wrong.

A widespread but anthropocentric view is that humans are completely different from all other animals. In reality, humans have far more similarities to animals than differences from them. Humans *are* animals, so the simple phrase 'humans and animals' is incorrect. Mechanisms of animal functioning include all mechanisms of human functioning and there is no part of human biology that is not animal biology. Consequently, in this book, the phrase 'humans and other animals' is used.

People have always wondered about the essential quality that makes us human. We have the same basic brain and bodily capabilities as other animals. Observations of their behaviour have long indicated that just like humans other animals need resources such as air, food and resting places, and that they are aware that other individuals have such needs (Broom, 2014, 2016a). However, we humans have always sought to differentiate ourselves, and efforts have been made to ascribe unique qualities to humans. In human societies, a soul, psyche or spirit has been attributed to people, or at least to some people, with the assumption that this quality helps to define a human being. When defined objectively, each of these qualities has components that are also thought of as components of sentience, so soul, psyche or spirit can mean the same as being sentient.

One of the reasons why people categorized the domestic and wild animals that they encountered as being completely different from humans was that this made it easier to use them, kill them or otherwise harm them. In the same way, groups of people have sometimes been able to persuade themselves that human enemies, slaves or despised groups were not really human. Moral actions are directed towards people, or other animal species, viewed as 'us' rather than 'them' (Broom, 2003). Many people now regard a wide range of non-humans, especially those considered as sentient (European Union, 1997; Broom, 2014), as moral entities and hence 'us'. This means that there are obligations to avoid causing their welfare to be poor. For a smaller number of people, other harms, in particular death, are also unacceptable. These issues are considered further below.

Sentient Beings

The term 'sentience' is usually taken to mean that the individual has the capacity to experience one or more of the various states we call 'feelings' (DeGrazia, 1996; Kirkwood, 2006; Broom, 2006b, 2014, 2016b). This capacity involves awareness and cognitive ability, and is hence located in the brain. A major change in attitudes regarding awareness and feelings in humans and other animals has occurred as studies of behaviour have become more detailed. Complex behavioural sequences can provide evidence for the presence of cognitive ability and emotional reactions. In addition, there are methods that allow advances in the study of brain mechanisms (e.g. electroencephalography (EEG), positron-emission tomography (PET-scanning), magneto-encephalography (MEG), and frequency-modulated magnetic resonance imaging (fMRI)). These methods for monitoring human brains have long required that the subject tolerate being inside a chamber, so were scarcely usable for non-humans, but new equipment is changing this.

Sentience implies having a range of abilities, not just feelings. Abilities associated with sentience, including some necessary cognitive abilities, are listed below. The abilities and the underlying concepts call for both definitions and evidence. A sentient being is one that has some ability to evaluate the actions of others in relation to itself and third parties; to remember some of its own actions and their consequences; to assess risks and benefits; to have some feelings; and to have some degree of awareness (Broom, 2006b).

During human evolution, when did sentience arise? The idea that some races of people alive today have significant genetic differences in their level of brain function, so that they are less intelligent, is now known to be incorrect. There is no evidence for differences between races in sensory abilities and feelings, such as the capacity to feel pain. The variation of human ability within each race is much greater than the variation across races. Some people have the idea that early humans were primitive in every way and very different from modern humans. The idea that humans living a few million years ago were substantially less able than humans today is not supported by written or archaeological evidence. The evidence from non-humans is that, during evolution, sentience arose before the first humans.

This does not mean that all humans are sentient. As discussed in detail by Broom (2014), when human cognitive and other abilities are compared with those of other species, the very young and some of the injured or old are clearly less able than many non-humans. At birth, a human child may have the potential to carry out impressive cognitive tasks later in life but has far less actual ability than many other animals have. During development, there is a point between the fertilized egg and the functioning child when the individual could be called sentient. Humans are certainly not sentient during early fetal development. Similarly, a person who has suffered substantial brain damage after an accident or a person with advanced senile dementia may be much less able to use their brains and have full capability to have feelings than a companion dog or a magpie in a garden, for example. Sentience is a capacity that normally grows during human development; it can also diminish and be lost. The same is true for other animals. The presence or absence of sentience, and our evaluation of sentience in an individual of the species, affects our ideas of individual value and acceptable treatment. The concept of sentience is relevant to ethical decisions about, for example, abortion, killing young at birth or hatching, and the use of anaesthetics and analgesics.

A sentient being has some concepts, some awareness about its world and some feelings. Awareness is a state during which concepts of environment, of self and of self in relation to environment result from complex brain analysis of sensory stimuli or constructs based on memory (Broom, 2014, chapter 6). There are different categories of awareness: perceptual awareness; cognitive awareness; assessment awareness; and executive awareness (Sommerville and Broom, 1998). The term 'consciousness' is best used in the sense of not being unconscious, so a conscious individual is one that has the capability to perceive and respond to sensory stimuli.

What categories of awareness do different kinds of animals have? The conditioning that has been shown in marine sea slugs would require at least cognitive awareness. Place learning by cockroaches and the formation of cognitive maps by bees and ants involve at least assessment awareness. Predatory fireflies, *Photuris*, mimic the signals of other firefly species, attract males and eat them. The flashing pattern used in this deception is changed to that of another potential prey species if the flashing of that second species is the most frequent in a given location. In addition, when prey use counter-measures, the predator changes signals and behaviour (Lloyd, 1986). The complexity of these responses cannot be accounted for by automatic processes so quite sophisticated cognitive ability is indicated. Stomatopod Crustacea, such as *Squilla*, also use deception in contests with other individuals (Caldwell, 1986). In studies of jumping spiders (*Portia*), by Jackson and colleagues, they were found to have a very sophisticated ability to evaluate when to jump, to assess where to jump accurately onto prey, and also to show deception and modify movements in accordance with the circumstances. During predation, *Portia* spiders deceive the prey while gaining information that optimizes their attack strategy (Jackson and

Cross, 2011). When a *Portia* individual is preparing to attack, it is clear that a sequence of movements is planned and then detours are executed which increase the chances of success. These spiders must have some awareness of themselves in relation to the environment and of an event that is expected in the future (i.e. the jump onto the prey) so again, executive awareness is implied. Rolls (2005) argues that the ability to exhibit flexible planning is evidence that the individual is not just using automatic brain systems but is aware of the world around it. If this is the threshold criterion for complexity of cognitive function, then these spiders are aware.

Many vertebrate animals have been demonstrated to have concepts of their own bodies in relation to their environment; their own abilities; aspects of what is likely to happen in the future; and the concepts that other individuals have (Broom, 2014, chapter 4; Broom and Fraser, 2015). Comparisons of learning ability have been possible using mazes. Kilgour (1987) used simple mazes for animals of different sizes. These mazes start with a decision point where there are two or more possible directions to take, one being towards a concealed target reached after two further turns. When the number of errors was measured, cows, sheep, goats and pigs performed less well than 5-year-old children but better than dogs, cats, rats, horses and several other mammals and birds. When speed of learning was compared in the same study, the sequence was very similar but dogs performed as well as the farm ungulates.

In tests, cows, sheep, pigs and fish learned rapidly to discriminate other individuals of their own species, or to discriminate between humans (Kendrick *et al.*, 1995). A variety of studies of learning by farm animals, fish and other animals are reviewed by Broom (2007, 2010, 2014). It has sometimes been assumed that farm animals are not very intelligent, but this has been shown to be untrue by many recent studies. Does a chicken have a concept of an object when it is not directly detectable? Studies by Rugani and colleagues (Rugani *et al.*, 2009) showed that not only could young domestic chicks go to objects hidden behind screens but that when two or three objects were hidden behind screens, the chicks went to the screen with the larger number of objects. Can animals remember and use a visual symbol for a resource? Langbein *et al.* (2004) found that goats could respond by carrying out an action, or operant, in order to get water when they saw one particular picture rather than others.

The complex array of concepts that pigs can have in their brains was evident from studies by Held *et al.* (2000). Pigs were put in a room and allowed to find hidden food. On the next day they were returned to the room and they went immediately to the place where they had found food. If another pig was watching, the pig waited and did not go to the food if that other pig was known from previous experience to be able to steal from it. If the other pig was known not to steal, the food was immediately approached. These pigs must have had a concept of an object in the absence of that object, a concept of a location, and an ability to predict that in the future it might have the food item stolen from it. The ability to learn what is in a mirror is demonstrated for only a few animals: humans, chimpanzees, capuchin monkeys, pigs, elephants, dolphins, parrots and magpies. Broom *et al.* (2009) exposed 4–6-week-old piglets to a mirror for the first time in such a way that they could see a food bowl otherwise out of view behind a barrier. The young pigs went behind the mirror to the apparent position of the food bowl. However, when given 5 hours' experience of a mirror, they responded initially to it as if to another pig, but later by looking at it as they moved. After this experience with the mirror, seven out of eight pigs tested moved away from the mirror and around the barrier to the food bowl. Location by odour was prevented by fans and the naïve controls had exactly the same olfactory situation. To use information from a mirror and find a food bowl, each pig must have observed features of its surroundings, remembered these and its own actions, deduced relationships among observed and remembered features and acted accordingly.

In recent years there have been many studies of cognitive ability that lead us to the conclusions that: (i) hardly any ability is uniquely human; (ii) the best bird brains allow greater cognitive ability than any mammal except man; (iii) learning by fish can be very complex; and (iv) cognition in cephalopods, jumping spiders, ants and bees is much more sophisticated than we had previously thought. Furthermore, communicating using symbols is possible for many animals, so language is not just human.

Emotion, which has long been viewed as necessarily separate from intellectual activity, is now shown to be a facilitator of learning and a consequence of learning. An indication of the possible awareness of own actions and functioning comes from the studies of Hagen and Broom (2004) on young cattle. The heifers were put in a pen, the gate of which could be opened by pressing a panel with the nose, thus giving access to food 15 m away. The heifers learned to do this and, at the time of learning, showed an excitement response of increased heart rate and jumping or galloping. This 'Eureka' effect was not shown by control heifers, that just gained access to the reward, or by heifers that had learned earlier how to open the gate. Evaluation of welfare can use the link between emotion and motivation or cognition, as in the case of studies of cognitive bias (Mendl and Paul, 2008).

The most widely studied feeling is pain. Pain is an aversive sensation and feeling associated with actual or potential tissue damage (Broom, 2001a,b). Its occurrence in animals is clearly demonstrated for all vertebrates, including fish, and for cephalopods, such as octopus and squid, and decapod crustacea such as crabs and prawns (Sneddon, *et al.*, 2014; Broom, 2016b). There is an evident need for an objective, reliable scoring tool that can be effectively used to recognize and assess pain severity. Facial expression scoring systems for pain assessment have been recently developed for use in rodents, rabbits, horses and sheep (Dalla Costa *et al.*, 2016; McLennan *et al.*, 2016).

The high levels of cognitive ability in sentient animals may often help them to cope with their environment. Hence a given level of a problem, such as pain, may be less in more complex animals than in simpler animals. There is also a possibility that more complex animals may have more fear of possible future adversity. Because of these two possible effects, the relationships between negative feelings, such as fear and pain, and the role of cognition in the coping abilities of the animal should be investigated further and considered when evaluating the risk of poor welfare. Cognitive ability should also be considered when designing methods of enriching the environments of captive animals.

A reasonable conclusion, in relation to the less complex animals, is that all animal life should be respected and studies of the welfare of even the simplest invertebrate animals should be taken into account when we interact with these animals. Even if we do not protect the animals by law, we should try to avoid cutting an earthworm in half, mutilating a snail or damaging the wing of an insect.

Ethics and Attitudes

Ethics is the study of moral issues and 'something is moral if it pertains to right rather than wrong' (Broom, 2003, p. 1). These are important parts of our everyday lives. Humans, like many other animals, live in social groups. It is not possible to live for a long period in a social group without behaving in a moral way towards others. Hence moral codes have a biological basis and the central part of widespread religions is a structure for moral codes (Broom, 2003). Long-lasting groups of dolphins, or monkeys, or cows, or wolves, or magpies, or babblers, or long-tailed tits have to recognize individuals, remember good and bad actions and respond to these. In other words, they have to know when they and others are behaving in a moral or less moral way. Morality is not just a human characteristic, and some behaviour is altruistic in all social animals.

There are many ways in which individuals can gain more food by responding to or collaborating with others (Box 2.1).

Wolves, pelicans and crocodiles are among the species that have been identified as collaborating in obtaining food. Vampire bats, ravens and chimpanzees are among those that share food (de Waal, 1989).

In addition to the more obvious kinds of cooperation, the commonest kind of altruistic behaviour in social groups, which is often reciprocated, is to avoid injuring other individuals. Great care is usually, although not always, taken by individuals in social groups to do this (Box 2.2).

The biological characteristics that are required in order to behave in a moral way and live in a group are described by de Waal (1996) and Broom (2003, 2014), among others. One characteristic that facilitates parental care and moral behaviour is empathy. The human desire to protect animals is promoted by empathy and compassion (Würbel, 2009). As Bentham said, people identify with and care about individuals that can suffer and this is still a widespread view (Dawkins, 1993). The term 'pathocentrism' is used by German-speaking scientists and refers to those who focus especially on suffering. People are more likely to show empathy with those perceived to have a capacity for feelings similar to that of humans. Griffin referred to 'a deep-seated sympathy for animals as sentient creatures' (1984, as cited in Broom, 2014, p. 18). People are also likely to show compassion only to those whom they perceive to need compassion. The treatment of various groups of animals used in some way by people is discussed by Serpell (1986, 1989).

The two major ethical positions used when people consider what action is right are the deontological and the utilitarian. Today, most people would say that if we use a living animal in

Box 2.1. Ways to gain more food by responding to or collaborating with others (after Broom, 1981).

Joining others who are likely to have found food
Observing others in order to find food sources or learn how to acquire food
Collaborating in hunting for food
Collaborating in acquiring food
Collaborating in handling and defending food
Collaborating in avoiding depleted food sources
Sharing food
Giving food to others

Box 2.2. Actions to avoid harms to others (after Broom, 2003).

To avoid collisions, thus benefiting the avoider as well as the avoided
Not to step on others
Not to injure them with horns or teeth
Not to push others out of trees, or over cliffs
Not to put others in danger from predators

a way that gives us some benefit, we have some obligations to that animal. The idea that we have duties, including duties to an individual that we use, is deontological. These duties are often considered to be independent of the value of the action to us. Using the utilitarian approach, the decision about what is right is taken by evaluating the consequences of the various possible actions and following the course with the maximum utility. When there is a particular treatment of an animal, the action may lead to costs or benefits to that animal, or to other animals including humans, or to the environment. If there is a cost to the animal, in terms of poor welfare or death, it may be judged that there is counter-balancing compensation for this in that there are benefits to others. Everybody uses cost–benefit analysis to some degree when making decisions. However, is this utilitarian approach sufficient to determine all obligations? After analysing various possible situations, the normal conclusion is that a deontological approach is also needed because there are some degrees of poor welfare that are never justified by benefit to others.

Broom (2003) proposes that all human behaviour and laws should be based on the obligations of each person to act in an acceptable way towards each other person and to each animal that is used, rather than involve the concept of rights. This is because many so-called rights can result in harm to others. There are occasions when people state that they have a right to say what they want, or drive as fast as they want, or carry a gun, or select the sex or genetic make-up of their children (Broom, 2006c). In each of these cases, the action could cause harm to others. This harm would be accepted by very few people. The argument based on a concept of rights can lead to a morally wrong or questionable outcome. Arguments based on the obligation of one individual towards others do not suffer from such problems. As far as animal rights are concerned, non-human animals do not normally have legal rights. On the other hand, there are many statements, codes of conduct, or widely accepted but unwritten rules that explain the obligations towards animals of people who use those animals. This argument, criticizing the use of the term 'rights', is also applicable to references to the freedom that an individual asserts, or that is supposed to be given to an individual. Broom (2014) presents arguments for the inadequacy of the concept of freedoms, whether five or any other number, in relation to animal treatment.

Public concern about animal welfare has increased in many countries during the last 30 years and especially in the last 10 years. Evidence for this is summarized in Box 2.3.

The attitudes of animal users depend upon early training, traditional practices, acquisition of knowledge from others subsequent to any training, personal experience, and general beliefs and philosophy. Training in animal-use businesses, did not, until recently, include much information about animal welfare except where it impinged on profitability. Today's training courses are more

Box 2.3. Evidence for increased concern about animal welfare (modified from Broom, 1999a).

1. Letters from the public, media coverage, social media activity
2. References in parliamentary discussions and government statements
3. Government requests for scientific evidence on animal welfare
4. Activity of scientific and other advisory committees
5. Funding of scientific research on animal welfare
6. Increased teaching and conferences
7. More legislation

likely to include information about the welfare of the animals. Some traditional practices undertaken by animal users result in poor welfare, so should not continue.

Animal Welfare

Scientists and legislators now use animal welfare as a term that is a scientific concept describing a potentially measurable quality of a living animal at a particular time. Such usage has rapidly become widespread during the last 30 years (Broom, 2011) and, like health, the concept is exactly the same for humans and for other animals (Garcia Pinillos *et al.*, 2015, 2016). However, the term animal welfare was not always used as a scientific concept, and indeed there are still many people who are not aware of this approach to the subject.

Ruth Harrison's book, *Animal Machines* (1964), pointed out that those involved in the animal production industry were often treating animals like inanimate machines rather than living individuals. As a consequence of this book, the British government set up the Brambell Committee in 1965, chaired by Professor F. Rogers Brambell, to report on the matter. One of its members was W.H. Thorpe, an ethologist at Cambridge University, who emphasized that an understanding of the biology of animals is important. He explained that animals have needs with a biological basis, including some needs to show particular behaviours, and that animals would have problems if their needs were not met (Thorpe, 1965). At this time, the emphasis of discussions was on animal protection, a human activity, rather than on animal welfare. In the 1970s and early 1980s, the term animal welfare was used but not defined and not considered scientific by most scientists. Animal welfare was often confused with animal rights and such confusion still occurs.

Much of the discussion about the use of animals, until relatively recently, centred on whether or not they should be killed. Philosophers and the public were often concerned with the ethics of killing animals for human food, human clothing, scientific research or as unwanted pets (Regan, 1990; Fraser, 2008). This is an important ethical question but it is not an animal welfare issue. The animal welfare issue is what happens before death, including how they are treated during the last part of their lives, and then the method by which they are killed.

Barry Hughes (1982) proposed that the term 'animal welfare' meant that the animal was in harmony with nature, or with its environment. This is a biologically relevant statement and a precursor of later views but it is not a usable definition. Being in harmony is a single state so it does not allow the use of scientific measures of welfare. The key question is how much the individual is in harmony. In the 1980s, the term 'welfare' was being used more and more in science, in laws and in discussions about the effects of the treatment of laboratory, farm and companion animals. Hence there was a clear need for a scientific definition. Broom (1986, p. 324) used this definition of welfare: '*the welfare of an individual is its state as regards its attempts to cope with its environment*'. This was further explained in a series of publications (Broom, 1988, 1991a,b; Broom and Johnson, 1993). The term 'welfare' refers only to animals, not to plants or inanimate objects. The OIE (World Organization for Animal Health; OIE 2011) followed the Broom definition in a description of what is meant by animal welfare. The OIE text is imprecise and is being revised. Words equivalent to welfare in other languages include *bien-être*, *bienestar*, *bem estar*, *benessere*, *Wohlergehen*, *welzijn*, *velfærd* and *dobrostan*. Well-being is an essentially equivalent term in English but is less precise in its usage, so scientists and legislators usually use the word 'welfare'. Welfare can be measured scientifically and varies over a range from very good to very poor. Welfare will be poor if there is difficulty in coping or failure to cope. Coping means having control of mental and bodily stability (Broom and Johnson, 1993). Feelings, such as pain, fear and the various forms of pleasure, are identifiable as biological coping mechanisms and an important part of welfare. All of the systems for coping with pathology, the state of which is health, are also key parts of welfare. If all of the coping systems are functioning well, welfare will be good and the individual will have good feelings and will thrive. Indeed, striving towards rewards and happiness is a major mechanism for coping. Quality of life means welfare, so quality of life can be measured using the wide range of welfare indicators. However, while we refer to pain or pleasure that lasts for only a few minutes or hours as affecting welfare, we do not use the term 'quality of life' for what happens to individuals during brief periods. In order that welfare can be good rather than poor, it is important to know the needs of the animal. These needs depend on the biological functioning of the animal and therefore vary somewhat from species to species. Most accounts of the welfare of a particular kind of animal start with a summary of its needs (e.g. European Food Safety Authority (EFSA) Scientific Reports, such as EFSA (2009), and Council of Europe Recommendations, such as Council of Europe (1999a)). The motivation system of each animal, including each human, functions to control interactions with the environment, promoting the occurrence of optimal responses and initiation of actions by means of a set of needs (Broom and Fraser, 2015, chapter 4). A need is a requirement, which is part of the basic biology of an animal, to obtain a particular resource or respond to a particular environmental or bodily stimulus (Broom and Johnson, 1993; Broom, 2008). The need itself is in the brain. It allows effective functioning of the animal and may be fulfilled by physiology or behaviour.

Some needs are for particular resources, such as water or heat, but control systems have evolved in animals in such a way that the means of obtaining a particular objective have become important to the individual animal. The animal may need to perform a certain behaviour and may be seriously affected if unable to carry out the activity, even in the presence of the ultimate objective of the activity. It has been shown that many animals will work, in the sense of carrying out actions that result in food presentation, even in the presence of food. Examples of needs are that pigs need to root in soil or some similar substratum, hens need to dust-bathe and both of these species need to build a nest before giving birth or laying eggs. Needs can be identified by studies of motivation and by assessing the extent of poor welfare in individuals whose needs are not satisfied and of good welfare when they are satisfied. In studies assessing motivational strength, the methodology depends on the cognitive ability of the animals. Unsatisfied needs are often, but not always, associated with bad feelings, while satisfied needs may be associated with good feelings. When needs are not satisfied, welfare will be poorer than when they are satisfied.

The idea of providing for 'the five freedoms' was first suggested in the Brambell Report in 1965. A list of freedoms or domains (Beausoleil and Mellor, 2015) just provides a general guideline for non-specialists. Animals have a range of needs and these have been investigated for many species. Hence the rather general idea of freedoms is now replaced by the more scientific concept of needs as the freedoms are not precise enough to be used as a basis for assessment of the welfare of a particular species or group of closely related species.

The overall need of any animal is to maintain the integrity of its functional systems, which include the brain and other organs, while growing and during adult life. The list of needs below is not in order of importance. Some needs require satisfying only at intervals of some hours, or only when young, or when adult. The causes of some problems of animals are multifactorial and related to more than one need. Some needs involve not only the avoidance of poor welfare but also increasing the likelihood of good welfare.

Example of the Range of Needs

To have sufficient oxygen and good air quality – Oxygen is needed to prevent the partial pressure of oxygen in tissues falling below a particular level. Aquatic and land animals show preferences that help them to avoid any harm that lack of oxygen may cause. Noxious gases are usually detected and avoided.

To carry out feeding to maintain themselves and grow – A level of energy input and a variety of nutrients are needed by animals. If any are lacking in the feed or there is dietary imbalance, there will be adverse consequences. Starvation is a problem and social factors can prevent adequate feeding. In addition to the need to ingest food, the animals need to carry out foraging behaviour and to avoid dietary toxins.

To have good environmental water quality (aquatic or partly aquatic animals) – Inappropriate water conditions can harm aquatic animals. Many toxic chemicals may be present in captive aquatic environments.

To maintain osmotic and other body fluid stability – In order that normal physiological functioning can occur in body cells and tissues, a range of homeostatic mechanisms maintaining stability need to work. Land animals need to obtain water by drinking or from food.

To receive appropriate sensory input – Stimuli perceived using the visual, olfactory and auditory systems are all important. The perceived conditions could be sub-optimal. For example, light may be too dim, or inappropriate in some other way, or of too short a duration during 24 hours. Very bright lights, very loud noise and certain other stimuli could also cause poor welfare. Too much sensory input in total or too little sensory input can cause poor welfare.

To rest and sleep – Animals need to rest and sleep in order to recuperate and avoid danger. Rest and sleep may be insufficient because of disturbance by other animals.

To exercise and have space for movement (swimming for aquatic and partly aquatic animals) – Exercise is needed for normal bone and muscle development. The amount of space required for normal functioning in water or on land depends on the species.

To have appropriate social interactions – Many animals are social. They associate and interact in a friendly way much more than in an aggressive way. They show by their normal behaviour the extent to which they choose to associate closely with other individuals. Some animals are able to tolerate the proximity of others but generally space themselves, even in confinement, so as to maximize inter-individual distance.

To avoid fear – Animals living in natural conditions are vulnerable to predation and still have anti-predator adaptations when in captivity. Their biological functioning is adapted to maximize recognition of danger and escape from it. There are responses to sudden events and approaches by humans or other animals perceived to be potentially dangerous with substantial sympathetic nervous system and hypothalamic–pituitary–adrenal changes. These physiological changes are followed by rapid and often vigorous behavioural responses. Fear is a factor in the life of many animals and has a great effect on their welfare, including suppression of feeding and reproduction.

To explore – An aspect of avoiding danger and reaching a suitable environment involves exploration. The exploration itself is a need for animals. An animal in a new environment needs to explore it and risks are minimized by intermittent exploration of surroundings.

To thermoregulate – Adverse temperature conditions can harm animals so they need to avoid them. Some degree of thermoregulation occurs in many cold-blooded animals and prevention of high or low body temperature by physiological and behavioural means is important in warm-blooded animals.

To carry out reproductive and maternal functions – Animals in reproductive condition make attempts to find appropriate partners. At this time they could be said to need sexual activity.

To maintain good health condition – All animals need systems and actions promoting avoidance of contact with pathogens that might cause disease. These involve various behaviours, anatomical adaptations and physiological responses. They also need to minimize the adverse impacts of pathogens, again using a range of responses.

To perform maintenance and eliminatory behaviour – Most animals need to groom and scratch themselves in order to keep the body surface free of harmful substances or organisms, including ectoparasites. Land animals select resting places that are dry and comfortable when possible and this behaviour tends to keep the body clean. Particular postures may be adopted to carry out defecation and urination.

To avoid pain and injury – All animals need to avoid any physical or chemical impact that causes tissue damage and may cause pain. This may include wounds resulting from attack by conspecifics, or predators, or by human handling.

Measuring Animal Welfare

Thousands of animal welfare scientists, studying diverse species, have used the concept of animal welfare explained above and assessed the welfare of the animals. Since there are many ways in which animals cope with their environment, a wide variety of measures of welfare are possible. Indeed, although any one measure could indicate very poor welfare, plans for welfare assessment are normally better if a range of measures is used.

Measures of the welfare of animals that may be affected by tourism are the same as those used for farm animals, laboratory animals or for humans. For humans, self-reporting is also used, even if this is sometimes less reliable. There may be greater difficulty in obtaining data from animals in their natural environment or in freely moving but captive conditions but all of the measures can be considered in any study of welfare.

One way of determining what animals need is to find out from them what they prefer. How hard will an individual work for a resource? For example, in work with rats that are given a choice of floors, one measure is how often they choose each floor. More information is obtained if the rats have to work in order to get to the floor of their choice. A rat can readily learn to lift a weighted door and the amount lifted gives an indication of its strength of preference for the resource (Manser *et al.*, 1996). Sophisticated strength of preference studies depend upon the use of operant and other techniques that exploit the abilities of animals to learn to carry out new procedures (Fraser and Matthews, 1997; Kirkden *et al.*, 2003). A second approach to assessing needs is to evaluate the welfare of animals that do or do not have a particular resource.

The use of a wide range of measures for the direct assessment of animal welfare is described in detail by Broom (2014, chapter 8) and Broom and Fraser (2015, chapter 6). The assessment of welfare should be carried out in an objective way, taking no account of any human-oriented ethical questions about the systems, practices or conditions for individuals that are being compared. Once the objective evidence about welfare has been obtained, ethical decisions can be taken.

Much of the evidence used in welfare assessment indicates the extent of the problems experienced by individuals but it is also important to recognize and assess good welfare (i.e. happiness, contentment, control of interactions with the environment and possibilities to exploit abilities). We should try to assess: the specific functioning of the brain when welfare is good in humans and other animals (Broom and Zanella, 2004); the methods of recognizing when welfare is, or is likely to be, good; and the factors that contribute to good welfare in humans and other species. Good welfare in general, and a positive status in each of the various coping systems, should have effects that are a part of a positive reinforcement system, just as poor welfare is associated with various negative reinforcers. There should be various recognizable effects on individuals of good welfare. We need to identify these so that the assessment of welfare is as effective at the good end of the range as at the bad end.

Each assessment of welfare for a human or other animal will pertain to a single individual and to a particular time range. In the overall assessment of the impact of a condition or treatment on an individual, a very brief period of a certain degree of good or poor welfare is not the same as a prolonged period. However, a simple multiplicative function of maximum degree and duration is often not sufficient because the most severe effect of poor welfare may be brief, while there is a more prolonged milder effect. If the intensity of the good or poor welfare is plotted against time, the best overall assessment of welfare for that individual animal is the area under the curve thus produced (Broom, 2001c).

Positive and negative effects on animal welfare which can be described include those of disease, injury, starvation, beneficial stimulation, social interactions, other forms of success in actions, living conditions, presence of humans who might be perceived as dangerous, deliberate or accidental ill-treatment, human handling, transport, injurious procedures, veterinary treatment, and genetic change by conventional or other breeding methods.

The general methods for assessing welfare are summarized in Table 2.1 and a list of measures of welfare is presented in Box 2.4. Most indicators will help to pinpoint the state of the animal wherever it is on the scale from very good to very poor welfare. Some measures are most relevant

Table 2.1. Summary of welfare assessment (modified from Broom, 1999b).

General methods	Assessment
Direct indicators of poor welfare	How poor is it?
Tests of: (a) avoidance	(a) What is the extent to which animals have to live with avoided situations or stimuli?
(b) positive preference	(b) To what extent is that which is strongly preferred available?
Measures of ability to carry out normal behaviour and other biological functions.	How much important normal behaviour or physiological or anatomical development cannot occur?
Other direct indicators of good welfare	How good is it?

Box 2.4. Measures of welfare (after Broom and Fraser, 2015).

Physiological indicators of pleasure
Behavioural indicators of pleasure
Extent to which strongly preferred behaviours can be shown
Variety of normal behaviours shown or suppressed
Extent to which normal physiological processes and anatomical development are possible
Extent of behavioural aversion shown
Physiological attempts to cope
Immunosuppression
Disease prevalence
Behavioural attempts to cope
Behaviour pathology
Brain changes
Body damage prevalence
Reduced ability to grow or breed
Cellular changes indicating system failure and ageing
Reduced life expectancy

to short-term problems, such as those associated with human contact or a brief period of adverse physical conditions, whereas others are more appropriate to long-term problems. These measures of welfare are objective, with their validity and robustness having been confirmed in many species.

Some signs of poor welfare arise from physiological measurements. For instance, increased heart rate, adrenal activity, or reduced immunological response following a challenge can all indicate that welfare is poorer than in individuals that do not show such changes. Care must be taken, when interpreting such results, to take account of the context and of other indicators. As a consequence of the high proportion of coping mechanisms that involve the functioning of higher centres in the brain, some welfare assessment should involve brain function measures (Broom and Zanella, 2004).

Behavioural measures are also of particular value in welfare assessment. The fact that an animal avoids strongly an object or event gives information about its feelings and hence about its welfare. The stronger the avoidance, the worse the welfare while the object is present or the event is occurring. An individual who is completely unable to adopt a preferred lying posture despite repeated attempts will be assessed as having poorer welfare than one who can adopt the preferred posture. Other abnormal behaviour such as stereotypies, self-mutilation, tail-biting in pigs, feather-pecking in hens, or excessively aggressive behaviour in dogs indicates that the perpetrator's welfare is poor. A variety of behavioural tests can be used to identify negative emotions (e.g. cognitive bias tests) (Mendl *et al.*, 2009). In some of these physiological and behavioural measures, it is clear that the individual is trying to cope with adversity and the extent of the attempts to cope can be measured. In other cases, however, some responses are solely pathological and the individual is failing to cope. In either case, the measure indicates poor welfare.

Disease, injury, movement difficulties and growth abnormality all indicate poor welfare. The welfare of any diseased animal is worse than that of an animal that is not diseased, but much remains to be discovered about the magnitude of the effects of disease on welfare. We have some information about how much suffering is associated with different diseases (Broom, 2006a). Pain may be assessed by aversion, physiological measures, behavioural changes such as grimace responses, the effects of analgesics (Duncan *et al.*, 1991; Stilwell *et al.*, 2009; McLennan *et al.*, 2016) or by the existence of neuromas (Gentle, 1986). Some measures of welfare are obtained after the period when welfare is affected so they are welfare outcome indicators such as injury frequency or extent of difficulty in walking. Whatever the measurement, data collected in studies of animal welfare give information about the position of the animal on a scale of welfare from very good to very poor.

The majority of indicators of good welfare that we can use are obtained by studies demonstrating positive preferences by animals. In operant tests, a cost is imposed upon access to the resource by requiring the subject to perform a task. Performance of the task requires time and effort, which could otherwise have been spent doing other things. The task may also be unpleasant to the subject. In choice tests, a cost is normally imposed instead upon consumption. The animal must allocate time and effort to one or other alternative.

In all welfare assessments it is necessary to take account of individual variation in attempts to cope with adversity and the effects that adversity can have on the animal. For example, confined pigs may show high levels of stereotypies or be very inactive and unresponsive.

The information presented here on the definition and measurement of welfare is now widely accepted by scientists, veterinarians and those who formulate laws and recommendations on the subject. Utilization within the tourism context of scientific measures of animal welfare is exemplified in the opinion pieces by Christopher Andrews, which focuses on aquaria, and by

Blakeway and Cousquer, which focuses on donkeys and mules. However, there are still many who are unaware of these scientific developments and who think that welfare has not been and cannot be defined or assessed in such a way. In addition to those who are unaware of all of the developments, there are others who wish to continue animal use unfettered by science and ethics and who therefore deny the scientific advances. Yet there may also be those who feel that a scientific assessment of animal welfare may miss the human perception of welfare. The problem with such a view is that it is inherently riven with personal human perspectives, yet to ignore it on these grounds alone potentially denies the complex, nuanced reality of the lives of all animals (human and non-human). Within this context, the immediate future for improving animal welfare affected by tourism clearly requires action based on precise thinking and full use of scientific studies of animal welfare. Looking beyond this, new methods for identifying happiness and careful evaluation of human perceptions of welfare may be required to fully understand and provide for the good welfare of all animals (see Chapter 6 by Lee Durrell).

Laws

Ideally, laws should reflect moral values in society and individuals' ethical values, rather than just protecting the property of the rich. The idea that animals used by people should not be treated like inanimate possessions, but should be protected from actions that might cause suffering, is very old and widespread in human society. Irrespective of any law, many people have condemned those perceived as being cruel to animals. On the other hand, cruelty has been part of some forms of human entertainment throughout history. In Europe, laws intended to prevent cruelty to dogs and horses were passed as long as 200 years ago and were gradually extended to other kinds of animals. Most early laws referred to companion animals and working animals but not to farm animals. Some laws protected animals against the forms of animal experimentation that were considered likely to cause substantial pain to the animals. Laws were also passed that proscribed some forms of entertainment involving animals as being cruel but others were still permitted. Laws aimed at preventing poor welfare in animals have become more wide-ranging, both in terms of species and different animal uses, and have been passed in more and more countries.

Many of the laws refer to animals that are kept, or are in captivity. Hence poor welfare of animals in the wild may not be legally prevented. In many countries, it is only comparatively recently that the capture or import or sale of wild-caught birds has been prohibited. Some laws make it illegal to disturb named wild animals, or wild animals in nature reserves. These laws were mainly aimed at conservation objectives but they also prevent the poor welfare associated with disturbance, capture or attempts to kill. The CITES conventions, agreed to in most countries, protect some rare species but not common species (refer to Chapter 16 by John Sellar, a former CITES Chief of Enforcement).

Laws relating to animals vary greatly from country to country (Cao and White, 2016). The enforcement of laws is also variable and in some countries with laws that seem appropriate for protection, animals suffer greatly because little effort is made to enforce them. In other cases, it is very difficult to enforce the laws, for example, the ill-treatment of animals at sea by the actions of people in boats is generally difficult to detect and prevent.

The term 'welfare' is now being used frequently in laws, as it has an established scientific and legal usage. As explained above, the concept is biologically based and is exactly the same in humans and in non-human animals. However, words are sometimes used in ways that belittle the animals and this can affect treatment in law and in all aspects of life. For example, if people refuse to accept that the term 'pain' can be applied in the same way to dogs and fish, those who might never cause pain to a dog might cause pain to a fish. The word 'harvest' should be applied only to plants but, by using this plant word in relation to killing animals, people may salve their consciences about what is done to the animals. We should say that we kill or slaughter animals but not that we harvest them. In humans, euthanasia has a clear meaning, 'the killing of an individual for its own benefit using a humane method', and it should have exactly the same meaning for non-humans. However, euthanasia is also often used to refer to the killing of an animal for the convenience of a person. Perhaps a pet owner can no longer look after a pet, or a person in a laboratory or farm no longer wants an animal. This may be humane killing, in that causing pain or other poor welfare to the animal is avoided, but it should then be called humane killing and not euthanasia unless it is done for the benefit of that individual animal. We should use all such terms in the same way for humans and non-humans. The decision about this common task of a vet rests with the humans with the power, but human owners are fearful of it, being driven to make it as a good friend and owner solely for the benefit of the animal.

Summary

This chapter has been focused on discussing the sentience of animals and their needs. This has identified that many animals are sentient beings and that they have a wide range of needs. It has also been argued that we, humans, have moral and ethical obligations to ensure that the welfare of all animals is as good as possible.

The chapter has also discussed how we can assess and measure the welfare of animals, focusing on the scientific measures available to us and identifying the importance of following these. The chapter has also raised the issue of the value of understanding human perspectives of animal welfare and the potential for considering these as well as the animal-based evidence in order to decide on policies for improving animal welfare.

Having provided a foundation for understanding animal welfare, the book now turns its attention to animal welfare within tourism.

References

Beausoleil, N.J. and Mellor, D.J. (2015) Advantages and limitations of the Five Domains model for assessing welfare impacts associated with vertebrate pest control. *New Zealand Veterinary Journal* 63, 37–43.

Broom, D.M. (1981; reprinted 2009) *Biology of Behaviour.* Cambridge University Press, Cambridge, UK.

Broom, D.M. (1986) Indicators of poor welfare. *British Veterinary Journal* 142, 524–526.

Broom, D.M. (1988) The scientific assessment of animal welfare. *Applied Animal Behaviour Science* 20, 5–19.

Broom, D.M. (1991a) Animal welfare: concepts and measurement. *Journal of Animal Science* 69, 4167–4175.

Broom, D.M. (1991b) Assessing welfare and suffering. *Behavioural Processes* 25, 117–123.

Broom D.M. (1999a) Animal welfare: the concept and the issues. In: Dolins, F.L. (ed.) *Attitudes to Animals: Views in Animal Welfare*. Cambridge University Press, Cambridge, UK, pp. 129–142.

Broom, D.M. (1999b) Welfare and how it is affected by regulation. In: Kunisch, M. and Ekkel, H. (eds) *Regulation of Animal Production in Europe*. K.T.B.L., Darmstadt, pp. 51–57.

Broom, D.M. (2001a) The evolution of pain. *Vlaams Dierqeneeskunde Tijdschrift* 70, 17–21.

Broom, D.M. (2001b) Evolution of pain. In: Soulsby, E.J.L. and Morton, D. (eds) *Pain: Its Nature and Management in Man and Animals. Royal Society of Medicine International Congress Symposium Series* 246, 17–25.

Broom, D.M. (2001c) Coping, stress and welfare. In: Broom D.M. (ed.) *Coping with Challenge: Welfare in Animals Including Humans.* Dahlem University Press, Berlin, pp. 1–9.

Broom, D.M. (2003) *The Evolution of Morality and Religion*. Cambridge University Press, Cambridge, UK.

Broom D.M. (2006a) Behaviour and welfare in relation to pathology. *Applied Animal Behaviour Science* 97, 71–83.

Broom, D.M. (2006b) The evolution of morality. *Applied Animal Behaviour Science* 100, 20–28.

Broom, D.M. (2006c) Introduction – Concepts of animal protection and welfare including obligations and rights. *Animal Welfare. Ethical Eye Series.* Council of Europe Publishing, Strasbourg, France, pp. 13–28.

Broom, D.M. (2007) Cognitive ability and sentience: which aquatic animals should be protected? *Diseases in Aquatic Organisms* 75, 99–108.

Broom, D.M. (2008) Welfare assessment and relevant ethical decisions: key concepts. *Annual Review of Biomedical Sciences* 10, T79–T90.

Broom, D.M. (2010) Cognitive ability and awareness in domestic animals and decisions about obligations to animals. *Applied Animal Behaviour Science* 126, 1–11.

Broom, D.M. (2011) A history of animal welfare science. *Acta Biotheoretica* 59, 121–137.

Broom, D.M. (2014) *Sentience and Animal Welfare*. CAB International, Wallingford, Oxfordshire, UK.

Broom, D.M. (2016a) International animal welfare perspectives, including whaling and inhumane seal killing as a public morality issue. In: Cao, D. and White, S. (eds) *Animal Law and Welfare – International Perspectives*. Springer International Publishing, Switzerland, pp. 45–61.

Broom, D.M. (2016b) Considering animals' feelings. *Animal Sentience*, 2016.005. Available at: https://pdfs.semanticscholar.org/2ba8/197ef88baccb99e96cec906c1b6b6ba22fe2.pdf (accessed 25 January 2018).

Broom, D.M. and Fraser, A.F. (2015) *Domestic Animal Behaviour and Welfare*, 5th edn. CAB International, Wallingford, Oxfordshire, UK.

Broom, D.M. and Johnson, K.G. (1993; reprinted with corrections 2000) *Stress and Animal Welfare*. Kluwer/Springer, Dordrecht.

Broom, D.M. and Zanella A.J. (2004) Brain measures which tell us about animal welfare. *Animal Welfare* 13, S41–S45.

Broom, D.M., Sena, H. and Moynihan, K.L. (2009) Pigs learn what a mirror image represents and use it to obtain information. *Animal Behaviour* 78, 1037–1041.

Caldwell, R.L. (1986) The deceptive use of reputation by stomatopods. In: Mitchell, R.W. and Thompson, N.S. (eds) *Deception*. SUNY Press, Albany, NY, pp. 129–145.

Cao, D. and White, S. (eds) (2016) *Animal Law and Welfare – International Perspectives*. Springer International Publishing, Switzerland. DOI: 10.1007/978-3-319-26818-7.

Council of Europe (1999) *Standing Committee of the European Convention for the Protection of Animals Kept for Farming Purposes (T-AP) Recommendation concerning domestic ducks (Anas platyrhynchos)*. Council of Europe, Strasbourg.

Dalla Costa, E., Dai, F., Lebelt, D., Scholz, P., Barbieri, S., Canali, E., Zanella, A.J. and Minero, M. (2016) Welfare assessment of horses: the AWIN approach. *Animal Welfare* 25, 481–488.

Dawkins, M. (1993) *Through Our Eyes Only*. Freeman, Oxford, UK.

DeGrazia, D. (1996) *Taking Animals Seriously*. Cambridge University Press, Cambridge, UK.

de Waal, F. (1989) Food sharing and reciprocal obligations among chimpanzees. *Journal of Human Evolution* 18, 433–459.

de Waal, F. (1996) *Good Natured*. Harvard University Press, Cambridge, MA.

Duncan, I.J.H., Beatty, E.R., Hocking, P.M. and Duff, S.R.I. (1991) Assessment of pain associated with degenerative hip disorders in adult male turkeys. *Research in Veterinary Sciences* 50, 200–203.

EFSA (2009) Scientific report on the effects of farming systems on dairy cow welfare and disease. (Also scientific opinions on the same subject.) *The EFSA Journal* 1143, 1–38.

European Union (1997) *Treaty of Amsterdam Amending the Treaty on European Union, the Treaties Establishing the European Communities and Certain Related Acts* (97/C 340/01). Available at: https://www.ecb.europa.eu/ecb/legal/pdf/amsterdam_en.pdf (accessed 25 January 2018).

Fraser, D. (2008) *Understanding Animal Welfare: The Science in Its Cultural Context*. Wiley Blackwell, Chichester.

Fraser, D. and Matthews, L.R. (1997) Preference and motivation testing. In: Appleby, M.C. and Hughes, B.O. (eds) *Animal Welfare*. CAB International, Wallingford, Oxfordshire, UK, pp. 159–171.

García Pinillos, R., Appleby, M.C., Scott-Park, F. and Smith, C.W. (2015) One welfare. *Veterinary Record* 179, 629–630.

García Pinillos, R., Appleby, M., Manteca, X., Scott-Park, F., Smith, C. and Velarde, A. (2016) One welfare – a platform for improving human and animal welfare. *Veterinary Record* 179, 412. DOI: 10.1136/vr.i5575.

Gentle, M.J. (1986) Neuroma formation following partial beak amputation (beak-trimming) in the chicken. *Research in Veterinary Science* 41, 383–385.

Griffin, D.R. (1984) *Animal Thinking*. Harvard University Press, Cambridge, MA.

Hagen, K. and Broom, D.M. (2004) Emotional reactions to learning in cattle. *Applied Animal Behaviour Science* 85, 203–213.

Harrison, R. (1964) *Animal Machines*. Vincent Stuart, London. Reprinted with commentaries (2013), CAB International, Wallingford, Oxfordshire, UK.

Held, S., Mendl, M. Devereux, C. and Byrne, R.W. (2000) Social tactics of pigs in a competitive foraging task: the 'informed forager' paradigm. *Animal Behaviour* 59, 569–576.

Hughes, B.O. (1982) The historical and ethical background of animal welfare. In: Uglow, J. (ed) *How Well Do Our Animals Fare? Proceedings of the 15th Annual Conference of the Reading University Agricultural Club*, pp. 1–9.

Jackson, R.R. and Cross, F.R. (2011) Spider cognition. *Advances in Insect Physiology* 41, 115–174.

Kendrick, K.M., Atkins, K., Hinton, M.R., Borad, K.D., Fabre-Nys, C. and Keverne, B. (1995) Facial and vocal discrimination in sheep. *Animal Behaviour* 49, 1665–1676.

Kilgour, R. (1987) Learning and the training of farm animals. In: Price, E.O. (ed.) *The Veterinary Clinics of North America* 3(2), 269–284.

Kirkden, R.D., Edwards, J.S.S. and Broom, D.M. (2003) A theoretical comparison of the consumer surplus and the elasticities of demand as measures of motivational strength. *Animal Behaviour* 65, 157–178.

Kirkwood, J.K. (2006) The distribution of the capacity for sentience in the animal kingdom. In: Turner, J. and D'Silva, J. (eds) *Animals, Ethics and Trade: The Challenge of Animal Sentience*. Compassion in World Farming Trust, Petersfield, UK, pp. 12–26.

Langbein, J., Nürnberg, G. and Manteuffel, G. (2004) Visual discrimination learning in dwarf goats and associated changes in heart rate and heart rate variability. *Physiology and Behavior* 82, 601–609.

Lloyd, J.E. (1986) Firefly communication and deception, oh what a tangled web! In: Mitchell, R.W. and Thompson, N.S. (eds) *Deception*. SUNY Press, Albany, NY, pp. 113–128.

Manser, C.E., Elliott, H., Morris, T.H. and Broom, D.M. (1996) The use of a novel operant test to determine the strength of preference for flooring in laboratory rats. *Laboratory Animals* 30, 1–6.

McLennan, K.M., Rebelo, C.B.J., Corke, M.J., Holmes, M.A., Leach, M.C. and Constantino-Casas, F. (2016) Development of a facial expression scale using footrot and mastitis as models of pain in sheep. *Applied Animal Behaviour Science* 176, 19–26. DOI: 10.1016/j.applanim.2016.01.007.

Mendl, M. and Paul, E.S. (2008) Do animals live in the present? Current evidence and implications for welfare. *Applied Animal Behaviour Science* 113, 357–382.

Mendl, M., Burman, H.P., Parker, R.M.A. and Paul, E.S. (2009) Cognitive bias as an indicator of animal emotion and welfare: emerging evidence and underlying mechanisms. *Applied Animal Behaviour Science* 118, 161–181.

OIE (2011) *Terrestrial Animal Health Code*. World Organization for Animal Health. OIE, Paris.

Regan, T. (1990) Animal rights. In: Clarke, S.R.L. and Linzey, A. (eds) *Political Theory and Animal Rights*. Pluto Press, London, pp. 176–186.

Rolls, E.T. (2005) *Emotion Explained*. Oxford University Press, Oxford, UK.

Rugani, R., Fontanari, L., Simoni, E., Regolin, L. and Vallortigara, G. (2009) Arithmetic in newborn chicks. *Proceedings of the Royal Society B* 276, 2451–2460.

Serpell, J.A. (1986) *In the Company of Animals*. Cambridge University Press, Cambridge, UK.

Serpell, J.A. (1989) Attitudes to animals. In: Paterson, D. and Palmer, M. (eds) *The Status of Animals: Ethics Education and Welfare*. CAB International, Wallingford, Oxfordshire, UK, pp. 162–166.

Sneddon, L.U., Elwood, R.W., Adamo, S.A. and Leach, M.C. (2014) Defining and assessing animal pain. *Animal Behaviour* 97, 201–212.

Sommerville, B.A. and Broom, D.M. (1998) Olfactory awareness. *Applied Animal Behaviour Science* 57, 269–286.

Stilwell, G. Carvalho, R.C., Lima, M.S. and Broom, D.M. (2009) Effect of caustic paste disbudding, using local anaesthesia with and without analgesia, on behaviour and cortisol of calves. *Applied Animal Behaviour Science* 116, 35–44.

Thorpe, W.H. (1965) The assessment of pain and distress in animals. Appendix III in *Report of the Technical Committee to Enquire into the Welfare of Animals Kept under Intensive Husbandry Conditions*. F.W.R. Brambell (chairman). London, HMSO.

Würbel, H. (2009) Ethology applied to animal ethics. *Applied Animal Behaviour Science* 118, 118–127.

3 The Position of Animals in Tourism

Introduction

In this chapter we aim to provide a discussion of the myriad ways in which animals exist within and in relation to tourism. As part of this, the chapter is concerned with identifying how animals can be, and often are, defined as objects that provide sources of entertainment for humans in their leisure time. Consequently, we talk about how these animals are used or consumed, dead or alive and sometimes both, and why people seek out animal experiences while they are on holiday. There is also explanation of how animals are increasingly being presented and utilized as employees and guests of the tourism industry. Many of the animals discussed in the chapter are those we, as humans, wish to see and potentially engage with. However, the tourism industry and the people it caters to have significant impacts on other animals. These animals and the impacts on them are also dealt with in this chapter when looking at the animals that the industry seeks to airbrush out of the tourism experience. Some of these animals are the ones that we hate or fear, while others are those that are, to employ the banal language of the modern-day military, simply collateral damage, an incidental cost of tourism development. The chapter builds towards an analysis of whether animal welfare and tourism are mutually exclusive or potentially inclusive of one another, the issue that is at the heart of the discussion in Chapter 4.

The Roles Animals Play in Tourism: Objects of the Tourist Gaze

If asked to consider the roles animals play within the tourism experience, it is likely that the first thing that comes to mind is images of animals in zoos or possibly aquaria, as depicted in Fig. 3.1. If asked to expand on this we may begin to think of donkey and horse rides, or camel and elephant rides. From there we may think of dog sled rides (see Fig. 3.2) or branch out into the viewing of animals in the wild. Within this context in an aquatic setting, whale watching, including orcas or dolphins, and coastal boat trips to watch seals or seabirds may come to mind. On land, we may think of trips to see bears, lions, tigers, kangaroos, koalas, gorillas, or giraffes, among many others. If asked to think further we may consider the position of animals in petting zoos (see Fig. 3.3) and farm tourism.

Not all animals are equally attractive to tourists. The charismatic animals lead the way as those that people most want to see and are both satisfied and entertained by seeing. The charismatic, or box office, animals are generally large, mammalian, furry, and are perceived to display intelligence. Such animals include the iconic panda, orangutans, black bears, and gorillas. While not furry, this group also includes aquatic animals such as whales and dolphins. These are the animals that attract people to zoos and aquaria and they are the animals that help to sustain the soft toy industry. They are also the animals around which animal welfare and conservation organizations, such as the World Wide Fund for Nature and Born Free, build their imageries and

Fig. 3.1. (a) London Zoo (2008); (b) the Vancouver Aquarium (2008).

Fig. 3.2. Dog sled rides in Whistler, Canada (2012).

agendas. These organizations care for far more than the charismatic animals, but just like zoos they see the value of these animals in drawing in people to a wider debate and agenda (for a detailed examination of the attractiveness of different species the reader is directed to Small, 2011, 2012; Frynta *et al.*, 2013 and Carr, 2016a,b,c).

The tourism experience also incorporates events ostensibly focused around animals but with many other components. Such events include sled dog races, such as the Iditarod and Yukon Quest and horse races such as the Grand National and the Melbourne Cup. Shifting away from the sports arena, farm and animal shows also fit into this category. Such events include Crufts dog show in England and the Royal Highland Show in Scotland. These are differentiated from the animal experiences noted already in this section because they are focused on the event and at least partially on the 'prowess' of the human participants rather than solely on the animal (see Hultsman, 2012, 2015 for a detailed discussion of why people take part in dog sports).

Animal-related tourism is not just about wishing to see and potentially interact with animals, sometimes it is about wishing to hunt and kill them. This form of tourism encapsulates everything from domestic tourism to high-cost international tourism and a host of animals both on land and in the water. The controversy around this type of tourism is huge, with both sides adopting passionate, and in their own way, persuasive arguments (witness Chapter 17 by Jane Goodall and Chapter 18 by Brent Lovelock later in this book). Hunting tourism arguably exists just about everywhere in the world though on land it is often largely hidden thanks to its contentious status and also, perhaps fortuitously, it being generally situated in wilderness areas, away from prying eyes. Yet despite hunters killing rather than taking pictures of or interacting in a

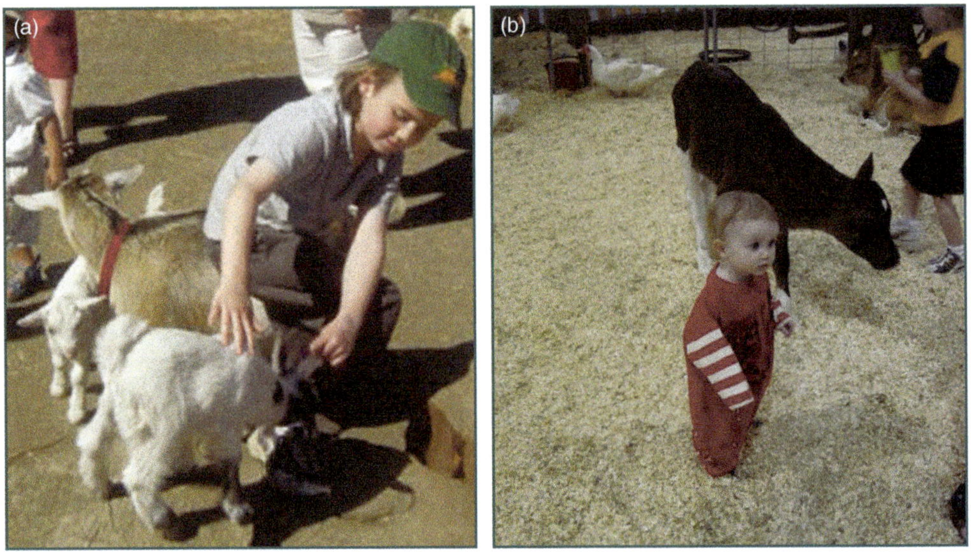

Fig. 3.3. (a) Petting zoo in Victoria, Canada (2005); (b) pop-up petting zoo in Brisbane, Australia (2003).

non-lethal way with animals, hunting tourism has something in common with the other tourism experiences noted above – they all perceive the animal as an object for the utilization by humans for their enjoyment. While traditionally focused on wild animals, contemporary hunting tourism includes a significant component of 'wild' animals that have been bred in captivity and released into enclosed areas specifically for the enjoyment of hunters. The canned hunts of animals such as lions in parts of Africa are perhaps the most notorious but the hunting of captive bred wild animals has a much longer history that includes deer and wild boar in central Europe and the fishing lakes around the world that are stocked with 'game' fish especially for human entertainment through fishing (see Cohen, 2014 and Ireland, 2002 for more discussion of the ethics of hunting in general and the canned hunt in particular).

So far all of these experiences and animals have one thing in common; they are all being utilized by tourists to give satisfaction to their human desires. In this way, all of these animals are objectified by humans for the entertainment of humans. Within this context, a very wide range of animal species is utilized by the tourism industry.

Why Do Tourists Wish to Have Experiences of or with Animals?

The desire of tourists to see and potentially interact with animals is certainly nothing new. The concept of the zoo can be traced back over 4500 years (Benbow, 2004) though they were originally perhaps more accurately seen as private menageries whose role was to indicate the power of the rulers of the time. Yet as a place of leisure for the masses, zoos have been around since the late 18th century when the creation of zoological societies, such the Zoological Society of London, gave a scientific *raison d'être* for zoos. Indeed, London Zoo was opened to the public in 1847. It, like many other modern zoos, may initially have been envisaged as a site for the scientific investigation of animals and not a public leisure attraction but just like all zoos today (Hallman and Benbow, 2006; Carr and Cohen, 2011), London Zoo became a significant tourist attraction that is highly dependent on tourists for its economic viability. Curiosity, a desire to see animals, partially driven, but also fed upon and reinforced by media representations of them in everything from zoo advertising to David Attenborough programmes and Disney movies is certainly a core reason why people visit zoos. This curiosity and desire is directly linked to the wish to be entertained by the experience of the zoo and the animals housed within it (Turley, 1998; Linke and Winter, 2011). In other words, zoos are, in the eyes of the public, a site of potential human leisure. Zoos offer an easily accessible way of seeing, hearing and smelling animals in the flesh rather than having to be satisfied with images on the television. The alternative of visiting myriad animals in their natural environments around the world is simply not a realistic option for the majority of people (Shani and Pizam, 2011). Yet for those who can afford to, such experiences are sought for similar reasons to why we go to the zoo and may actually be reinforced by visiting a zoo.

It has also been hypothesized that we like to see and interact with animals, in zoos and beyond, because in our contemporary urban world we are more disassociated from animals than at any time in the past of humanity (Curtin, 2009; Ferguson and Litchfield, 2018). The zoo offers an opportunity to get back in touch with nature. More recently, zoos have attempted to rebrand themselves, reacting to changing social values regarding the keeping of animals in confined spaces for the purposes of human entertainment. As part of this rebranding, zoos have highlighted their potential to act as repositories of endangered species and their ability to aid the re-introduction into the wild of such animals. They have also, within this context, sought to stress their potential to educate the public about the need for, and value of preserving, not just endangered species but also their natural environments. Buying into this social responsibility, zoo visitors may now talk not just of the entertaining possibilities of a visit to the zoo but also of its ability to educate them, and particularly their children. In this way, the zoo has been redefined not just as a site of fun and entertainment, but also of education and learning (Carr and Cohen, 2011). A similar, though arguably less distinct, morphing of all animal experiences beyond the zoo into learning as well as entertainment opportunities may be said to have taken place for exactly the same reason it has in zoos.

The wildlife tourism industry that offers guided tours, with the aim of encountering wild animals, is a more recent development than the zoo but it arguably offers and provides fundamentally similar experiences to tourists and meets the same needs/desires. Aquatic wildlife tourism providers, including those offering the chance to view orcas, dolphins, other whales, sharks, seals, penguins, etc. all offer a mix of entertainment and education. In addition, they offer tourists the opportunity to experience something unique, something memorable, and something that offers them the opportunity to add to their social capital or kudos (Curtin, 2005).

The importance of this kudos in driving human behaviour cannot be underestimated in our consumerist economy. A visit to the zoo provides relatively low social capital, as zoos are fairly common and are designed to ensure that viewing the animals is relatively easy. More social capital is on offer for animal experiences that are out of the ordinary or where the viewed animals, particularly in their natural environment, are rare, exotic or endangered. This all, of course, entails a financial cost that can be said in many ways to be proportional to the social capital value. Consequently, more social capital may be experienced in a zoo via an animal interaction or behind the scenes experience. However, even more will be gained via a journey into Uganda or Rwanda to witness the critically endangered mountain gorilla in its natural environment. Whatever the social capital sought, proof of the experience undertaken must be gained in order to cash in on the social capital. Previously, this meant taking photos and then showing them to friends and relatives after they had been developed and the holiday was completed. In today's digital and social media age, pictures are taken and uploaded immediately onto the internet to be shared with followers. In the age of the 'selfie', we see an increasing desire of tourists to be pictured with the animal: witness the rage for selfies with the quokka of Rottnest Island in Western Australia, for example.

It is also worth pausing to consider which animals tourists do not wish to see or interact with. Relatively few people wish to see or interact with the 'creepy crawlies', the creatures that haunt our nightmares and feature in cheap old horror B movies. Co-author Neil Carr has a vivid memory of his eldest son in Durrell Wildlife Park attempting to get visitors to the Park to interact with the Madagascar hissing cockroach he was taking care of, with zero success. The mundane also tends to be of little interest to tourists (Carr, 2016b; Young and Carr, 2018). The latter is not exciting and taking a photo of it to show to friends or post on social media offers no social capital. Gerald Durrell berated this situation when noting the fate of the 'little brown job' (Durrell Wildlife Conservation Trust, 2015), small inconspicuous creatures who are no less important than the flagship species but who are unable to excite the public, not because they are scary but rather because their appearance is mundane, anonymous. The Meller's duck arguably fits into this category. To the casual eye there is little to distinguish it from a common mallard duck and yet it is one of the rarest animals on the planet. While it may, under its brown feathered surface, meet the characteristics of 'rare' and 'exotic' to appeal to tourists it fails to gain attention because of its appearance.

A precursor of modern wildlife tourism was the guided hunting tour, which is itself an extension of the hunting that has played a long-term role during human evolution. Initially undertaken for sustenance and survival, tourism hunting is about the 'thrill' of the hunt and the earning of the right to brag about killing a particular animal. The hunt, like virtually all forms of tourism, is also about escapism from reality. Finally, as an activity that has, at least historically, been dominated by men, another reason for partaking in hunting tourism may be identified as a desire to reinforce hegemonic, masculine identity. Such an identity is associated with the 'hunter' providing for the family, or dominating nature, and conquering the apex or biggest creature in the natural environment. Conquering such animals is not in itself sufficient though, a permanent display of this dominance is required, hence the presence of severed heads on the walls of stately homes throughout the world. Although severed heads may no longer be present on the walls of the homes of many hunters, the underlying reasons for the hunt have not changed at all. Rather, the severed heads on the walls have been switched for the pictures of the killed animal with the victorious hunter lording over it now displayed on personal Facebook sites. In all of this, the animal is once again an object (refer to Chapter 17 by Jane Goodall and Chapter 18 by Brent Lovelock on hunting and tourism, and Lovelock (2015) for more detailed perspectives on this aspect of the tourism industry).

The desire to hunt animals may be reinforced, just like the desire to see animals, by what we see on television. Contemporary fishing and hunting shows promote and glorify such experiences. A prime example of this would be the series of fishing programmes by Robson Green. Through Mr Green we learn that catching some fish is more desirable and contributes to higher social capital than others. The size of a fish may also have similar significance, bigger always appearing to be better (Shiffman *et al.*, 2014), along with the rarity of the fish and the difficulty associated with catching it. The latter harks back to the notion central to fox hunting in the UK, at least prior to its banning, of a desirable hunt being a one where the fox provides a good-quality chase. In this way, it is not sufficient to merely catch the fish. Rather, it must put up a good 'fight' that challenges the skills and stamina of the fishermen. In this way, the fish, by being challenging, transforms the fishing exercise into a competitive sport, at least in the eyes of the fisherman. Those who hunted foxes or deer, on horseback using packs of hounds, were often able to persuade themselves that the fox or deer enjoyed the competitive aspect of the chase. These same people were disturbed or disbelieving when presented with evidence of extreme fear and stress induced in the chased animals (see the Chapter 4 section headed 'Fishing and trophy-hunting tourism', p. 54). On land there are also clearly some animals that are more prized than others by hunters. Desirability is calculated in a similar manner to that associated with fish, as is the social capital on offer at the end of a successful hunt.

Hunters often have codes of practice in relation to which actions are acceptable in their perceived competition with their prey and which are not (Serpell, 1986). Today, hunters also talk of themselves as environmental stewards, protecting the natural environment from introduced species and consuming ethically sourced meat while at the same time still reinforcing their imagery of hegemonic masculinity (again, not dismissing the fact that some women are involved in these 'sports') and human dominance over nature. This is then fed back to them and the public in general via shows such as *NZ Adventure Hunters* (http://www.nzhunteradventures.co.nz/adventures/index.html). The introduced species are often respected less than native species, even though their capacity to suffer is the same. Yet some of the introduced species, on land and in water, are only present because previous generations of hunters brought them into the country.

Fishermen also talk of their ethical behaviour, both in terms of their role in controlling introduced species and how they handle the fish they catch (Mordue and Wilson, 2018). Today, many people who fish for sport pride themselves on a policy of catch-and-release, a process often enforced by authorities to protect fish populations. Yet such a process is not without its critics due to the pain and stress inflicted on the fish. As our scientific knowledge about animal sentience and the ability of fish and other kinds of animal to feel pain continues to increase, questions are likely to continue to be raised regarding the ethics of catch-and-release practices. These questions must be balanced against the reality of fishing as one of the world's most popular sports/leisure pursuits. Given its scale, banning fishing as a leisure pursuit is highly unlikely to ever occur and, in this context, consideration must be given to whether a painful catch-and-release is preferable to the death of the caught fish. This type of question is examined in detail in Chapter 4.

The desire to see animals in the wild pre-dates the creation of the wildlife tourism industry. It dates back at least to the Romantic Movement, which includes the poems of William Blake, the paintings of Henri Rousseau and the animal-centred books of Ernest Thompson Seton and Henry Williamson, that has been widely identified (Lane, 2009; Holden, 2016) as kick-starting the urban population's interest in the rural environment and the wilderness that lies beyond it. This movement can be seen to be at least partially responsible for the conceptualization of the National Park, an entity that has spread, since the first one was created in the USA (Yellowstone National Park in 1872), to virtually every country in the world. The myth-making at the heart of the Romantic Movement was mirrored in a myriad of subsequent developments that would have a significant impact on how the public viewed wild animals and their desire to see them and get close to them. The bear is an ideal example here. A resident of many North American National Parks, the bear was transformed from a wild and potentially dangerous animal into the teddy bear (see Fig. 3.4), whose form evolved to be more child-like (Hinde and Barden, 1985). The anthropomorphization of the bear was furthered through the creation of Yogi Bear and the presence of Winnie-the-Pooh in the writings of A.A. Milne and his consequent transformation into the central character in various movies. The result was that, virtually as soon as they were opened, National Parks in North America were witnessing people keen to see and get as close as possible to a bear. Feeding bears was a favourite activity, driven by images of cute teddy bears that wiped away the reality of a wild animal capable, if pushed, of killing a human. It is also arguable that this positioning of the bear as an adorable animal led to its positioning in many zoos around the world. Bears are not the only animals to have been influenced in this way. The television series *Flipper,* about a dolphin, has also been highly influential in the stocking of aquaria with dolphins for the attraction of tourists. The North American National Parks and the aquaria then bought into and fed back to the public the myths society had created around these animals. For example, the Parks encouraged bear feeding (see Biel, 2006 for a history of bears in North American National Parks), and utilized and reinforced their anthropomorphic personification in the form of *Smokey Bear* (a creation of the US Forest Service) to warn visitors of the dangers of forest fires.

Seeing animals seems not to be enough for many people; they wish to interact with them as well. Witness the dog owner (Neil) sitting at home typing this chapter with his 3-month-old pup (Ebony) on his lap. To stroke her is a simple pleasure, an interaction between animal and human that then extends to walking and playing together. Ebony and Neil are, of course, not in a tourism environment but this desire to have contact with an animal for the joy, thrills and peace it gives can arguably be transferred into such an environment and begin to influence our desire for animal contact. As hinted earlier in this section, the desire for animal contact can be partially traced to social constructions of particular animals (witness the points made about bears). These constructions are wrapped up in everything that is wrong with anthropomorphism, of seeing the animals as fur-covered humans (often babies or young children) and then imposing human thought characteristics onto their actions. The desire to touch and interact with animals can also be related to the concept of social capital, with such experiences being perceived to be worth more than merely seeing an animal. Finally, perhaps we simply wish to touch some animals because we derive pleasure from certain touch stimuli. Such touching and interaction encompasses everything from the acceptable and sanctioned (horse trekking and walking dogs in animal shelters while on vacation) to the illegal, at least in some countries (e.g. holding onto the fins of dolphins while in the water with them).

Marketing plays on all of the issues discussed above, buying into them and feeding them back to tourists and potential visitors: we see tourist destinations construct their brands around animals that they know visitors are keen to see (see the bus in Fig. 3.5). In this way, the nations of Southern Africa have strongly identified themselves with safari tourism focused around the Big Five (lion, elephant, buffalo, leopard and rhino), while, Kaikoura in New Zealand is

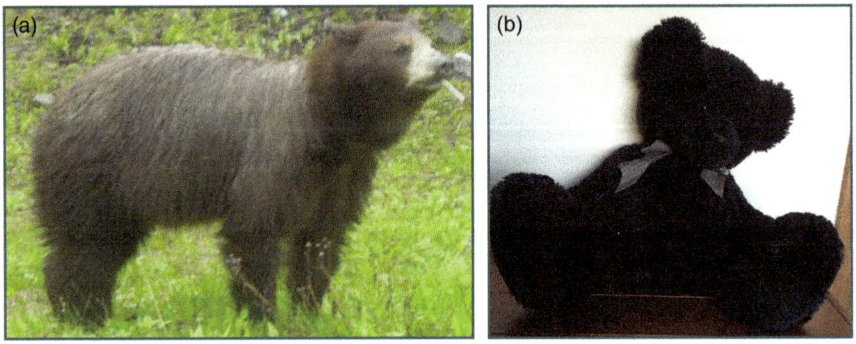

Fig. 3.4. (a) A black bear in Waterton Lakes National Park, Canada (2005); (b) an anthropomorphized black bear (or cute and cuddly teddy bear) in New Zealand.

Fig. 3.5. Public bus in Banff, Canada (2008).

synonymous with whale-watching and Churchill in Canada with polar bear tourism. The common issue across the diverse marketing campaigns is their utilization of animals that appeal to people, as noted earlier. The only exception being when they deliberately use animals perceived to be scary to appeal to people's desire for excitement linked to danger, something that may be referred to as a 'sneaky thrill'.

Consuming Animals and the Tourism Industry

When looking at the position of animals in tourism, we need to consider not just those that we wish to see or engage with but also those that we eat. The consumption of meat in the tourism experience ranges from the mundane to the exotic. The former is concerned with the consumption of meat of a type and quantity that is similar to what the tourist consumes within their home environment. The latter is all about the consumption of something different. So for the tourist from Europe visiting various parts of Asia, it may be about the consumption of meat from snakes or dogs (see Podberscek, 2007 for discussion of attitudes to dogs as food). However, visitors to New Zealand from China, for example, may categorize lamb as an exotic meat.

One of the primary reasons for undertaking a holiday is to escape from the mundane and to explore the exotic, to engage in something different. It is within this context that meat products not normally consumed at home may be deliberately sought in the holiday environment. Furthermore, the hospitality industry may deliberately seek to entice tourists with the promise of an exotic meal. An example of this is highlighted in Fig, 3.6, which depicts the entrance to a restaurant in Banff, Canada. The menu includes, among other things, such non-mundane items as buffalo and caribou.

In addition to providing tourists with animal-based food, restaurants may utilize animals in their marketing to tourists. Indeed, the restaurant noted in Fig, 3.6 does exactly this, employing the most famous of wild animals in the Canadian wilderness – the grizzly bear. A similar utilization of the bear is depicted in Fig. 3.7. While they may not affect wild animals directly, depictions like these (and others used in various marketing campaigns associated with produce sold in the hospitality sector) reinforce anthropomorphized images of wild animals in the minds of people. These images, in a continuous feedback loop, may influence people's desires to see and interact with wild animals during their tourism experiences. It is not, of course, only wild animals that are used in this way. Domestic animals are also often used in the marketing of products for the hospitality industry (see Carr, 2014 for an examination of the position of the dog in alcohol marketing).

Restaurants and other food outlets may also utilize animals as a source of entertainment. Such labelling may be attached to restaurants that display live animals that customers can pick from to decide which they will eat. Such an experience can be gained with a variety of animals, including fish, crustaceans, and snakes, among others.

The tourism industry does not only provide visitors with the opportunity to eat animals. Instead, visitors are also offered the opportunity to buy a myriad range of animal and animal-related products. Animal fur (the most common, but certainly not the only example, being the sheep's fleece), leather goods (including shoes, jackets, and handbags, among others) from the hides of various animals (not just cattle), sea shells, and ivory carvings are among just some of the trinkets tourists can buy in some parts of the world when on holiday. If some of these products, such as ivory, are illegal in some countries that does not mean they are not for sale, or that tourists do not buy them and smuggle them home. In contrast to the sale and purchasing of ivory, some animal products are positioned in the tourism market as not just being socially acceptable but even as aiding the preservation of native wildlife and habitats. This is the way that the selling of possum fur products in New Zealand has been presented to the world. Possums are an introduced species in New Zealand where they are identified as a pest responsible for the destruction of native wildlife. They have been the subject of long-term eradication attempts that have included selling their fur to tourists. In this way, the killing of possums is identified as being environmentally responsible. No mention is made of the welfare of the individual possum when it is killed. This mirrors the points made earlier in the chapter in relation to hunting.

Fig. 3.6. Restaurant in Banff, Canada (2008).

Fig. 3.7. Restaurant in Canmore, Canada (2008).

The Rise of the Animal Tourism Employee

What differentiates an object from an employee? When we are talking about humans the distinction may be easy to make; a sentient being is an employee, not an object. Yet even in the case of humans this is not, sadly, always the case. Consider, for example, the abusive situations in which many women find themselves trapped within the sex industry. These women are not employees, no matter how people may choose to dress it up by calling them 'sex workers'. Rather, they are objects, utilized by clients and 'owners'. This is not to say that everyone in the sex industry is an object, far from it, but this is the reality for many across the globe.

If animals are not generally seen as sentient beings and lack the legal rights of humans, can we apply a humanistic label like 'employee' to them? Furthermore, to be an employee suggests that the individual is paid. Certainly, there are few people who would classify themselves as an employee if they were not paid by an employer. Yet despite this, there is an increasing number and range of animals being identified by humans as employees within the tourism industry. Prime among these animals is the dog. This is unsurprising given their long association with humanity and their diverse skills. These animals can now be found in airports around the world where they are employed to sniff out everything from explosives, to narcotics and food substances. In addition, dogs that have been variously labelled as 'meet-and-greet dogs', 'canine ambassadors' and 'therapy dogs' are now to be found in airports. The 'job' for these dogs, irrespective of their title, is to calm the nerves of harassed or frightened fliers by allowing themselves to be stroked and patted. Similarly, some hotels and other types of accommodation now have animals working to meet and greet guests. Dogs may be prime among them, but cats are also utilized in this role. There are also the search-and-rescue dogs whose role is to find missing people.

It may be suggested that sniffing out substances and saying 'hello' to people are roles for which dogs are perfectly suited and that undertaking them is more akin to play than work for them. Is it not, after all, obvious that dogs love to be patted and said hello to, and to seek things with their noses? The evidence is right in front of Neil, whose pup (at the time of writing) had a wonderful morning saying hello to everyone she possibly could and sniffing out every discarded banana skin on the university campus. It was clear that she loved it all: the attempt to initiate interaction with other humans and the interaction itself was all filled with significant joy for her, as was the discovery of each banana skin. Yet meeting people and sniffing out things can be stressful and are tiring. Neil's pup, as he wrote this part of the book, was, after her morning activities, fast asleep on her beanbag, too tired to even bother chasing the cat. The stress, especially for dogs, as opposed to pups, who know no better, is associated not just with the constant interaction with strangers in airports and hotel lobbies but the knowledge that they must act in the correct manner irrespective of how the humans meeting them act. To be a sniffer dog requires intense concentration, something that a dog who has been bred and trained can do. However, while searching things out with its nose is within a dog's capabilities, it is seldom naturally required to the level demanded by humans. Consequently, the sniffer, the search-and-rescue, and the meet-and-greet dogs all need extensive training to ensure they will do their 'work' correctly and to the required standard.

If these animals are not paid to work in the tourism industry, then can they be defined as 'employees'? The lack of pay would suggest that they cannot, but this does not necessarily return them to the category of object. Human volunteers who work in a vast array of roles, both inside and outside of the tourism industry are not paid (in a capitalistic sense) for their work. Similarly (and ironically) emeritus professors receive no salary from their universities but undertake many, if not all, the roles that paid academics do, publishing material in journals and books, advising students, acting as mentors to paid staff, and lecturing. The key point here is 'may': the volunteer and the emeritus professor have the choice to do the work or not, they are not required to do it. If an animal is neither paid to undertake a role nor given the option of not undertaking it, then it can hardly be thought of as an employee as opposed to an object or tool to be utilized for the enjoyment of the customer and the financial gain of the owner. In the next chapter we shall explore how, and to what extent, the tourism industry has managed to deal with this issue and consequently whether it can be said that there are actually any animal employees or even volunteers in the tourism industry.

The Rise of the Animal as Guest

Today, the tourism industry is increasingly catering to, and branding itself as accepting animals as guests. Accommodation providers may now offer the opportunity for dogs to stay in their guest rooms. In addition, they may provide treats for dogs upon arrival, in a similar manner to which some hotels have historically offered gifts to young children upon arrival. Furthermore, accommodation providers may offer meal options for canine guests as may some restaurants while others may allow dogs into their venues and at least provide water for them (see Fig. 3.8 and Carr, 2014 for a more detailed discussion).

The rise of the animal as guest has been focused on the dog, reflecting the historically and increasingly close bond between people and dogs. Many people now see their dogs as members of the family and would no more leave them at home than leave their children. Yet it is not only dogs that are welcomed: hotel operators in Whistler, Canada, for example, reporting that while most of their non-human guests are dogs, they have also catered for a variety of other small animals.

Yet are these animals really 'guests'? This demands an examination of what we mean by 'guest', which in turn requires an understanding of the concept of 'hospitality'. This book is not the place for an extended discussion on these topics, so interested readers are instead directed to work by such authors as Conrad Lashley (2015) and David Scott (2015), among others. However, we may view a guest as a 'person' (for in our human-centric world a guest has traditionally been defined as a human) towards whom hospitality is extended. Following on from this, hospitality may be defined as the reception and provisioning of guests in a friendly and welcoming manner. Outside the hospitality industry, such provisioning falls outside the remit of a cash-for-services exchange. However, within a capitalist system the provisioning of guests within the hospitality industry requires the payment by guests for the welcome, services and provisions they are provided with. In this way, within the industry, hospitality becomes an act that is intimately bound up with the economic system, and the guest is also the client and purchaser and those working in the hospitality industry the employee and servant of the guest.

Fig. 3.8. Dog water on offer at a food outlet on the Isle of Arran, Scotland (2004).

So if within the hospitality industry a guest is at least partially defined by their ability to pay for services received, then it may be argued that an animal cannot be a guest. After all, they have no money of their own and no understanding of the value of money, something that is arguably required in order to be able to purchase a service or provision. However, many children do not have the ability to pay for services or goods they consume within the hospitality industry and they are clearly accepted as guests of the hospitality industry. Indeed, they have been recognized as important and potentially valuable guests (see Carr, 2011). The reasons behind this are largely related not to the children themselves but their parents. There is the recognition that parents seek to take their children on holiday with them and in the process to engage in a range of hospitality services. Catering successfully to the significant family market is economically advantageous and doing so requires ensuring that the children are happy with the experiences they encounter. Failure to satisfy or please children may result in a negative family holiday experience and consequently dissatisfied parents who are unlikely to act as return tourists or provide positive word-of-mouth recommendations to friends and family members. Thus, the children are identified as guests in an economic sense because of the financial advantages, which are controlled by parents, or other adults with a direct link or responsibility to the child, that may accrue from doing so. This logic can be applied to animals, particularly pets and especially pet dogs, who are increasingly assuming a central role in the lives and families of many people. In this sense, the hospitality industry operator who fails to meet the needs of the dog will potentially feel the wrath of dissatisfied dog owners in just the same way they would if they failed to meet the needs of children.

However, when talking of satisfying needs, we have to ask whose needs are being catered for? In this context, it is important to recognize the distinction between what animals actually need and want, what is good for them, and what human owners or companions want for their animals. These distinctions again raise the question of whether an animal can be a guest of the hospitality industry. Can they be a guest if their presence on holiday is a result of the need of their owner rather than themselves, and if what is required of the hospitality industry is a result of the desires of owners rather than the needs of animals? In an absolute sense, the answer may be no, but from a perception-based perspective, the answer may be yes. In other words, even if a human guest is the one demanding services and products for their pet rather than the animal needing them, the industry must still buy into the image of the pet as a guest or face the potential wrath of the human owner. It is also clear that an animal can be a guest when its needs are being catered to, irrespective of whether it is paying for them in cash or not. However, as will be discussed in the next chapter there may be very different welfare issues and implications underlying these very different types of animal guests of the hospitality industry.

While some companion animals may be guests in tourist situations, many are not taken on holiday, so the tourism of their human companions has consequences for their welfare while the pets are separated from their owners. This separation may have a relatively small effect because the pet remains in the same physical environment with other familiar human companions and sometimes with familiar non-human companions. Another good environment for companion animals, such as dogs or cats, while owners are away is a frequently visited home where there are people, and often other dogs or cats, with whom there are previously established good relationships. However, companion animals are often put in an unfamiliar environment, such as commercially run kennels, during owner holidays, where the situation may be somewhat or very disturbing. Some consequences for welfare are described in Chapter 4. Yet today, many kennels are presented as holiday destinations for pets (see Carr, 2014 for a discussion of the evolution of the pet hotel for dogs) that play on and contribute further to the centralization of pets within the human family.

The welfare of owned animals other than companion animals may also be affected by owners going on holiday. For example, a farmer or owner of working animals may arrange for the care of these animals while on holiday and the care may range from very good to very poor. Some of these animals may have a social bond with particular people and may be adversely affected by the absence of those people even if the temporary carer is entirely conscientious in their work. Some animal owners who depart for their tourism experience do not wish to think about negative consequences for the animals for which they are responsible, while others are very careful to consider the welfare of the animals.

Tourism, Animals and Sanitization

The tourism experience has often been identified as something that offers an escape from everyday reality in a liminal space (Carr, 2002; Hall, 2003). As part of this, it is no surprise that the tourism industry has been accused of offering up a sanitized experience bereft of the realities of life (Law, 2002). The examples are myriad but include ensuring that wealthy visitors to the beaches of Africa, Central America and the Caribbean are kept away from the poverty of many of the people living in these areas. Perhaps more mundane, but no less significant, is the constant attempts by local authorities to ensure that tourist centres are clean, while rubbish may pile up on the back streets not frequented by tourists. Yet perhaps the ultimate example of a sanitized tourist destination is that to be found in Disneyland. All the rough edges of reality have been smoothed over here, anything that has the potential to offend sensibilities has been airbrushed out.

Why is it that the tourist industry engages in such airbrushing? Despite claims to the contrary, by various academics (e.g. Wearing *et al.*, 2010) attempting to rarefy tourism, claiming that tourists are increasingly in search of the 'authentic', an experience where the grit of reality is still in place and on view, the majority of people still desire a holiday devoid of the harsh realities of life. Consequently, it may be suggested that the tourism industry is simply responding to consumer demand in attempting to ensure that the sensitivities of tourists are not offended during their holiday experiences.

Why does this matter for animals? Clearly if animals or aspects of their behaviour may offend the sensitivities of tourists, then it matters a great deal, as the tourism industry may seek to airbrush them or their offending behaviours out of the tourism experience. Evidence of such actions by the tourism industry abound. The animals we 'love' and desire to see are embraced by the tourism industry, and opportunities are provided for the tourists to see and interact with them, as seen earlier in this chapter. In contrast, those animals we 'hate' are removed, not uncommonly via the use of lethal force, from the tourism experience. At the mundane level, all we have to do is consider how many spiders we have seen when staying in a hotel. Spiders consume many animals that may be damaging to people but, because some people are disturbed by them, many are killed. All other creepy crawlies are likewise banned from the hospitality industry. If we step out of our hotel and onto the streets of the destination, we see further attempts to airbrush out undesirable animals. For example, there have been plenty of reported instances of local authorities removing and killing stray dogs in order to make their cities look more attractive to international visitors. It was, for example, reported that authorities in the Ukraine rounded up and destroyed stray dogs in the build up to their hosting of the 2012 European Football Championship (Osborn, 2011).

If we continue the walk through our imaginary resort we may end up at the beach where more airbrushing has been and is underway. The local contractors have worked on the beach in the early hours to ensure that it is pristine and golden for the day. In the process they have removed the debris and flotsam brought in by the tide. Some of this was undoubtedly human waste but a portion was also natural materials such as seaweed, decaying logs, and dead animals. The latter, of course, must be removed as images of death can easily upset people. Indeed, we often go to significant lengths to hide the reality of mortality from our eyes and minds. The smell of living or rotting material might offend as the sun rises. However, by removing the rotting vegetation we create a desert by the sea, destroying a natural ecosystem in the process and banishing the animals that depend on the materials deposited on the beach by the sea. Standing on the pristine beach we may be enticed into the sea; it is, after all, a warm day and the water sparkles with a vivid blue hue. So in we plunge, probably in the blissful ignorance that we are safe from the sharks that would naturally frequent this area. Instead, these sharks are kept out of the area by a ring of nets.

Of course, these nets do not simply keep the sharks away from the area we wish to swim in. Instead, they have the potential to kill them, and a variety of other sea creatures. Yet these deaths, which may offend our sensitivities, are hidden from our view, not least of all because the tourist industry has no desire at all to upset its clients. This is the same as the process associated with the removal of the stray dogs from the streets of the destination. In both instances, some of us want the animals removed from 'our' tourist experience. They may offend our sensitivities or frighten us. Images of malnourished, injured or diseased stray dogs are upsetting for most people. It does not matter whether the fear is based on a real risk. All that matters is the mistaken perception that a shark will always try to eat me if I go in the sea or that a dog will always attack me if it is on the loose and may subject me to the threat of diseases such as rabies. However, do we want to see either animal killed? Generally, the answer is 'no'. Rather, we just want them 'out of our way', as if they have never been there in the first place. However, the reality is that the solution to 'out of the way' is often the killing of the offending animal/s (see Chapter 14 by Darci Galati for a discussion of these issues). What is more, tourists often know this. However, by allowing the tourism industry to deal with these animals out of sight of the tourist the latter is offered, and thankfully grasps at, culpable deniability.

Having enjoyed our swim in the sea, time at the beach, and stroll through the sanitized streets of the resort, we are now hungry. It is time to go and find our lunch. Just as at home, when we enter the restaurant as a practising omnivore, we are able to eat various meat dishes without having to witness the transformation of a living animal into the juicy peppered steak, gloriously smelling bacon sandwich, or dog stew. We do not have to witness the living animal paraded past us, or hear and see its death and dismemberment. We may be 'treated' at a certain class of restaurant to the chef cooking the meat in front of us but by then it is 'meat' and no longer 'animal'. We know the meat we eat was once a living, breathing animal, but we are offered, and grasp at, the ability to hide this knowledge from ourselves by the way society hides abattoirs and what goes on behind their closed doors. Yes, I hear you argue, what about the fish, crabs, oysters, and other crustaceans that are displayed in tanks of water in some restaurants where we can pick which one we wish to eat, or other animals treated in the same way? There is nothing hidden here, surely? While that may be true, as humans, we create a smoke screen to hide behind; that these animals are somehow lesser than those we have to send to abattoirs. People persuade themselves that these animals do not feel pain, do not experience fear, and are of lesser value, so there is no harm in simply picking them, alive, from the menu.

What of the dog on the menu? As noted in Carr (2014) there is a long history of the consumption of dog meat around the world, sometimes out of necessity, but at others as a luxury cuisine. There is huge controversy associated with the provision and consumption of dog meat. Why? After all, if we are happy to eat cow, pig, chicken or fish, for example, why should we be offended by the idea of eating dog? Yet this is, of course, not the only animal whose consumption has the potential to offend our sensitivities. We also get upset at the idea of the consumption of whale meat and would doubtless hate the idea of black bear, panda, turtle or tiger being served at a restaurant. All of these animals are consumed, yet not without controversy. The controversy is associated with how we view these animals and have identified them with human emotions and levels of intelligence. It is also associated with the rarity of the animal and our social construction of the need for and desirability of protecting the species from extinction. For example, we may be happy to see the extermination of entire species of 'pests', such as the mosquito, while seeking to preserve butterflies. Dogs we have constructed as a companion and friend of humans. Whales we have constructed as having an intelligence on a par with our own, a beautiful and rare animal that our world would be lessened without. Bears are, of course, just living incarnations of our childhood teddy bears. Tigers, turtles, pandas and clown fish are not only loveable, and characterized in Disney movies, as such *Kung Fu Panda* and *Finding Nemo*, but also identified as rare iconic species. Consequently, eating all of these species is socially constructed as being wrong. So as part of the sanitization process where such consumption does take place, it does so out of the public gaze.

Having eaten our socially acceptable lunch and having been assured that the restaurant has a local authority hygiene rating and its kitchen is therefore devoid of cockroaches, rats, mice or any other vermin, we may now decide to visit the local zoo. Here we shall be offered the opportunity to see a wide array of 'wild' animals. Yet once again what we are seeing is sanitized for us, probably with our blessing. Once we are in the zoo and wandering around we may or may not notice that all the animals are fit and healthy. Zoos are castigated in the media and by various authorities if they are home to any unwell animals. Sick animals are properly kept in hospital conditions, not on display to the public, but in good zoos, feeding is good and veterinary care ensures that few are sick. Yet the reality is that, in the wild life is tough and animals often are injured, do have scars, and are thinner than when well fed. However, zoos are constructed only as a place to see the ideal animal, a beauty pageant for the wild. Carnivores and omnivores need meat in their diet and in the wild they would spend a not-inconsiderable amount of their time hunting and killing it. Yet such behaviour is not to be displayed to the visiting public, at least not in a western, socially acceptable zoo. Such is the sensitivity associated with feeding meat to animals in zoos that it is rarely shown as even a complete dead animal (Cushing and Markwell, 2011). So, if animals must be fed in view of the public, then the meat best be in a state akin to that which we see each day in the supermarkets and butchers. If this is not possible, then best that the animal be fed behind the scenes. So if the lions are to be fed the remains of a zebra or giraffe, it is perhaps best to ensure that the butchering of the animal is not undertaken in public and that the hide is removed before it is fed to them (more discussion of this issue is provided in the next chapter). In this way, it is just another joint of meat, the viewing public can simply be left to believe it is a cow if they wish. After all, if it is fine for a human to eat a cow, then surely there is nothing wrong with a lion eating a beef steak (witness how Marty the lion's meat is always depicted in the movie *Madagascar*).

Finally, on our journey through the zoo, we note that the operator is proud to talk about its efforts to breed various endangered species. There are tales of mating partners and of mums and dads and babies. Yet this is all skirting around the central fact of what is going on here: sex. We live in a sex-saturated world, where it is difficult to make it through a day without being exposed to a variety of sexualized instances, yet at the same time we remain generally rather prudish, preferring not to see what we may secretly like to see. Is it fear of offending visitor sensibilities that contributes to zoos doing all they can to make sure that sex among their animals takes place away from the gaze of their visitors. In just the same way, visitors, although perhaps not children, who have no social chains on their views, prefer not to see any other bodily functions being undertaken by animals in zoos. In just the same way that we will close the door on the toilet, be it a public one or in our own home, we prefer not to witness the zoo animals defecating or urinating.

So it is that we reach the end of our day in the holiday destination in which animals have been airbrushed out of it or primped and preened into a shape and form that is acceptable to our sensitivities. The implications for animal welfare are multitudinous and, in many instances, obvious. Nevertheless, further discussion of these implications is provided in the next chapter.

Tourism, Animals and Collateral Damage

Animals are directly affected in myriad ways by tourism. In addition, many animals are indirectly impacted where tourism development takes place. In these instances, the developer usually has no interest in using animals as a tourist attraction or protecting them from over-eager tourists. The destruction of the natural habitat of animals that used to live along coastal strips of the Mediterranean and Caribbean, for example, bear witness to this. The destruction of sand dunes to make way for high-rise apartments and hotels have robbed animals of places to breed, lay their eggs, and survive and thrive. Areas of mangrove are home to a wide range of animals and plants, yet they are being destroyed faster than almost any world habitat. The pollution caused by tourism developments has the potential to further push animal populations to extinction.

It is not just at the local development level that tourism has the potential to adversely affect the lives of individual animals and entire species without such disasters being deliberately planned. Setting aside those few people who still mistakenly cling to the forlorn hope that global warming is a myth, we must realize the significant contribution that travel by tourists makes to this process (see Hall and Higham, 2005 and Scott *et al.*, 2012 for a detailed discussion of the link between tourism and global warming). The implications for animal populations of global warming are potentially huge. In terms of scale, the continuing destruction of the Great Barrier Reef is probably the largest example of the impact of global warming on animals. Another iconic example is the melting of ice in the Arctic that is threatening the survival of the polar bear. Such destruction endangers the future of the tourism industry surrounding the Reef and the bears, while also driving tourists to visit such attractions in ever-greater numbers while they can, in a form of last-chance tourism. Of course, such demand can, and often does hasten the ongoing destruction.

Animals and their natural environments are also potentially under threat from invasive species unwittingly brought in by the tourism industry. For example, global warming combined with the increasing popularity of the Antarctic as a tourist destination is leading to concerns about the potential for tourism to bring in invasive species to the continent. Where previously such species may not have survived the cold of winter, climate change is altering this and in the process endangering native ecosystems. Rats, carried accidentally but carelessly, aboard cruise ships, are also a common threat to isolated islands. Examples include the myriad small islands off the coast of New Zealand's main two islands and the Galápagos Islands.

Exotic animals brought into a location to educate or titillate tourists also pose an indirect threat to native wildlife and their environments. Such tourist attractions and the animals they house are increasingly dangerous in an era of global warming in the same way that the threat of invasive species is increasing in Antarctica. Examples are myriad but can be said to include butterfly attractions (see, for example, the one in the Otago Museum in Dunedin, New Zealand) which house animals in heated buildings because in theory they will not survive the local temperate and climate. However, what if they do escape at a mild time of year and manage to breed, what then are the implications for the native ecosystem and the animals it is home to? What of the wallabies, muntjac deer and sika deer roaming the British countryside as a result of escapes from zoos. They may look cute but they are certainly not native to the UK. They are, however, capable of adapting to climates different from their native ones,

Summary

The aim of this chapter has been to throw light on the many ways in which animals are a part of the tourism experience. Within this, some animals are most clearly seen as objects of tourists' desire, entertainment or attraction. Others are more accurately seen as workers in the tourism industry or even guests of it. For the touring public, not all animals are equal. There are some animals that tourists want to see, there are others that they have no interest in, and there are some they actively loathe. The tourism industry panders to and reinforces these positions, giving access to the animals that tourists wish to see and ensuring that the others are barred from the holiday environment. The examples provided in this chapter are not meant to be all-encompassing. They are intended to raise the issues that surround animals in relation to tourism and provide a grounding for the reader to explore examples from their own experience or the wider literature in more detail if they wish to.

The chapter hints at the welfare implications for animals in relation to tourism. This issue takes centre-stage in the next chapter when examining whether animal welfare and tourism are mutually exclusive or potentially inclusive. This is a question that reflects the complexities and diversity of the tourism industry, and the ways in which humans perceive non-human animals.

References

Benbow, M. (2004) Death and dying at the zoo. *Journal of Popular Culture* 37(3), 379–398.

Biel, A.W. (2006) *Do (Not) Feed the Bears: The Fitful History of Wildlife and Tourists in Yellowstone*. University Press of Kansas, Lawrence.

Carr, N. (2002) The tourism-leisure behavioural continuum. *Annals of Tourism Research* 29(4), 972–986.

Carr, N. (2011) *Children's and Families' Holiday Experiences*. Routledge, Abingdon, Oxfordshire, UK.

Carr, N. (2014) *Dogs in the Leisure Experience*. CAB International, Wallingford, Oxfordshire, UK.

Carr, N. (2016a) An analysis of zoo visitors' favourite and least favourite animals. *Tourism Management Perspectives* 20, 70–76.

Carr, N. (2016b) Star attractions and damp squibs at the zoo: a study of visitor attention and animal attractiveness. *Tourism Recreation Research* 41(3), 326–338.

Carr, N. (2016c) Ideal animals and animal traits for zoos: general public perspectives. *Tourism Management* 57, 37–44.

Carr, N. and Cohen, S. (2011) The public face of zoos: balancing entertainment, education, and conservation. *Anthrozoos* 24(2), 175–189.

Cohen, E. (2014) Recreational hunting: ethics, experiences and commoditization. *Tourism Recreation Research* 39(1), 3–17.

Curtin, S. (2005) Nature, wild animals and tourism: an experiential view. *Journal of Ecotourism* 4(1), 1–15.

Curtin, S. (2009) Wildlife tourism: the intangible, psychological benefits of human–wildlife encounters. *Current Issues in Tourism* 12(5–6), 451–474.

Cushing, N. and Markwell, K. (2011) I can't look: disgust as a factor in the zoo experience. In: Frost, W. (ed.) *Zoos and Tourism: Conservation, Education, Entertainment?* Channel View Publications, Bristol, UK, pp. 167–178.

Durrell Wildlife Conservation Trust (2015) *The Gerald Durrell Story*. Available at: http://www.durrell.org/about/gerald-durrell/ (accessed 11 May 2015).

Ferguson, M. and Litchfield, C. (2018) Human-wild animal leisure experiences: the good, the bad, the ugly. In: Carr, N. and Young, J. (eds) *Wild Animals and Leisure: Rights and Welfare*. Routledge, Abingdon, Oxfordshire, UK.

Frynta, D., Simkova, O., Liskova, S. and Landova, E. (2013) Mammalian collection on Noah's ark: the effects of beauty, brain and body size. *PLoS ONE* 8(5), 1–12.

Hall, C.M. (2003) Introduction to Tourism: Dimensions and Issues, 4th edn. Pearson Education, South Melbourne.

Hall, C.M. and Higham, J. (eds) (2005) *Tourism, Recreation and Climate Change*. Channel View Publications, Clevedon, UK.

Hallman, B.C. and Benbow, M. (2006) Naturally cultural: the zoo as cultural landscape. *The Canadian Geographer* 50(2), 256–264.

Hinde, R.A. and Barden, L.A. (1985) The evolution of the teddy bear. *Animal Behaviour* 33, 1371–1373.

Holden, A. (2016) *Environment and Tourism*, 3rd edn. Routledge, Abingdon, Oxfordshire.

Hultsman, W. (2012) Couple involvement in serious leisure: examining participation in dog agility. *Leisure Studies* 31(2), 231–253.

Hultsman, W. (2015) Dogs and companion/performance sport: unique social worlds, serious leisure enthusiasts, and solid human–canine partnerships. In: Carr, N. (ed.) *Domestic Animals and Leisure*. Palgrave Macmillan, Basingstoke, UK, pp. 35–66.

Ireland, L. (2002) Canning canned hunts: using state and federal legislation to eliminate the unethical practice of canned 'hunting'. *Animal Law* 8, 223–241.

Lane, B. (2009) Rural tourism: an overview. In: Jamal, T. and Robinson, M. (eds) *The SAGE Handbook of Tourist Studies*. Sage Publications, London, pp. 354–370.

Lashley, C. (2015) Hospitality and hospitableness. *Research in Hospitality Management* 5(1), 1–7.

Law, C. (2002) *Urban Tourism: The Visitor Economy and the Growth of Large Cities*, 2nd edn. Continuum, London.

Linke, S. and Winter, C. (2011) Conservation, education and entertainment: what really matters to zoo visitors? In: Warwick, F. (ed.) *Zoos and Tourism: Conservation, Education, Entertainment*. Channel View Publications, Bristol, UK, pp. 69–81.

Lovelock, B. (2015) Troubled-shooting: the ethics of helicopter-assisted guiding trophy hunting by tourists for Tahr. In: Markwell, K. (ed.) *Animals and Tourism: Understanding Diverse Relationships*. Channel View Publications, Bristol, UK, pp. 91–105.

Mordue, T. and Wilson, S. (2018) Angler and fish relations in the UK: ethics, aesthetics and material semiotics. In: Carr, N. and Young, J. (eds) *Wild Animals and Leisure: Rights and Welfare*. Routledge, Abingdon, Oxfordshire, UK.

Osborn, A. (2011) Ukraine accused of culling stray dogs ahead of Euro 2012. *The Telegraph*. Available at: http://www.telegraph.co.uk/sport/football/competitions/euro-2012/8931419/Ukraine-accused-of-culling-stray-dogs-ahead-of-Euro-2012.html (accessed 11 November 2013).

Podberscek, A.L. (2007) Animals as food: dogs and cats as food in Asia. In: Bekoff, M. (ed.) *Encyclopedia of Human–Animal Relationships*. Greenwood Press, London, pp. 24–34.

Scott, D. (2015) The practice of everyday life performed away from home: a reflexive ethnography of a group tour. Unpublished PhD thesis, University of Otago, Dunedin, New Zealand.

Scott, D., Hall, C.M. and Gossling, S. (2012) *Tourism and Climate Change: Impacts, Adaptation and Mitigation*. Routledge, Abingdon, Oxfordshire, UK.

Serpell, J.A. (1986) *In the Company of Animals*. Cambridge University Press, Cambridge, UK.

Shani, A. and Pizam, A. (2011) A typology of animal displays in captive settings. In: Warwick, F. (ed.) *Zoos and Tourism: Conservation, Education, Entertainment*. Channel View Publications, Bristol, UK, pp. 33–46.

Shiffman, D., Gallagher, A., Wester, J., Macdonald, C., Thaler, A., Cooke, S. and Hammerschlag, N. (2014) Trophy fishing for species threatened with extinction: a way forward building on a history of conservation. *Marine Policy* 50, 318–322.

Small, E. (2011) The new Noah's Ark: beautiful and useful species only. Part 1. Biodiversity conservation issues and priorities. *Biodiversity* 12(4), 232–247.

Small, E. (2012) The new Noah's Ark: beautiful and useful species only. Part 2. The chosen species. *Biodiversity* 13(1), 37–53.

Turley, S. (1998) Exploring the future of the traditional UK zoo. *Journal of Vacation Marketing* 5(4), 340–355.

Wearing, S., Stevenson, D. and Young, T. (2010) *Tourist Cultures: Identity, Place and the Traveller.* Sage Publications, London.

Young, J. and Carr, N. (2018) Introduction: domestic animals, humans, and leisure – rights, welfare, and wellbeing. In: Young, J. and Carr, N. (eds) *Domestic Animals, Humans, and Leisure: Rights, Welfare, and Wellbeing.* Routledge, Abingdon, Oxfordshire, UK.

4 Animal Welfare and Tourism: Are the Aims Mutually Exclusive or Potentially Inclusive?

Introduction

In this chapter we build on the previous two, which looked at the concept of animal welfare and the position of animals in the tourism experience, to discuss and provide evidence of the extent to which the aims to ensure that animal welfare is good and to promote tourism are mutually exclusive or can be potentially inclusive of one another. In other words, the chapter is focused on assessing whether a tourism experience and industry does, or can, exist that takes into consideration and meets the needs of animals so that their welfare is good. To do this, the chapter begins by exploring some topics where we have information about the history and current situation of animal welfare in tourism. This section builds on Chapter 2 by recognizing that, as well as having a scientific grounding, concern for animal welfare is a social phenomenon and as such varies culturally and has varied over time as attitudes have changed. This raises the point that we must be careful to avoid claims of cultural imperialism when examining animal welfare issues in different human cultures. There is also a need to view the historical position of animals in relation to tourism through the social values of the time rather than through a contemporary lens. The next part of the chapter explores linkages between animal welfare, conservation and sustainability within the context of tourism. The differences between these concepts are discussed, together with the overlaps between them, as there is a need to ensure that a holistic and sustainable approach is adopted in relation to both welfare and conservation.

The next focus in the chapter is on whether or not tourism and animal welfare are mutually exclusive. In doing so, it draws on and expands many issues that have already been raised. The section provides many examples that speak to the inclusivity of continuing tourism and ensuring good welfare, and also many that indicate areas of conflict. It is clear that it is important to look beneath the surface of a tourism experience in order to judge the intent of the tourists and operators regarding animal welfare. The last part of the chapter turns to the question of who is responsible for championing animal welfare in tourism and ensuring that it is good. This section considers the roles of all actors: the tourism industry, tourists, local people within the tourism destination, public authorities, people in general, and animal protection organizations in promoting animal welfare in and through tourism.

Animal Welfare in Tourism: Topics

Context

Chapter 2 provides a scientific rationale for animal welfare. Yet we also need to recognize that concern for animal welfare is grounded within a human constructed social and cultural reality. Social and cultural values, which underpin human behaviour, and laws, rules and standards, both written and unwritten, may be influenced by scientific evidence but they are not entirely governed by it. Within this context, while welfare is an animal characteristic and its assessment should be scientific, people have concerns about animal welfare and make ethical decisions about it so there are social as well as scientific aspects to the discussion of it. Recognizing this means that we need to consider the temporal and spatial specificity of social values when looking at the history and geography of animal welfare and tourism.

If we look at history solely through our contemporary eyes and with our contemporary mindset, we are likely to come away disappointed in our ancestors. We are likely to be disappointed, even disgusted at much of their behaviour and many of their decisions. For example, we now feel little sympathy for systems across history that have rationalized and promoted slavery, that have viewed women, those of colour, and those identifying as something other than heterosexual as being markedly inferior to the dominant white, Anglo-Saxon Protestant heterosexual male. To espouse such beliefs today is widely considered to be highly inappropriate and is likely to be met with social sanctions. Yet these sanctions are socially constructed, just like the views they are designed to counteract. In other words, views that today result in social censure if publicly espoused have historically existed in the mainstream of social thinking. In former times, to criticize these views would have resulted in having to face the moral outrage of society.

What does this mean for looking at the history of animal welfare in general and specifically in relation to tourism? It means that we should take care not to simply adopt a position of moral righteousness born of the privileged position of living now rather than then. Instead, we should try to look at history in its context. This is not to say that whatever happened in a historical period was right or justified by the prevalent social values of the time but that we should take care to not judge people and their actions and positions purely in the context of the social values of today.

Just as we recognize that social values are prone to change over time, we must also note the spatial specificity of such values. In this way, it is important to recognize that geography matters, even in an age of unparalleled globalization, when considering social values and moral standpoints. Ignoring this fuels claims of imperialism and may hamper debates about contentious issues such as animal rights and welfare.

Zoos

Broadly speaking, the history of animal welfare in tourism mirrors the broader history of animal welfare across society and the economy. In other words, the concerns of tourists and the tourism industry with animals and their welfare have changed in the same way as general society concerns with animals. This means that, historically the tourism industry has a poor record of animal welfare if judged by today's standards, but that, in some ways and in some places, it is improving. An example of this change is the zoo. Chapter 3 has already provided some discussion of the history of zoos, noting their existence across several thousand years. The original zoos created by European royalty were mainly concerned with the displaying of animals as trophies. These animals were objects, utilized as a means of indicating dominance, over nature and over the states who had gifted the animals in the first place. In this way there was little, or no concern for the welfare of the animals.

Following on from this, the animals became items of amusement, curios to be displayed for their entertainment value (Carr and Cohen, 2011). Still there was no concern about the welfare of the animals, though those charged with ensuring they did not die undeniably felt a certain amount of pressure associated with their work, especially given the very limited knowledge of animal nutrition and other needs in the early centuries of the zoos. Yet this concern did not extend to what, as noted in Chapter 2, we would define as welfare today. Rather, it was about survival of the animals for the continued enjoyment of their human owners. In this way, the animals were little different from the suites of luxury cars kept today by some of the mega-rich.

Such cars are serviced, polished and maintained with a huge amount of care and attention to detail. There is, however, no real care for the car – why should there be? After all, they are merely objects. Instead, all the care lavished on the cars is for the benefit of the owner. In the same way, the early zoos, while developing skills in the maintenance of animals under their control that increased animal lifespans, did nothing more than they would have done if looking after any other prized object. Yet if we remember to take off our contemporary glasses, through which society may view such history with distaste, even disgust, we must see that such a positioning of zoo animals was entirely in keeping with societal constructions of animals at the time. They were objects, to be owned by humans for the benefit of humans. How they were kept and treated within zoos was entirely appropriate, in the eyes of society at that time.

By the 1950s we see the beginnings of a different social mindset regarding animals. Here we see the spreading of the idea of animals as sentient beings and the rise of debates surrounding animal rights and welfare. Zoos did not begin this change but they certainly had to respond to it and continue to have to do so (Beardsworth and Bryman, 2001). They have had to shift away from the objectification of animals purely for human entertainment and begin to consider animal welfare. The extent to which zoos have engaged with this shift is linked to the strength of the rise of animal welfare concerns in the geographically specific social context in which each zoo is located. People who knew about the biology, and especially the behaviour, of animals, began in the 1970s to criticize zoos that did not provide for the needs of the animals. The zoos initially largely ignored this view but put more effort into justifying their policies in relation to their collections. They started to provide more information about the lives and functioning of the animals and to advocate conservation of animals in the wild. However, they seldom referred to the welfare of the animals.

In the 1980s, zoos were more strongly criticized by animal protection groups, in particular Zoo Check, now the Born Free Foundation (see Jamieson, 1985). Scientific publications had reported for many years on the extreme abnormal behaviour of some zoo animals. As explained by Kiley-Worthington (1990) and Broom (2002): first, when wild animals are brought into captivity their welfare is very poor and they show extreme responses, often including immunosuppression and consequent mortality from latent pathogens. Second, close confinement results in poor welfare in most vertebrate animals. Poor welfare when kept in some degree of confinement is much more likely in animals that are not domesticated than in domesticated animals. Where the needs of animals are not met in zoo conditions they may show behavioural abnormalities such as apathy involving reduced responsiveness, stereotypies, self-mutilation or increased aggression. It seems that elephants are one of a group of species whose individuals find zoo conditions particularly difficult. Others in this group are most bears, active small carnivores, many primates and cetaceans (Jantschke, 1997). In addition, many zoos fail to provide for the needs of the animals, so that welfare is usually poor in social animals deprived of adequate social contact, grazers unable to graze, excavators unable to excavate, animals that are frightened of humans or conspecifics but unable to hide from them, and all animals in barren environments (Broom, 2002). Broom emphasized that locomotion is important to many animals, so, as a general principle, captive condition space should be related to the locomotion shown by an actively moving or moderately disturbed individual, so all animals should be able to show normal locomotion for at least 5 seconds.

Clubb and Mason (2003) reported that animals that range over large areas in the wild are less well able to adapt to zoo environments and concluded that many of such species should not be kept in zoos as their welfare could never be good. For example, while brown bears, American mink and snow leopards adapted quite well to zoo conditions, clouded leopards and polar bears were likely to show stereotypies and other abnormal behaviour and physiology. The needs of some small animals and some domesticated animals can be met and their welfare can be good in zoos. However, the needs of many animals are not met in most zoo conditions. When animals are obviously adversely affected by the conditions in zoos, members of the public may refuse to visit the establishments, exhibits or performances (Margodt, 2000). While this is the case, there are still plenty of people willing to visit zoos, as evidenced by the continuing popularity of these tourism attractions.

The conclusions reached about zoos by Broom (2002) were as follows:

(i) The welfare of animals of some species is too poor in zoos to justify ever keeping them.
(ii) Zoos should keep other animals only when the negative aspects of welfare are adequately counterbalanced by the positive value of zoos.
(iii) The major value of zoos is in education.
(iv) People who experience animals in zoos, especially in good conditions, are more likely to care about animals, including their conservation.
(v) The major impact of zoos on conservation is via education.
(vi) The direct impact of zoos on conservation in the wild (i.e. by breeding and releasing animals), has, to date, been negligible for most species. In only a few species has the wild population been affected by zoo breeding.
(vii) Breeding is better done in specialist places with no public access; this is because of the negative effects of exposure to humans and difficulties in providing experience about food finding and predator avoidance.
(viii) A further positive aspect of zoos is that they have therapeutic benefits for people who feel better because of contact with the animals.

In a clear sign of the societal shift towards greater awareness of the needs and rights of animals, some people today voice an opinion that zoos are a dated concept that can never be dissociated from the objectification of animals and should be closed down. Some see all attempts by zoos to improve the welfare of their animals as nothing more than a distraction designed to hide the ongoing abuse of animals that they think should not be in captivity at all. An opposite perspective is that some zoos are increasingly concerned with the welfare of their animals and the conservation of each species and are doing everything they can to ensure good welfare in the animals in their establishments and the conservation of their wild brethren. As part of this process, we have seen a shift away from traditional zoo cages to larger enclosures that incorporate natural elements, both to stimulate animals and to allow them to hide from the unremitting gaze of visitors when they wish. Interacting with animals is either prevented or is undertaken in strictly controlled settings, with visitors banned from feeding animals or treating them as toys during encounter sessions. The result today is that zoos are still very popular tourist attractions, even among those people who are concerned about the welfare of animals in such places (Curtin and Green, 2018).

The evidence from scientific studies (e.g. Hill and Broom, 2009) is helping zoos, tourism companies and the public to decide, first, which species of animals can be kept in captivity without negative effects on their welfare and which cannot and, second, what conditions and treatments in zoos generally result in good welfare and which do not. Individual tourist and tourism companies are then in a position to adopt policies as to which zoo, aquarium or other wildlife exhibits to visit and which to avoid. In addition, where appropriate laws exist, national and local government agencies can use the evidence to close down some zoos and exhibits but permit the continuation of others. Those who manage or otherwise work in zoos can use scientific information about animal welfare to evaluate their own animal conditions and management methods and to present information to the public in an informed and unbiased way.

Some animals have much more difficulty in adapting to captivity than others (Mason, 2010). There is now a substantial list of animals, including those noted earlier in this section, that do not adapt well enough to captivity to warrant keeping them in zoos, aquaria or other animal exhibits or otherwise presenting them in captivity as a tourist attraction. Elephants are a prime example. In zoos they frequently show abnormal behaviour, such as stereotypies and aggression, that indicates poor welfare. The animal that causes the largest number of deaths in zoo staff is the elephant. Animals in captivity are protected from starvation, predation, disease and other impacts of conditions in natural environments so their life expectancy should be greater than that of animals in the wild. However, if their needs are not met and their welfare is poor, life expectancy is reduced. Clubb *et al.* (2008), who studied 4500 elephants, found that their median lifespan in European zoos was only half that of elephants in protected populations in range countries. The ability of captive elephants to reproduce is lower in zoo conditions than in natural conditions (Clubb *et al.*, 2009) and elephant populations in captivity, whether in zoos or not, are not sustained by births in captivity. As a result, captive populations, whether in zoos or in 'working' conditions, have to be supplemented by young elephants taken from the wild. These elephants are almost always 'trained' using violent methods such as a knife in the neck (see also Chapters 10 and 11).

There is also evidence about life expectancy in captivity, and hence welfare, for some dolphin and whale species. When these animals were brought into captivity and kept in what were essentially swimming pools designed for humans, their life expectancy in captivity was very much shorter than in the wild. Many died within a year. Longevity of orcas in the wild is reported to be 60–70 years for females and 50–60 years for males. Median survivorship in the wild, according to one calculation taking account of early mortality, is 15 years. Jett and Ventre (2015) carried out an analysis of 201 orcas in zoos and aquaria. For those entering captivity before 1985, the median survival estimate was 4 years. However, with more large aquaria and better care, after 1985 the orca survival was 12 years. Another study with smaller samples and somewhat different conclusions is that of Robeck *et al.* (2015). In addition to this evidence about welfare from life expectancy, there is evidence about the extent of abnormal behaviours that are indicators of poor welfare. Orcas show stereotypies and other abnormal behaviour in zoo conditions. High level of aggression is an abnormal behaviour and orcas have several times killed other orcas, zoo staff or other persons. This would seem to be anomalous behaviour associated with captivity, as no wild orca has ever been recorded to seriously injure a human (Marino and Frohoff, 2011).

Many efforts have been made in zoos to enrich the environment and hence to improve welfare. Many of the early attempts did not consider what the animals need but were aimed more at what human visitors might like to see. Pictures of the natural environment generally did not improve the life of the captive animals. However, some recent attempts have been more biologically sensible and often do have the effect of reducing stereotypies and other abnormal behaviour (Swaisgood and Shepherdson, 2005; Alligood and Leighty, 2015). Other attempts are based more on guesswork than science and may or may not have any useful effect (Law and Kitchener, 2017). Enrichment attempts may involve objects, tasks with food as a reward, gross structure of the exhibit, human contact, or contact with members of their own species. Tourists will not always easily understand what is being done for the animals so explanation is needed. Other ways of improving the welfare of the animals are to give better food, deal with health problems better and shield animals from undesirable human contact, or sometimes all human contact. Again, explanation for the viewing public is necessary. The greatest problem for the animals occurs when animal accommodation and management cannot be modified in such a way that the welfare is good. In that case, the animal should ideally be moved to a different zoo or aquarium where its needs can be met. If this cannot be done and return to the wild is impossible, it may be more ethical for it to be humanely killed than for it to be kept in conditions where its welfare is very poor, though this is a highly emotive issue. In any of these cases, no further animals of the species should be kept in the inadequate circumstances.

Today, animal encounters in zoos and visits to the zoo in general, while still clearly a leisure activity, are now often wrapped up in educational messages aimed at wildlife and natural habitat preservation (World Association of Zoos and Aquariums, 2005). Furthermore, many zoos now have active programmes aimed at wildlife preservation in the wild. Does this mean zoos are now fully engaged with animal welfare debates? It is more accurate to say that most are now far more interested in animal welfare for the sake of the animals than has historically been the case. However, there are good examples and bad examples of zoos, as defined by the dominant global social values of today, and there are no perfect examples.

It is clearly the case that concern for animal welfare must exist alongside the economic reality that zoos cannot make a financial loss if they are to survive. In this way they are the same as all animal tourism experiences. They exist within the neo-liberal capitalist reality; in order to survive and have a chance of contributing to the preservation of wild animals and their habitats they must generate income. For virtually all zoos, the primary source of such income is tourists who, despite changing social attitudes, still primarily go to zoos and engage with other animal tourism experiences in order to be entertained.

So what does a good example of a 21st-century zoo look like? Such zoos, while still funded through visitors who seek entertainment, may be seen, and certainly portray themselves as, sites for education and learning about the importance and value of the conservation of animals and their natural environments. Through this, zoos and related associations argue, societal change may be driven. These zoos also act as breeding sites for endangered animals and engage in natural environment preservation and re-wilding programmes. While even these zoos are still guilty, to varying degrees, of pandering to the entertainment desires of visitors, there are some, in various parts of the world, including Asia and the Middle East, where entertainment is still the primary, and indeed often the only, rationale for a zoo. In such zoos, animals and their welfare are arguably stuck in 19th- and 20th-century thinking, where the animals are still seen as objects to be used for the satisfaction of human leisure desires. In this context, any good welfare is still because of the entertainment and economic value the animals represent rather than because they are important and of value in their own right.

Circuses

People who are on holiday are a significant part of the audience in circuses. Furthermore, even though many visitors to the circus may not be tourists they are all engaging in a leisure experience. In this way, it is important to recognize the close practical and conceptual links between tourism and leisure (Carr, 2002) and the implications for animal welfare. In the past, most circuses included 'animal acts' and some still do now. Animal welfare problems for animals in circuses include: poor living conditions while travelling; poor living conditions during periods when there is no travelling; harsh training methods; and the circus acts in front of the public (Regan, 2004). The accommodation on vehicles that can be moved from place to place as the circus travels is necessarily small for the larger animals. Lions, tigers, elephants etc. must be in small cages if they are to be driven down a road. In some cases, circus animals are tethered or kept in small spaces in 'winter quarters' as well. Close confinement results in poor welfare in most vertebrate animals. Poor welfare when kept in some degree of confinement is much more likely in animals that are not domesticated than in domesticated animals. Where the needs of animals are not met in circus conditions, they may show behavioural abnormalities such as apathy involving reduced responsiveness, stereotypies, self-mutilation or increased aggression (Kiley-Worthington, 1990). In a study of elephants kept in circus winter quarters and often harshly treated, stereotypies occupied much of the waking life of some individuals. For example, one elephant showed stereotypies for 57% of the daylight period, while in another it was 71%. There was variation among individuals in the extent to which the stereotypies were interrupted by people in the vicinity, social contact with other elephants, or provision of food (Broom, 2002, describing a study by Kirkden and Broom). The needs of an animal like a lion or an elephant clearly cannot be met when the animal is living for some weeks in a circus truck. Circus elephants studied by Friend (1999) in the United States were tethered by the leg throughout the time that they were not performing in the circus ring and showed various behavioural abnormalities.

The training of animals like horses and dogs can be carried out in a way that does not result in poor welfare. Hence some circus acts may be an entertainment for the animal as well as for the public watching. However, it is unlikely that any training of non-domesticated animals such as lions, tigers, bears and elephants, can be carried out without some degree of cruelty to the animals. This also does not mean that just because domestic animals can be trained in a manner that is not cruel, this is always the case. Circus owners always claimed that they trained animals in a kind way. For example, Mary Chipperfield, of the famous Chipperfield circus, in an interview with Palmer, stated that

> people who criticise circuses rarely know what they are complaining about. They never actually come and see the animals being trained. They imagine that we beat them into submission. We are training tigers at the moment. If I were to beat them to go over to where they must sit, all they would do is hide under the seat on which they are supposed to mount. When animals are your livelihood you are hardly likely to be cruel to them. (Palmer, 1983, p. 32)

However, covert filming of such training has on several occasions resulted in trainers in high-profile circuses, including Mary Chipperfield, being convicted for cruelty to the animals. The result of the evidence about poor living conditions for circus animals and cruel training practices in order to get the animals to perform in the circus ring has resulted in members of the public in more and more countries refusing to go to circuses that have animal acts. In addition, some countries and some local authorities have banned circuses with animal acts. In other instances, once famous circuses, such as the Ringling Brothers, have closed down in the face of the shift in public opinion and declining visitor numbers (Kiley-Worthington, 1990). There has been public pressure to bring about these changes, some from tourists. However, many countries still allow various animal acts and tourists continue to have a role to play in preventing the continuation of those that are associated with poor welfare of animals. The problem with animal acts is that they are not restricted to circuses. Instead, they have a long history in zoos, though today they are presented to audiences as demonstrations of natural animal behaviour for the education of the public. However, it is links like this that help to fuel anti-zoo sentiment and why the blending of education and entertainment (i.e. edutainment) in zoos must not be allowed to veer too far towards entertainment that is associated with circuses.

Donkeys

Other forms of animal tourism that mirror the history of zoos regarding animal welfare concerns abound. The position of donkeys in the tourism experience would be one such example. These creatures were to be found on the beaches of the seaside resorts of the UK during much of the

19th and 20th centuries, where people would pay to ride on them. The welfare of these animals was of minimal concern when compared with the desire to profit from them. Any care provided was focused on maintenance of the donkey as a tool rather than a sentient being. This contrasts today with such tourist attractions as the Donkey Sanctuary in Devon, UK. Here, as at the beaches, donkeys are still a tourist attraction from which money is generated. The difference is that it is a sanctuary; its reason for existing is the welfare of donkeys, not to profit by them. Funds generated from visitors are utilized to improve donkey welfare within the sanctuary and beyond. This is an issue that is hard to specify but very important: it is not the position of an animal in the tourism experience that determines whether its welfare is good or poor but the underlying rationale for its position in the industry. This matters even where, for example, a donkey providing rides on the beach is well cared for and whose owners conform to all the legal animal welfare guidelines compared with a donkey at a sanctuary who meets and interacts with visitors and whose owners meet all the same guidelines. In one case, the donkey may still simply be a tool from which to profit, while in the other the donkey may be viewed as a sentient animal to whom we, as humans, have obligations. We can never have the same kinds of obligations to objects. The tricky point is that even the person who owns the donkey that gives rides on the beach may see the animal as being sentient. Thus, it is the context behind the surface that matters in determining the treatment of the animal and hence its welfare, not just the activity in which the animal is engaged as part of the tourism experience.

Donkeys and mules are also used to carry tourists in many other countries. For example, on the small path leading to a glacier in the French Pyrenees, paths to archaeological sites in the Andes and many tourist routes in mountainous areas of Nepal. Some of these donkeys can carry their human rider and walk sure-footedly on the path with no difficulty. Others may have a rider who weighs as much as they do, or more. The tourists may find it amusing to see the little donkey carrying the big fat tourist. However, the risk of injury and the extent of fatigue for the donkey or mule may result in physiological responses, tissue damage and other pathology at a level that, in some countries, could result in a prosecution for cruelty. In many parts of the world, donkeys and mules carry heavy luggage for tourists, again with the risk of poor welfare ranging from very low to very high. In most countries there is no donkey sanctuary to which the sick, injured or aged animal can go. The people who own the donkeys may try hard to avoid problems for the donkeys or mules, in particular because they depend on the animals for their livelihoods, but they may be too poor to pay for veterinary care. International animal protection organizations like SPANA (Society for the Protection of Animals Abroad), World Horse Welfare, the Brooke and the Donkey Sanctuary arrange veterinary care for draught animals and education of their owners, thereby improving welfare for many animals. However, the majority of draught animals that carry tourists need welfare standards to be imposed by tourist organizations and by individual tourists themselves. Tourists who see an overloaded donkey whose welfare is clearly poor, or indeed an overloaded and perhaps elderly human carrying bags for a tourist who could easily carry them himself, should refuse to pay for such action and perhaps try to change the situation (see Chapter 13 for more on donkeys and mules).

A recent problem for donkeys, and for the owners of donkeys, is that in some countries the skin of donkeys has been marketed as having aphrodisiac or other miraculous properties. The result of this is that a trade has developed, somewhat like the rhinoceros horn trade. There is suddenly a great demand for donkey skins and not enough donkeys are dying naturally, so they are being killed for their skins. In some African countries there are reports of donkeys, often owned by poor people, being killed and the carcasses left after the skin has been taken off. In the worst cases, the donkey is immobilized by having its Achilles tendons cut and the skin is removed from a live animal. At a meeting of representatives from African countries in 2017 there was an agreement that attempts to deal with this problem would be an animal welfare priority for all of the countries. While this may not be directly a tourism issue, it is arguably the responsibility of tourists (as discussed elsewhere in this book) to support efforts to stop it and ensure they do not directly or indirectly do anything to encourage the activity.

Tourists viewing and engaging with marine mammals at sea

Marine mammals number about 120 species including cetaceans (whales, dolphins), pinnipeds (seals, sea-lions), sirenians (manatees, dugongs), sea otters and polar bears. All of these may be viewed by tourists during commercial tourism activities, although polar bear watching in Arctic Canada mainly occurs on land. How can the welfare of these mammals be affected by the tourism activities? One effect to consider is that the profits of tourism can be sufficiently large that local people and governments do not want the animals killed and there is public pressure for the marine habitats to be protected in order to conserve the animals. Since most marine mammal-chasing and -killing procedures cause very poor welfare for long periods in some animals (Broom, 2013, 2016), avoidance of killing reduces the amount of poor welfare in the animals. Most countries now protect some or all marine mammal species and many communities where there was formerly hunting of the animals now make much more money from keeping the animals alive and organizing tourist visits to see them. This has not entirely prevented the continuation of the hunting of a variety of animals (e.g. whales and dolphins) for economic gain even in the face of protectionist policies and activities, though it may have helped to kerb such activities.

Boat approach for observation, chasing and swimming with marine mammals may cause avoidance behaviour, reduced time for foraging, social disruption, injury, increased disease, reduced breeding success and reduced life expectancy. All of these are indicators of poor welfare. However, well-controlled observation methods may cause no negative effects on the animals (Higham and Bejder, 2008; Higham *et al.*, 2009, 2014). When a boat carrying tourists arrives in an area where whales are feeding or resting, the animals can sometimes easily move away. However, short-term avoidance consequences for cetaceans close to tourists may include less time for feeding and social disruption (Higham *et al.*, 2014). On occasions when the whales have just surfaced after a long dive, perhaps searching for food by echo-location at great depths (Johnson *et al.*, 2004), they may need to rest because of exhaustion or nitrogen narcosis management (Hooker *et al.*, 2012). They may not then be easily able to move away from a tourist boat, so failure to move away from the boat does not necessarily mean tolerance of boat proximity. There are also concerns about the potential for noise pollution caused by cruise ships to disrupt aquatic mammal welfare, even though they are simply transiting an area rather than deliberately searching for animal encounters for their passengers. Of course, such disruption is not restricted to cruise ships but it is a concern given the increasing scale of this segment of the tourism industry.

When mother harp seals with pups were subjected to close contact with tourists, many of the mothers were found to desert their pups for some time and pups often showed freezing behaviour (a defensive behaviour akin to the more widely known fight-or-flight response) for a while (Kovacs and Innes, 1990). These observations indicate some degree of poor welfare and, if the behaviours were prolonged, more serious effects would occur. Dolphin populations have sometimes been found to decline where dolphin watching occurred but there was no decline where there was no dolphin watching (Higham and Bejder, 2008).

Where tourists were allowed to swim with dolphins, afterwards there was increased avoidance of swimmers in the study by Constantine (2001). Similarly, Lundquist *et al.* (2013)

reported more avoidance of people and boats and some disruption of social groups after people had been swimming with whales. Whether on the boat or swimming with the animals, tourists have expectations of getting very close to the animals and show their disappointment if they do not. Because of this, many boats chase the animals (Marino, 2013). Actions by those controlling the boat are sometimes inconsistent, depending on the demands of the tourists, and hence are difficult for the whales, dolphins or seals to predict. If the distance between boats and the animals and between swimmers and animals is sufficient and predictable, the negative effects on welfare may not occur. The distance required to prevent poor welfare in the observed animals varies with species and previous experience with humans (see Chapter 7 for a discussion of the impacts of tourism on dolphins).

Boat trips with the aim of encountering marine mammals can provide an opportunity for education of tourists about conservation and animal welfare. This can be a good effect of marine mammal-watching trips. But do the tourists want to be educated? Studies by Lück (2003, 2015) suggest that many do. However, there is a great range in the quality of information given (Curtin *et al.*, 2009). It is often poor, making no mention of the effects on the welfare of the animals, and tends to be uncritical of the tourist company in particular and the tourism industry more generally. The issues associated with education of tourists on this kind of trip are similar to those related to zoos.

There should always be codes of practice, and ideally laws, regulating marine mammal-watching trips. Unregulated whale-watching and penguin-watching has caused many problems for the animals. People coming close to turtles and operators offering shark cage diving experiences can also cause poor welfare if the tourists and tour operators do not abide by strict codes of practice (see Chapter 8 on shark cage diving). Many countries have no laws or scientifically based codes of practice, while others, such as Canada, do have such controls. Canadian legislation on the observation of marine life prohibits boats from approaching closer than 100 metres from a whale and prohibits staying in the vicinity of a whale for more than 30 minutes. Yet at the same time in Canada it is legal to keep marine mammals such as dolphins and orcas in restricted pools within aquaria.

Fishing and trophy-hunting tourism

The methods used during commercial fishing, whaling, or other wild animal hunting are starting to be considered in relation to their impact on the welfare and conservation of the animals. Methods that lead to long periods of pain before death are condemned while humane killing, where death is instantaneous, is promoted. Some of the initially considered impacts are on non-target species. For example, commercial fishing with nets kills some marine mammals through drowning.

Those associated with the killing of animals in tourism for pleasure have similarly, to an extent, begun to consider animal welfare. In particular, sports fishing has begun, as noted in Chapter 3, to promote catch-and-release policies and many authorities now strictly enforce such behaviour in relation to iconic sports fishing species. Trophy-hunting tourism on land has not, however, engaged with the idea of humane killing, though it is more difficult when the activity does not take place in the controlled environment of the abattoir but out in the 'wild'. Fishing and trophy-hunting tourism can also have an adverse impact on non-target species. Fishermen and those who control the fishing sites may kill or prevent the reintroduction of animals such as seals, otters and cormorants that are perceived as competitors for the fish. On land, grouse and pheasants that are reared to be shot in the wild by tourists are protected from predators, often by killing the latter.

A central issue for tourism is where the main objective of the tourist visit is to kill or deliberately harm animals. Fishing or hunting by people in a subsistence economy, who need to eat the fish or other animals that they catch in order to survive, would be condemned by few who are concerned about animal welfare. Where possible, even the poorest people should use methods of capture and killing that minimize negative effects on the welfare of the animals. The same cannot be said for where the main objective is, as in the case of tourists, to kill an animal for the pleasure and social kudos to be gained by doing so.

Fishing is a major tourist activity in some countries (e.g. Scotland and New Zealand). Most of the fish are caught using a hook and line. Most biological scientists now accept that the pain system in fish is very similar to that in humans. The region of the brain where the analysis of the pain stimuli occurs is different but the sensory, transmission and analysis systems are extremely similar (Braithwaite, 2010; Broom, 2014, 2016). The emergency physiological responses of fish to very dangerous situations, such as being taken out of water, are the same as those of mammals in very dangerous situations. As a consequence, catching fish for entertainment purposes using a hook that damages tissue and causes pain, and taking fish out of water causing stress and immunosuppression, are unacceptable activities to more and more people. However, this must be set alongside the fact that fishing is one of the world's most popular leisure activities (Mordue and Wilson, 2018). The impact of the catching procedure on welfare would be the same if the fish was humanely killed but the question of whether or not the whole procedure is ethical would depend upon whether the person was fishing for vital food or just for entertainment.

There is, today, wide condemnation of any person who shoots a lion or rhinoceros because the shooter finds the act exciting, or to impress others (see Chapter 17 for more about hunting). On the other hand, many hunters persuade themselves that the animals do not feel pain, or that animal welfare is an unimportant matter, or that the animals are there for human benefit, or that hunting by humans is a natural activity and therefore all consequences are acceptable. Many hunters have their own codes of practice (Serpell, 1986), the aim of which is to minimize poor welfare though not to eliminate it if doing so would preclude the hunting activity (see Chapter 18 on ethical hunting). When an animal is shot, death can be instantaneous or occur very rapidly after the shooting. Deer shot accurately in the head or neck show low levels of physiological response (Bateson and Bradshaw, 1997). However, professional shooters may injure the animal rather than killing it and tourist hunters are much more likely to do this. An injured animal may be killed by the hunter soon after the first shot or it may escape and hide. Many shot animals which escape will die slowly of their wounds with very high levels of pain and other poor welfare. Hunting with guns or bows for amusement is an activity with high welfare costs to the hunted animals. This is also true for the shooting of wild boar, deer or African animals bred and kept in reserves so that tourists can pay to shoot them, or animals bred and released in order to be shot by tourists.

Although not a mainstream component of tourism, hunting foxes, deer or other animals on horseback with packs of dogs, something that is clearly a leisure activity. The extreme fear of the hunted deer or fox is evident from its behaviour in the latter stage of the hunt when the chased animal realizes that the large numbers of dogs and humans behind it are likely to catch it. The measures of cortisol and several other indicators of poor welfare in deer at the end of a hunt (Bateson and Bradshaw, 1997) were higher than those recorded anywhere else in deer (Broom, 1999). The extremely poor welfare of these hunted deer was much worse than that of all cleanly shot deer. Those defending hunting with dogs have suggested that the physiological and behavioural changes merely indicate the excitement of the deer in its contest with the pursuers, but the emergency responses are much greater than during excitement and the behaviour is different. Such information has contributed to the banning of hunting with dogs in some countries. Yet there are still people who strongly object to governmental intrusion on their leisure activities (e.g. the hunting ban in England; see Carr, 2014 for more discussion of animal welfare and fox hunting).

Tourist photography and impact on animals

Among the tourists of a century ago it was not uncommon to wish to kill mammals and birds and have them stuffed for displaying in houses or other places. The ultimate example of this desire is related to the safari parks of Southern Africa in the 20th century. Now, the desire of tourists to get close to animals is more commonly linked to the desire to take photographs of the animals. The nature of the photos taken has been associated with the available technology. In order to get close enough to take the perfect photo, many tourists have attempted to get closer to animals, both wild and domesticated, than is healthy for either themselves or the animals. Even with the advent of the telephoto lens, a proportion of tourists still wished to get closer to wild animals than was safe.

The desire to photograph and be photographed with animals has led to many instances of poor animal welfare and abuse. The infamous tiger temple in Thailand is an example of where animals are abused for the benefit of tourists. While an extreme example, the tiger temple is not alone in offering tourists the opportunity to take photos with wild animals. Some zoos around the world offer similar experiences, including Singapore Zoo, which offers the opportunity to have photos taken with orangutans, and Lone Pine Koala Sanctuary in Brisbane, which offers tourists the chance to have their photo taken with a koala. While in these examples the animals are in the care of expert staff, operating under specific rules regarding animal welfare, the potential for animals suffering stress is still clear. Furthermore, while the gains for tourists (satisfaction of desire) and tourism operators (economic gains beyond the price of entry to zoos and sanctuaries) are clear, there is no apparent potential gain for the animals that may offset the potential detrimental impacts on their welfare.

Tourist visits to wildlife reserves may help conservation and welfare of the animals but certain practices of tourists and for tourists may have negative effects. Some tourists in hides, vehicles or boats make much noise and cause animals to have to move away from resources that may be important to them. Some guides drive too close and may separate animals from groups, making them vulnerable to predators. These practices have sometimes been demonstrated to cause the death of young or other animals. Where the objective is to see and photograph birds, guides may use playback of bird sounds to encourage birds to come close enough to be seen. This may have only a trivial effect in that the cost to the bird is a small increment in energy expended. However, if done too often or in difficult circumstances for the bird, it may have the effect of preventing it from getting enough food to survive, impeding its ability to feed its young, causing fear when the proximity of humans is detected, or exposing it to a high risk of predation that would not exist if it had stayed in a safe place. Hence the tourists wanting to see the birds may sometimes cause poor welfare or even the deaths of those birds. Another practice that helps tourists to see and photograph birds and other wildlife is to provide food for the animals. Where this is a table with feeders for birds, this leads to a high density of individuals in the vicinity of the food supply because individuals are recruited to the area from elsewhere by the food. This may lead to a very competitive environment for the birds and poorer welfare for some as a consequence. If the food supply is withdrawn, some individuals may have difficulty finding a suitable feeding area and food supply. Predators may learn that many prey individuals can be found near the food provision area so the prey species may be subject to attacks. The same problems apply to provision of food for fish or cetaceans. Both playback of sounds and food provisioning should be prohibited in circumstances where harm to the animals is possible. Where there is evidence that it does not cause harm, they should be used carefully.

With the advent of digital photography and social media, as noted in Chapter 3, we have seen the advent of the 'selfie' of the photographer with the animal. These selfies are bringing wild animals and people into even closer proximity than was the case in the pre-digital camera era. Humans are perceived as potential predators by most wild animals and are more frightening if they are close. This may lead to many of the issues noted earlier in this chapter with the disruption to aquatic mammals by tour boats. In addition, it may lead to animals acting in a defensive manner that may harm the tourist. In these instances, there is the danger that the animal will subsequently be killed by authorities concerned more with the welfare of tourists than the animals they may disturb.

An example of the harm that can be caused by this craze was reported by the animal charity Equinac in the summer of 2017. At the resort Mojácar in southern Spain, tourists found a baby dolphin swimming in shallow water but separated from its mother. They caught it and a series of people handled it, photographed it in the water and took 'selfies' of themselves holding the dolphin out of the water. The young dolphin was handled for some time before any help was called, and it consequently died.

Professional wildlife photographers are usually much more careful to avoid actions that might have bad effects on their animal subjects, or themselves. They may be catering to a tourist audience, or to a 'stay at home and marvel at nature' audience, but they are generally concerned to preserve what they want to photograph. Clear examples of this are the BBC teams who produce films such as *Life on Earth*. Presenters like David Attenborough have well-publicized concerns about conservation and animal welfare and the photographers have high standards in their attempts not to damage the wildlife that they portray. Yet it is important to note that the motivation of tourists and professional photographers to gain a picture of an animal are very different. Most of the people, like David Attenborough, who are making films have much more knowledge than the average person taking a 'selfie', who would probably be appalled to know that they had contributed to an animal's death. In this respect, education and availability of information about animal welfare in tourist sites is important. If the local government, tourist guide or hotel owner in an area is deriving benefit from the enthusiasm of tourists for the presence of animals, each of those organizations and people have an obligation to provide information to tourists in order to prevent harms to animals. If the young dolphin died in your town, you the local government and citizens of the town are, to some extent, to blame if you did not provide effective warnings and information to tourists.

Conclusions

While social attitudes and values may change at a particular speed it is necessary to recognize that infrastructure constructed during one era often cannot easily be changed when a new component of moral conscience develops. Again, the example of the zoo is a useful one to employ. The older zoos of the world (look at London Zoo and Tiergarten Schönbrunn for example) were initially created at a time of very different social values to that which exist today. A look at the history of any of these zoos shows attempts by them to both lead change and also a need to respond to change. This has involved numerous rebuilding and renovation initiatives to change the living conditions of the animals they house. Yet the problem of course is that space and money is limited. The arguably simplistic solution is to close zoos but if we reject this then we have to recognize that there is always likely to be a lag between the rate of social change and changes in infrastructure designed to house animals in places like zoos. Moving on from recognizing the spatial and temporal specificity of the social construction of animal welfare and its implications for animal-related tourism, the rest of the chapter now focuses on the issue of whether tourism and animal welfare are mutually exclusive or potentially inclusive.

Animal Welfare, Conservation and Sustainability Within Tourism

Beginning at the most generalist level, a discussion of the link between tourism and animal welfare must consider issues of conservation and sustainability. The concept of sustainability is not a new one, having been widely discussed elsewhere both in general and with specific reference to tourism (see Swarbrooke, 1999; Hall *et al.*, 2015). When we talk of sustainability, we have the idea that we should consider the future and utilize the resources of the Earth in such a manner as to allow future generations to achieve a similar standard of living to that which we have now. A definition of sustainability is: a system or procedure is sustainable if it is acceptable now and if its expected future effects are acceptable, in particular in relation to resource availability, consequences of functioning and morality of action (Broom, 2014). A system might be unsustainable because of: inefficient usage of world food resources; adverse effects on human health; poor welfare of animals; harmful environmental effects such as low biodiversity or insufficient conservation; unacceptable genetic modification; not being 'fair trade' in that producers in poor countries are not properly rewarded; or damage to rural communities. One problem with the ways in which the term sustainability has been used is that they tend to be human-centric. The standard of living and acceptability referred to are invariably human. Animals, if they feature at all in definitions of sustainability are either openly, or more commonly implicitly, seen as resources. There is no real suggestion that the concept of sustainability must be set within, or be able to create, a different economic reality from that which presently exists in current human society. Consequently, sustainability is generally seen to exist within the current neo-liberal capitalist system. This problem with the concept of sustainability has parallels with those for the concept of conservation. Initially that concept, in a wild animal context, may have been focused entirely on ensuring that species do not become extinct. Yet such a focus has come to be seen as overly simplistic and instead it has been recognized that to conserve a species we must also conserve their natural environment and the complex ecosystem of which they are a part. More recently, wildlife conservation organizations have gone further to recognize that, to be successful, conservation must be grounded in the wider reality of sustainability. Such a recognition is highlighted in Chapters 9 and 11 and also in the approach that the World Wide Fund for Nature now follows, as detailed on their website (https://www.worldwildlife.org). Yet, this in itself may not be sufficient if it does not take into account the notion that sustainability must not be about preservation of the status quo. Rather, recognizing that systems are constantly changing and fluctuating, the focus must be on the resilience of systems. In this way, in order to be successful, conservation of species must be focused on the resilience of them and the ecosystems they exist within to change. This shifts early concepts of sustainability as fixed to one where it allows systems to constantly change, without ever being destroyed (Oyarzun, 2017).

Arguably the difference between conservation on the one hand and welfare on the other is the focus of the former on the species level and the latter on the individual. However, this does not mean that there is no overlap between the two, far from it. Conservation studies are significantly devalued, and potentially less relevant, if they do not consider the welfare of the individual as well as conservation at the species level. Following a similar argument, animal welfare concerns that fail to address the survival of species can be devalued. It is within this context that it is important to address questions of the link between tourism and the conservation of species within the framework of sustainability.

Does tourism positively influence animal conservation? We have already seen in the previous chapter a range of ways in which the tourism industry has adversely affected the viability of individual species and their natural habitat. However, it is clear that the tourism industry can aid animal conservation. A powerful example of this is whale-watching tourism, with its potential to educate people about the value of live whales, as opposed to dead ones killed in the name of cuisine, fashion or science, and to provide former whaling communities with an alternative source of income and hence a rationale for engaging in whale conservation. There are, of course, a variety of other examples of conservation through tourism that are associated with different species. They include the mountain gorillas of Africa, the tigers of India, and the orangutans of Borneo and Sumatra. These examples all have one thing in common: the repositioning and rebranding of animals in human thinking by the tourism industry.

In this way, the tourism industry is at least partially responsible for the rebranding of various species as being worthy of conservation rather than as pests to be exterminated or matters of little importance. In this way the industry has often been a helper of various wildlife preservation groups and societies. The European wolf, bears, sea otters, orcas, lions, tigers, the European beaver and elephants are just a few of the animals that have been considered as pests or dangerous animals by humans and, in some cases, have subsequently been targeted for extermination. The animals were thought of as pests due to the perceived impact they have on farming or fishing. Yet wildlife tourism repositions them as 'must-see' animals that are thus socially and economically important to keep alive. Thus, the animals become positioned as being valuable in their own, individual right. They are then part of a broader collective that includes humans and gain a viable niche in the neo-liberal capitalist reality in the process. However, the success of efforts to remove the stigma of 'pest' are variable at best and it is certainly not only the tourism industry that is responsible for such efforts or to blame for any continued frictions between humans and animals that result in those animals still being defined as a pest by at least a portion of humanity. There is only a limited number of winners in this instance. The animals that the tourism industry is helping to transform from pests, or vermin to be exterminated, into those to be venerated and preserved are being placed into the same groupings as those noted in Chapter 3 when discussing animal attractiveness. In contrast to this situation, the tourism industry's vigilance in removing what it defines as pests from the holiday experience reinforces in the minds of tourists and society in general the identification of these animals as unwanted vermin to be destroyed. Mice, cockroaches, rats and flies are all examples of animals whose identification as pests is reinforced rather than repudiated by the tourism industry.

While some zoos are clearly profit-oriented, it is clear that others are more interested in preservation of endangered species and their natural environments. One of the latter is the recently renamed Jersey Zoo (see Chapter 6 for a discussion of the logic behind the renaming) that was created by the late Gerald Durrell. Indeed, Durrell (1976, p. 20) noted when talking about the zoo he planned to build, and eventually did on Jersey:

> Ideally, it [a zoo] would be a scientific research and breeding station, not open to the public, but I knew this to be impossible. We needed the visitors to provide us not only with the running expenses, but also the cash to repay the loan and the interest [used to start the zoo]. The zoo, therefore, would have to be sited either within easy reach of a large population, or else in a place that had a large influx of holidaymakers.

This speaks of a realization, at a comparatively early date, of the need to ground conservation within the neo-liberal capitalist reality.

Tourism in general and particularly animal-related tourism, just like the rest of society, has become increasingly good at speaking the language of conservation, of preserving wildlife and the natural habitats they need in order to survive. However, both are often guilty of focusing on specific animal types. As discussed in the previous chapter, people are drawn to particular types of animals and repelled by others. We are therefore happier to actively engage in conserving the former than the latter, and there is a tendency to encourage and support tourism operations to do so. With viable animal tourism businesses focused on animals that visitors wish to see, the conservation activities of the tourism industry are likewise unbalanced. This is potentially problematic when set alongside the recognition that a natural environment represents a diverse and complex ecosystem made up of a wide range of animals. For such an ecosystem to thrive, all its members should be present, not just those we happen to like. The tourism industry argues, not unfairly, that while they may focus on certain species, they use these as a way of protecting natural environments and this has positive implications for all animals, not just the ones we like the look of. Despite not being strongly encouraged by society to do so, the tourism industry can focus its efforts on less attractive animals. An example of this would be the work undertaken by Durrell Wildlife Park to return the red-billed chough to the island of Jersey. Here is a clear example of a tourism operator, a zoo in this case, aiding the conservation of a species that was not a significant tourist attraction. The key point is that Durrell did not undertake this programme to maximize profits. Hence the chough programme sits partially outside the neoliberal capitalist setting. This suggests that where the motivation is strong enough, tourism operators can take a step outside this setting to drive a conservation agenda. However, the action may have a reputation value for the tourism operator and the money required to fund such a programme still has to come from somewhere.

As noted earlier, discussions of conservation and sustainability in general should not take place without consideration of individual animal welfare. Good welfare of animals is a component of the sustainability of any system that has an impact on animals. Survival of a species at the expense of the welfare of the individual animal should not be acceptable. Within this context, while animal tourism organizations such as zoos champion their conservation credentials, they should also place emphasis on animal welfare as well as other aspects of sustainability. Indeed, zoos have a better potential to be able to do this than other animal tourism experiences. The reason is that the star attractions of zoos have, for generations, been individualized, given names and personal identities. This may rank as anthropomorphism but it may well help to facilitate a concern for individual animal welfare. Yet zoos are also not above placing species survival above individual welfare concerns. Sometimes rare animals used for breeding are kept in small cages, away from the public gaze, that are just sufficient for survival and breeding but the welfare of the animals is very poor.

Zoo objectives, including those aimed at conservation may not coincide with the protection of the lives of individuals. In the past, unwanted animals that could not be sold to other zoos were often quietly killed without any public announcement. If this is done humanely, there is no animal welfare issue, as explained in Chapter 2. However, there is ethical concern about the killing of animals and the difficulties for zoos in some situations were made public by the killing of Marius the giraffe in Copenhagen Zoo in 2014. Individually there was nothing wrong with Marius, and he was a healthy, young animal. However, in the often dry vernacular of scientifically driven conservation he was surplus to requirement and not considered appropriate for a breeding programme and therefore he had to be removed from the stock. Here we had species conservation and individual value colliding in a very public manner. Those who would hold the life of every individual as sacrosanct were appalled that Marius could be killed like this with no thought for him as an individual. Such views arguably at best skim the edges of all that is wrong with anthropomorphism, but also all that is right with human compassion and the 'obligations' we have to animals as defined in Chapter 2. Many people were even more disturbed when Marius's carcass was examined in public and his remains fed to the carnivores of the zoo.

Yet the counterpoint here, made clearly by the zoo, is that such a public process was designed to be an educational one and that those who felt angst at it were distant from the reality of death and the consumption of meat in the 21st century. Is there really anything wrong with the feeding of the meat to the carnivores? After all, carnivores need to eat meat and that meat has to come from somewhere and by using the meat from Marius, the zoo arguably was acting in a sustainably appropriate manner. If these carnivores did not eat this giraffe, several other animals would be killed for them to eat. Yet what the zoo was doing was to kill and allow other animals to eat a named individual, something human society is very uncomfortable with. Should killing and eating nameless others be different from killing and eating Marius? Another question relates to how we balance conservation, where the concern is the species or environment type, and animal welfare, where the concern is the individual. Such a balance is necessary in the ongoing search for a truer form of sustainability. Such questions may not benefit Marius at all, but they may benefit the lives of countless other animals, individually and collectively. In other words, what Copenhagen Zoo offered was a learning experience and the challenge is to learn from it rather than merely to castigate it and strive to ensure that it never happens again.

Some Impacts of Tourism on Wild Animal Welfare

Following on from the discussions so far in this chapter and Chapter 3 it is clear that there is no simple answer to the question of what is the impact of tourism on animal welfare. Evidence in support of the negative has already been touched on elsewhere in this book but we can expand on it here. There are numerous examples today of where individual animal welfare is made worse by the actions of tourism. Close encounters with bears, or tourists inappropriately storing food and waste while hiking in North America, have been blamed for the deaths of bears that had been described as being habituated. Within aquaria we can question the welfare of dolphins, belugas and orcas, among others, that are kept in enclosures that are too small for their needs (refer to Chapter 5 on aquaria). The same can be said for animals such as elephants kept in relatively small spaces within zoos.

The desire among most tourists to be free from the presence of creepy crawlies when visiting countries where they abound has also contributed to the deaths of innumerable animals. Australia is a fine example here, a country replete with such bugs where hotels are regularly 'protected' by 'pest' control companies that ensure an invisible (but deadly) barrier is set up and maintained between the visitor and the arachnids of the country. All of these examples, and others touched upon elsewhere in the book suggest that the tourism experience is not about animal welfare and that where animals are part of the tourism experience it is for the benefit of the tourist either primarily or exclusively rather than the welfare of individual animals.

While there are many instances within the tourism industry where we can question the negative impacts on the welfare of animals there are also examples of major concerns about animal welfare within the tourism industry. Chapter 5 to 8 all provide examples of the desire among wildlife tourism operations to consider carefully the welfare of the very animals that their industry depends on for its survival. They all talk of the balancing of economic pressures with animal welfare but of the primacy of the latter at all times. Similarly, a bear tourism operation in Whistler, Canada, has constructed itself around the idea of being concerned primarily with ensuring good welfare of bears rather than turning a profit. The logic here is that by offering tourists views of the bears that they want, in a manner that is controlled by experts, the bears and tourists will survive unscathed.

Impacts on the Welfare of Animals as Workers in Tourism

Even where animals are employed as workers in the tourism industry, questions can be raised about their welfare. Perhaps the ultimate example here is a trainee sniffer dog that got loose at Auckland airport and when nobody was able to get it back under control, it was shot and killed.

Many, in some ways not unreasonable, justifications were subsequently given for why the dog had to be destroyed. However, at the root of the issue appears to be the point that the dog was disrupting the normal business of the airport. Human employees are not treated like this, but tools or objects are. Less lethal but still problematic is the stress, as noted in the previous chapter, that we impose on animals like sniffer or meet-and-greet dogs at airports.

Similarly, it is possible to raise questions about the welfare of animals as guests of the tourism industry. This relates back to the question of whether animal guests are really 'guests' in their own right or appendages of their human owners, as noted in the previous chapter. If it is the latter, is the welfare of the animal being compromised to cater to the desires of the human? This question is arguably an extension of evolving crazes to treat dogs as fluffy children and/or fashion accessories. Both fail to see the dog for what it is: a dog, with welfare needs that are distinct to dogs. In this way, it must be asked if it is in the welfare interests of dogs, and other animals, to take them on holiday with us. Doing so may expose them to significant travel-related stress and may cause additional stress by placing them in unfamiliar situations. Furthermore, offering them luxury foodstuffs while on holiday, in a manner akin to the eating habits of many tourists, may not be giving them the treat human owners think but instead may be compromising their physical well-being in the short and long term.

The need to make sufficient money to care for the animals in their care was noted by the owner of a sled dog operation in Switzerland in 2013. She, and her husband, ran an animal boarding operation and had, over the years, been asked to take in huskies whose owners had found them unsuited to life as a pet. The result was that eventually the couple found themselves with a large group of huskies that were placing a significant burden on their finances and in need of exercise. The result was the development of a dog-sled operation that, although making money, was not originally designed for the owners' profit. Rather, it was to provide the dogs with appropriate exercise and better welfare. As the Swiss dog-sled operator noted, there are plenty of such operators who, unlike them, place profit before animal welfare.

While noting potential welfare concerns with animal employees within the tourism industry, it is also necessary to recognize that many of these animals are extremely well cared for, often as sentient beings rather than prized tools. The meet-and-greet dogs that are volunteered at airports are handled and cared for by devoted owners. These are not fashion accessories or fluffy humans in their eyes. The dogs may be doing a hard job, but the owners are there in the background to ensure that their animals' welfare is always being considered.

Impacts on the Welfare of Companion Animals in Tourism

As the dog is an integral part of the family, many dog owners recognize their obligation to give their dog exercise and sufficient social stimulation throughout every day and owners of other kinds of pets take care to provide for their needs. They may take their pet on holiday with them, often constraining their own holiday desires to ensure that they consider their obligations to the animal and all of its needs (Carr and Cohen, 2009). Sometimes, travel necessitates a period of quarantine and frequently pet animals are left in boarding kennels. What is the effect on the companion animal of spending time in such an establishment? Some of the problems are considered by Broom and Fraser (2015, chapters 37 and 38). Lack of environmental complexity is much more of a problem for dogs living in boarding kennels or quarantine kennels than for dogs in a human home. When dogs had lived in kennels for more than 6 months, they rested for longer, played less with people when given the opportunity, played more with objects, and showed more barking and growling at strange dogs. Cats require a relatively complex environment during the time that they are active if their welfare is not to be poor (Rochlitz, 2005). Cats kept in groups prefer to be able to sit on a raised platform or shelf rather than on the ground. Some cats are disturbed if another individual is in very close proximity and the welfare of many cats is not good unless they have the opportunity to hide. Specific resources are of importance to cats, for example, material that allows them to scrape with their claws such as rope or string wrapped around a post. Cats also need to be undisturbed by humans when they are resting. A cat in a small cage, repeatedly passed by unfamiliar humans, is always disturbed and responds by lying down and moving very little, an indicator of poor welfare. When a cat from a human home has been in a cage environment for some time, for example; when in quarantine for 6 months, its behaviour becomes more and more abnormal and behaviour towards familiar humans changes (Rochlitz *et al.*, 1998). The changes in behaviour and welfare are profound enough to make it clear that a 6-month quarantine period in the life of a cat is a severe imposition. The avoidance of rabies introduction, the main reason for the quarantine in some countries, is better achieved by vaccination and careful monitoring. While most holidays are of a shorter duration than 6 months the potential implications of staying in boarding kennels or catteries for these companion animals are still clear. What is less clear, is how successful are modern cat and dog 'hotels' (refer to Chapter 2; Carr, 2014) at maintaining good animal welfare.

Animal Welfare and Tourism: Who is Responsible?

We have already identified the all-pervasive nature of animals in the tourism experience, that animals are sentient beings, and that in a human-dominated world we have obligations to them regarding their welfare. Given the variety of ways in which tourism and animal welfare are, and can be, mutually exclusive and inclusive, who is responsible for the welfare of animals in the tourism experience? After all, it is only by knowing this that we may be able to ensure that tourism and concern about animal welfare are inclusive.

These questions are discussed in various ways in a number of the opinion pieces later in this book (Part II), including those authored by Jane Goodall (Chapters 9 and 17) and Jan Schmidt-Burbach (Chapter 11). On the one hand, it may be argued that it is incumbent on tourists to be aware of the needs of animals. How to be aware of whether the needs of an animal are being met is discussed by Stephen Blakeway and Glen Cousquer in their opinion piece, which focuses on donkeys (Chapter 13). Fuelled with this knowledge, the argument goes, tourists should only engage in animal tourism experiences that do not prevent these needs from being met and welfare from being good. Yet such an approach is of course dependent on tourists being knowledgeable and, even when they are, it requires them to act in a manner that prioritizes that knowledge over any other desires the tourists have relating to animals. The irony is that one potential route to this knowledge may be the tourism experience (more on this later in this chapter). Ideally, tourists will spend their money on animal tourism operators who care for the welfare of animals and also actively avoid operators who engage in practices that result in poor welfare of animals. In order to achieve this, there has to be accessible information for the tourist from government agencies, hotels, other tourist information services and consortia of tourist operators. This approach to animal welfare in tourism may share some of the concepts espoused under the umbrella of ecotourism (Fennell, 1999; Ceballos-Lascuráin, 2003). However, there is no call to confine animal welfare to ecotourism or to claim that only ecotourism can improve animal welfare. Rather, animal welfare is a concern to all types of tourism and must be dealt with in all of them.

Tourists acting collectively, just as with any social group, can drive change. In the age of social media, Ismail Shaheer from the University of Otago is studying the nature of tourism boycotts linked to animals inside and outside the tourism experience. These boycotts are a potentially strong tool for encouraging tourism operators and destinations to engage with the concerns about animal welfare. They include boycotts against aquaria that house dolphins or orcas; Japan for its whaling and culling of dolphins; and Spain for the practice of bull-fighting. What we see here is how tourist-led activism can change the tourism industry and also how boycotts of the tourism industry and of visits to whole countries can initiate moves towards wider societal change. Such boycotts are already greatly reducing the numbers of visitors at some aquaria and there are probably hundreds of thousands of people refusing to go to Japan and Spain for these animal welfare-related reasons (see Shaheer *et al.*, 2017 and Valentin, 2009 for discussion of the impact of boycotts on the tourism industry and tourist destinations).

In pushing for change in how societies and individual tourism operators within them engage with the concept of animal welfare, we run the risk, as noted at the beginning of this chapter, of being accused of cultural imperialism. Who are we to tell others how to value animals and to say that cultural practices where animals play a central role, or indeed any role, should be banned because of effects on animal welfare? If this is a major moral issue for us, is it an absolute moral issue that is valid everywhere or is it associated with one culture but not with others? In order to answer this, we have to ask whether the avoidance of cruelty to animals is a universal moral issue. Surveys in very many countries suggest that it is (see, for example, the Eurobarometer surveys reported by Broom, 2017). Despite this, it is clear that concerns for animal welfare are not homogeneous across the world. Take, for example, the case of bull-fighting in Spain. This is identified as a cultural tradition, a core component of the cultural identity associated with many parts of the country. Attempts by those from outside of the bull-fighting centres of Spain, including other parts of Spain, to ban the 'sport' have long been met with significant resistance and umbrage that anyone can demand the cessation of an aspect of the culture of a country or people. To date, only Catalonia has banned bull-fighting. While it is not reasonable to demand that people conform to a particular mindset at the expense of cultural heritage, there is a need to recognize the human-centric thinking at play here. Here we have the desires and right of people to preserve their culture taking precedence over animals and concerns about their welfare. While concerns about animal welfare can be said to be a human construct and therefore of no more, or less, value than concerns about preserving such activities as bull-fighting, the intrinsic value of the animals themselves is a separate matter. The solution may be to focus on animal welfare for the benefits of animals rather than the placating of human morals and the balancing of human preferences. This leads us back to the concept of obligations and the need to focus on our obligations to animals rather than on either our human cultural heritage or our anthropomorphic guilt when we see animals being treated cruelly. When looking at attempts to change animal welfare through tourism, we must consider the difference between those attempts focused on animal-centric obligations and those centred on human-centric guilt or even on squeamishness at the sight of blood. The human-centric focus is not sufficient by itself. The problem is that it is easier to gain the buy-in of people to a human-centric focus than an animal-centric focus. This encourages the utilization of the former as a way of gaining advances in animal welfare. However, such an approach is only likely to lead to resistance and angst among the affected human population.

While in the age of social media, we may suggest that boycotts have a life of their own, it is still the case, as it was in the pre-social-media age, that the initial thought about suggesting a boycott and the original call for one must come from somewhere. In this way, it is recognized that boycotts are in many ways driven by and a part of wider publicity campaigns that aim to raise public awareness of specific issues and drive social change. The campaigns and boycotts may be driven by individuals, or, in the case of animal-related boycotts, by one or more animal-protection groups. To some extent, these groups act as the conscience of society, constantly prodding us to do better and reminding us of the horrors that we normally hide behind closed doors. Winter and Young (2015) talk about this in relation to horse racing. Yet, as Turner notes in his opinion piece later in this book (Chapter 10), raising awareness of animal welfare concerns in the hope of changing public opinion or industry practice may not work, and indeed may be problematic if it results in the branding of the messenger as an extremist to be ignored by fair-minded members of society. Consequently, as Turner notes, some organizations, like the Born Free Foundation, have begun to work with associations and businesses to create with them an environment for change. This has required a change of mindset from seeing businesses as the enemy to seeing them as a partner for change for the betterment of animal welfare. Yet at the same time, examples of change resulting from publicity campaigns and boycotts do exist. Prime among them is the current move by many aquaria around the world to abandon the practice of keeping cetaceans (i.e. whales and dolphins) in captivity. Examples include the decisions by Barcelona Zoo to cease housing dolphins in 2016 and Vancouver Aquarium to cease this practice in 2017.

Education is seen as a key component of encouraging people to care about the welfare and conservation of animals (see all the work that zoos undertake to inform and teach visitors about the importance of preserving species and their natural environments). It is fair to point out that people cannot be expected to be concerned about animal welfare issues, or feel that they have obligations to these creatures, if they are not aware of welfare concerns and the entire issue of obligations. This takes us back to the raising of awareness by organizations like the Born Free Foundation. This is clearly a form of education, but it is by no means the only one available. The tourism industry itself can also be a source of education and, as noted earlier, good-quality zoos attempt to be such a source. Such tourist attractions offer people the opportunity to gain a connection with animals and, through that, to engage with the notion that they should be concerned about animal welfare and should take an active role in promoting good welfare. In a similar manner, at least some whale-, dolphin-, shark- and bear-watching operators offer an educational component to their visitors that is clearly designed to raise awareness of the issues facing these animals and the need for humans to do something to help them. While, as noted above, some organizations may find their voice going unheard if they are labelled as extremists, the same problem may occur with tourism operators. The messages about conservation and animal welfare presented in zoos are disparaged by the extreme anti zoo movement that will forever see zoos as prisons for animals and therefore always bad. In addition, the work of the good zoos can all too easily be undermined by the others whose primary or sole focus is on profit through the objectification of animals for the entertainment of visitors. Here we have a case of guilt by association and one of the stated reasons why Durrell Wildlife Park abandoned the use of 'zoo' in its name (see Chapter 6 by Lee Durrell for a more detailed discussion).

Within zoos that offer educational opportunities, like all tourism establishments, they face the tricky balancing act of providing education in an entertainment setting. They are not schools and visitors are primarily there because they want to enjoy themselves. Therefore, to have a useful effect, any educational opportunities offered must be entertaining. The problem is that, if such offerings become too entertaining then the educational message can become lost. If this happens, such events reinforce the position of the anti-zoo lobby. An example of edutainment gone wrong was an event in Calgary Zoo in the summer of 2005 when an 'educational' animal encounter was, as depicted in Fig. 4.1, downgraded into a kindergarten sing-along.

If tourism operators must be responsible in relation to animal welfare then we must ask, just as in the case of boycotts, how successful they can be, not just at encouraging good animal welfare and conservation behaviour but also discouraging bad behaviour. This must be asked with the kind of objective approach noted in Chapter 2, and in Chapter 13 by Stephen

Fig. 4.1. Calgary Zoo (2005) animal encounter.

Blakeway and Glen Cousquer that sets aside human-centric emotive debates. Following this approach, we have the tools to assess animal welfare in animal tourism experiences. However, this is only one part of any assessment that must occur to truly identify whether the animal experiences that tourists are offered are fully meeting our obligations to the animals. It is insufficient for the individual animals to either suffer no harm or actually benefit from a tourism experience. Rather, all animals must potentially gain. Here we return to the issue of education and the linked concept of learning. Unfortunately, it is not sufficient to simply say that a tourist operator meets their obligations to animals if they offer an educational component to their animal tourism experience. Instead, we need to know that tourists have learned something from the experience and that this learning will result in people being more concerned about animal welfare and consequently behaving differently, not just on holiday but after they return home. Unfortunately, at the current time there is no definitive proof about whether this happens or not. Indeed, within the context of zoos, a long-running debate continues about whether they are capable of educating the public about animal welfare and conservation issues. The result is that we continue to hear people calling for the closure of zoos for their perceived failure to provide learning opportunities that lead to change. We used to hear, and sometimes still do, that animals must be assumed to lack sentience because there was insufficient proof to the contrary. Are we to close zoos and other animal encounters because of a lack of proof of their ability to change people's minds?

Other evidence of the difficulties the tourism industry faces in changing public behaviour in relation to animal welfare is provided by a continued desire, among at least some tourists, to approach animals more closely than they should if there is to be no harm to the welfare of the animal or the person. Some people try to touch the animals. Signs, like those depicted in Fig. 4.2, show attempts by authorities to stop tourists from approaching wildlife too closely or

Fig. 4.2. Signs indicating appropriate behaviour around wild animals: (a) Alberta, Canada (2008); (b) Glacier National Park, USA (2005); (c) Columbia Icefields Centre, Canada (2008).

feeding them. Yet reports of tourists still seeking close encounters with bears abound. For example, the two pictures in Fig. 4.3 were taken in Revelstoke, Canada. The one at the top shows warning signs that had been placed at the beginning of a hiking track to warn people of the dangers of a bear with cubs who had been spotted in the vicinity. On the next page is a picture of an entry in a notebook for visitors positioned at the head of the same trail. The disappointment the writer had in not seeing the very bears they had been warned about speaks of a failure to educate these tourists. The message of 'dangerous bear' had been completely overwritten by the tourists' desire to see bears. The tourism industry, as noted in the previous chapter, is at least partially responsible for this desire that has proven to be extremely difficult to change since it emerged decades ago.

Zoos also regularly provide signs to tell visitors not to touch animals or bang on glass enclosures (Fig. 4.4). However, at least a small number of visitors are still to be found in zoos around the world attempting to feed, touch, or gain the attention of animals (see work by Carr, 2018 for a more detailed discussion of this issue). A struggle for zoos, as with the wild bears, is to overcome the desire of visitors to get close to animals. Zoos are increasingly risking sending out mixed messages about touching or not touching animals by offering carefully managed interactive experiences while attempting to ban people from interacting with animals outside of these experiences. However, such interactive experiences are said to bring two benefits: increasing zoo income and providing a higher-quality learning experience for the visitors willing and able to pay the extra cost. Overall, tourism operators providing educational material about animal welfare and trying to guide tourist behaviour in a more animal-friendly direction face several barriers, including the desire of tourists to see and interact with animals, something that is at least

Fig. 4.3. Bear warnings and desires, Revelstoke (2008).

partially a historical construct of the industry, and the lack of desire among many tourists to be treated as if they were in school while on holiday.

The tourist attractions themselves are not the only part of the industry concerned with animal welfare. Just as we see zoos increasingly engaging with animal welfare concerns, some travel agencies are now also active in this area. Both the tourist attraction and the travel agency may be driven by altruism, obligation-focused reasons or threats to income streams resulting from changes in social attitudes. So, just as we have seen Sea-World Entertainment launching their inaugural corporate responsibility report in 2016 to highlight their commitment to animal welfare, we have also witnessed the World Wide Fund for Nature announcing a 5-year partnership with Royal Caribbean Cruises. In addition, we have seen Thomas Cook, one of the world's largest travel agencies, stop selling tickets to wildlife tourist attractions with questionable animal welfare standards, and the travel company Responsible Travel has become the first to withdraw from sale any trips that include visits to zoos. In addition, several airlines have now stated they will not carry the souvenirs of trophy hunters, recognizing that this is one way they can help to contribute to the cessation of such activities while also gaining kudos from a general public that widely vilifies this tourism experience.

There is one other group that needs to be taken into consideration when thinking about who is responsible for animal welfare within the tourism environment. These are the local people who live in tourist destinations. In Chapter 11, Jan Schmidt-Burbach talks of these people in relation to elephant tourism in Asia, as do Rizzolo and Bradshaw (2018) in their book chapter about elephant welfare. There is, as both pieces note, no point in talking about animal welfare within tourism without also talking about the people it affects, because it is clear that our obligations to animals are not free of charge. Such a recognition is firmly situated within the contemporary understanding of sustainability and conservation discussed earlier in this chapter. What must also be recognized is that the costs of animal welfare are borne more often by local people than by tourists, industry owners or activists. Recognizing this is necessary for the sustainability of animal welfare agendas, as it is only with the buy-in of local people that such agendas have any hope of working. In addition to the local people, the governments and related public institutions that govern our lives have a role to play in driving animal welfare concerns and debates within tourism. They act mainly as a regulatory mechanism, enforcing socially defined positions on animal welfare. This is a reactive function that is driven by social values related to animal welfare rather than a proactive function that drives change and the betterment of animal welfare. This may not be surprising, as such institutions are bastions of the dominant social conscience of the

Fig. 4.4. Do not touch the animals signs: (a) Singapore Zoo (2013); (b) O'Keefe Ranch, Canada (2008); (c) Kamloops Wildlife Centre, Canada (2008).

day rather than drivers of change. Yet if they are to be useful rather than becoming irrelevant, such organizations must balance their inherent desire to maintain the status quo with an open attitude to changes in the social conscience that enables them to aid rather than resist such change.

Overall, it is clear that the answer to the question posed at the beginning of this section (i.e. who is responsible for the welfare of animals in the tourism experience?) is 'everyone'; tourists, the general public, tourism operators, activist groups and non-governmental organizations, governmental offices, and local people living next to and affected by animal tourism experiences all have a role to play in ensuring good welfare of animals within the tourism experience.

Summary

Tourism and animal welfare are sometimes mutually inclusive and sometimes exclusive and there are several different relationships between animal welfare, conservation and sustainability. There is no simple answer to the question of whether tourism and good animal welfare can coexist. The easy path is to identify particular types of tourism as being incompatible with animal welfare needs and others as being inclusive of such needs. However, this would lead to a gross and erroneous oversimplification of a much more complex and nuanced reality.

In reality, as the work in this chapter and the preceding one has shown, it is not the shop-window presentation of a tourism experience that needs to be examined when assessing its relation to animal welfare. Instead, we need to look at the underlying philosophy that drives each tourism operation. It is here that we find either a commitment to animal welfare that views animals as sentient beings or the prioritization of profit to such an extent that any concern for animal welfare is focused on the animal as a tool or object around which a tourism industry can be constructed. Building on contemporary understandings of the notion of sustainability, we must recognize that the tourism experience and the industry that caters to it exist in a neo-liberal capitalist system. As a result, all tourism operations must, at the very least, generate sufficient financial income to remain solvent. Consequently, any mutual inclusivity between tourism and animal welfare needs to exist within this reality. This does not mean that animal welfare should be secondary to economic income, but that it cannot exist outside of the need to generate such income. Animal welfare is not just a human social construct but is firmly situated within a human-centric world. We have to consider exactly what our obligations are. Humans and animals may exist in a human-dominated world, but that does not negate the possibility of animal needs being met. Rather, it is the responsibility of all people involved as tourists or tourism operators to ensure that the welfare of all animals is good. This is the concept of obligation in action. As this chapter has shown, all actors in the tourism experience – tourists, tourism industry operators, governmental organizations, local people in tourist destinations, animal welfare organizations, etc. – have a role to play in helping to ensure the welfare of animals involved, whether directly or indirectly, in the tourism experience. This raises questions about whether bans on selling tickets to animal attractions are justified and whether those engaging with such operations can improve their animal welfare record.

References

Alligood, C. and Leighty, K. (2015) Putting the 'E' in SPIDER: evolving trends in the evaluation of environmental enrichment efficacy in zoological settings. *Animal Behavior and Cognition* 2, 200–217.

Bateson, P. and Bradshaw, E.L. (1997) Physiological effects of hunting red deer (*Cervus elaphus*). *Proceedings of the Royal Society of London B* 264(1389), 1707–1714.

Beardsworth, A. and Bryman, A. (2001) The wild animal in late modernity: the case of the Disneyization of zoos. *Tourist Studies* 1(1), 83–104.

Braithwaite, V. (2010) *Do Fish Feel Pain?* Oxford University Press, Oxford, UK.

Broom, D.M. (2002) Welfare in wildlife management and zoos. Proceedings of the 4th International Congress on the Physiology and Behaviour of Wild and Zoo Animals. *Advances in Ethology* 37, 4–6.

Broom, D.M. (1999) The welfare of vertebrate pests in relation to their management. In: Cowan, P.D. and Feare, C.J. (eds) *Advances in Vertebrate Pest Management*. Filander Verlag, Fürth, Germany, pp. 309–329.

Broom, D.M. (2013) The science of animal welfare and its relevance to whales. *Animal Welfare* 22, 123–126.

Broom, D.M. (2014) *Sentience and Animal Welfare*. CAB International, Wallingford, Oxfordshire, UK.

Broom, D.M. (2016) Fish brains and behaviour indicate capacity for feeling pain. *Animal Sentience*, 2016.010.

Broom, D.M. (2017) *Animal Welfare in the European Union*. European Parliament Policy Department, Citizen's Rights and Constitutional Affairs, Study for the PETI Committee, Brussels. DOI: 10-2861/891355.

Broom, D.M. and Fraser, A.F. (2015) *Domestic Animal Behaviour and Welfare*, 5th edn. CAB International, Wallingford, Oxfordshire, UK.

Carr, N. (2002) The tourism–leisure behavioural continuum. *Annals of Tourism Research* 29(4), 972–986.

Carr, N. (2014) *Dogs in the Leisure Experience*. CAB International, Wallingford, UK.

Carr, N. (2018) Zoos and animal encounters: to touch or not to touch, that is the question. In: Carr, N. and Young, J. (eds) *Wild Animals and Leisure: Rights and Welfare*. Routledge, Abingdon, Oxfordshire, UK.

Carr, N. and Cohen, S. (2009) Holidaying with the family pet: no dogs allowed! *Tourism and Hospitality Research* 9(4), 290–304.

Carr, N. and Cohen, S. (2011) The public face of zoos: balancing entertainment, education, and conservation. *Anthrozoos* 24(2), 175–189.

Ceballos-Lascuráin (2003) Preface. In: Lück, M. and Kirstges, T. (eds) *Global Ecotourism Policies and Case Studies: Perspectives and Constraints*. Channel View Publications, Clevedon, UK, pp. viii–xii.

Clubb, R. and Mason, G. (2003) Animal welfare: captivity effects on wide-ranging carnivores. *Nature* 425, 473–474.

Clubb, R., Rowcliffe, M., Lee, P., Mar, K.U., Moss, C. and Mason, G.J. (2008) Compromised survivorship in zoo elephants. *Science* 322, 1649.

Clubb, R., Rowcliffe, M., Mar, K.U., Lee, P., Moss, C. and Mason, G.J. (2009) Fecundity and population viability in female zoo elephants: problems and possible solutions. *Animal Welfare* 18, 237–247.

Constantine, R. (2001) Increased avoidance of swimmers by wild bottlenose dolphins (*Tursiops truncatus*) due to long-term exposure to swim-with-dolphin tourism. *Marine Mammal Science* 17, 689–702.

Curtin, S. and Green, E. (2018) Consumer perceptions of keeping wild animals in captivity. In: Carr, N. and Young, J. (eds) *Wild Animals and Leisure: Rights and Welfare*. Routledge, Abingdon, Oxfordshire, UK.

Curtin, S., Richards, S. and Westcott, S. (2009) Tourism and grey seals in south Devon: management strategies, voluntary controls and tourists' perceptions of disturbance. *Current Issues in Tourism* 12, 59–81.

Durrell, G. (1976) *The Stationary Ark*. Collins, London.

Fennell, D. (1999) *Ecotourism*, 3rd edn. Routledge, London.

Friend, T. H. (1999) Behaviour of picketed circus elephants. *Applied Animal Behaviour Science* 62, 73–88.

Hall, C.M., Gossling, S. and Scott, D. (eds) (2015) *The Routledge Handbook of Tourism and Sustainability*. Routledge, Abingdon, Oxfordshire, UK.

Higham, J. and Bejder, L. (2008) Managing wildlife-based tourism: edging slowly towards sustainability? *Current Issues in Tourism* 11, 75–83.

Higham, J., Bejder, L. and Lusseau, D. (2009) An integrated and adaptive management model to address the long-term sustainability of tourist interactions with cetaceans. *Environmental Conservation* 35, 294–302.

Higham, J., Bejder, L. and Williams, R. (eds) (2014) *Whale-Watching: Sustainable Tourism and Ecological Management*. Cambridge University Press, Cambridge, UK.

Hill, S.P. and Broom, D.M. (2009) Measuring zoo animal welfare: theory and practice. *Zoo Biology* 28, 531–544.

Hooker, S.K., Fahlman, A., Moore, M.J., de Soto, N.A., de Quirós, Y.B., Brubakk, A.O., Costa, D.P., Costidis, A.M., Dennison, S., Falke, K.J., Fernandez, A. *et al.* (2012) Deadly diving? Physiological and behavioural management of decompression stress in diving mammals. *Proceedings of the Royal Society B* 279(1731), 1041–1050.

Jamieson, D. (1985) Against zoos. In: Singer, P. (ed.) *In Defence of Animals*. Basil Blackwell, Oxford, UK, pp. 108–117.

Jantschke, F. (1997) Zoo- und Zirkustiere. In: Sambraus, H.H. and Steiger, A. (eds) *Das Buch vom Tierschutz*. Enke, Stuttgart, pp. 402–423.

Jett, J. and Ventre, J. (2015) Captive killer whale (*Orcinus orca*) survival. *Marine Mammal Science* 31, 1362–1377.

Johnson, M., Madsen, P.T., Zimmer, W.M., de Soto, N.A. and Tyack, P.L. (2004) Beaked whales echolocate on prey. *Proceedings of the Royal Society B* 271(Supplement 6), S383–S386.

Kiley-Worthington, M. (1990) *Animals in Circuses and Zoos: Chiron's World*. Little Eco-Farms Publishing, Basildon, UK.

Kovacs, K.M. and Innes, S. (1990) The impact of tourism on harp seals (*Phoca groenlandica*) in the Gulf of St. Lawrence, Canada. *Applied Animal Behaviour Science* 26, 15–26.

Law, G. and Kitchener, A.C. (2017) Environmental enrichment for killer whales *Orcinus orca* at zoological institutions: untried and untested. *International Zoo Yearbook* 51(1), 232–247.

Lück, M. (2003) Education on marine mammal tours as agent for conservation – but do tourists want to be educated? *Ocean and Coastal Management* 46, 943–956.

Lück, M. (2015) Education on marine mammal tours – but what do tourists want to learn? *Ocean and Coastal management* 103, 25–33.

Lundquist, D., Sironi, M., Würsig, B., Rowntree, V., Martino, J. and Lundquist, L. (2013) Response of southern right whales to simulated swim-with-whale tourism at Península Valdés, Argentina. *Marine Mammal Science* 29, E24–E45.

Margodt, K. (2000) *The Welfare Ark: Suggestions for a Renewed Policy in Zoos*. VUB University Press, Brussels.

Marino, L. (2013) Humans, dolphins, and moral inclusivity. In: Corbey, R. and Lanjouw, A. (eds) *The Politics of Species: Reshaping Our Relationships with Other Animals*. Cambridge University Press, Cambridge, UK, pp. 95–105.

Marino, L. and Frohoff, T. (2011) Towards a new paradigm of non-captive research on cetacean cognition. *PloS PLoS ONE* 6(9), e24121.

Mason, G.J. (2010) Species differences in responses to captivity: stress, welfare and the comparative method. *Trends in Ecology & Evolution* 25, 713–721.

Mordue, T. and Wilson, S. (2018) Angler and fish relations in the UK: ethics, aesthetics and material semiotics. In: Carr, N. and Young, J. (eds) *Wild Animals and Leisure: Rights and Welfare*. Routledge, Abingdon, Oxfordshire, UK.

Oyarzun, F. (2017) Exploring the prospects for adaptive co-management of wildlife tourism: the case of shark cage diving on Stewart Island, New Zealand. Unpublished PhD thesis, University of Otago, Dunedin, New Zealand.

Palmer, J. (1983) *Working Dogs*. Patrick Stephens Ltd, Cambridge, UK.

Regan, T. (2004) *Empty Cages: Facing the Challenge of Animal Rights*. Rowman & Littlefield Publishers, Inc., Oxford, UK.

Rizzolo, J. and Bradshaw, G. (2018) Human leisure/elephant breakdown: impacts of tourism on Asian elephants. In: Carr, N. and Young, J. (eds) *Wild Animals and Leisure: Rights and Welfare*. Routledge, Abingdon, Oxfordshire, UK.

Robeck, T.R., Willis, K., Scarpuzzi, M.R. and O'Brien, J.K. (2015) Comparisons of life-history parameters between free-ranging and captive killer whale (*Orcinus orca*) populations for application toward species management. *Journal of Mammalogy* 96, 1055–1070.

Rochlitz, I.R. (2005) Housing and welfare. In: Rochlitz, I.R. (ed.) *The Welfare of Cats*. Springer, Berlin, pp. 177–203.

Rochlitz, I., Podberscek, A.L. and Broom, D.M. (1998) Effects of quarantine on cats and their owners. *Veterinary Record* 143, 181–185.

Serpell, J.A. (1986) *In the Company of Animals*. Cambridge University Press, Cambridge, UK.

Shaheer, I., Insch, A. and Carr, N. (2017) Tourism destination boycotts – are they becoming a standard practise? *Tourism Recreation Research* 43, 129–132. DOI: 10.1080/02508281.2017.1377385.

Swaisgood, R.R. and Shepherdson, D.J. (2005) Scientific approaches to enrichment and stereotypies in zoo animals: what's been done and where should we go next? *Zoo Biology* 24, 499–518.

Swarbrooke, J. (1999) *Sustainable Tourism Management*. CAB International, Wallingford, Oxfordshire, UK.

Valentin, A. (2009) The role of political awareness in backpackers' destination decision-making: a case study of the Burma travel boycott. Unpublished PhD thesis, University of Otago, Dunedin, New Zealand.

Winter, C. and Young, W. (2015) Fatalities and fascinators: a new perspective on thoroughbred racing. In: Carr, N. (ed.) *Domestic Animals and Leisure*. Palgrave Macmillan, Basingstoke, UK, pp. 241–258.

World Association of Zoos and Aquariums (2005) *Building a Future for Wildlife: The World Zoo and Aquarium Conservation Strategy*. WAZA Executive Office, Bern, Switzerland.

Part II

Tales from the Front Line: Animal Welfare Organizations and Animal Tourism Providers

This section of the book provides opinion pieces from a variety of animal welfare organizations and individual leaders in the area, tourism industry organizations, tourism operators and academic experts, which examine the relationship between tourism and animal welfare. They explore a variety of specific cases and issues but all are unified around the questions of how tourism and animal welfare sit alongside one another and what, if anything, can be done to ensure that the two are mutually inclusive rather than mutually exclusive. In this way, they talk of the complex reality of the position of animals in relation to tourism and consequently how their welfare is handled and positioned.

These opinion pieces are not designed to give definitive answers, but rather to allow differing perspectives on animal welfare in relation to tourism to be given voice. They are designed to give the reader the opportunity to consider diverse views and, in the process, determine their own position regarding animals in tourism and their welfare. In other words, the opinion pieces are designed to help the reader define their own ethical position regarding animal welfare in tourism. As has already been seen, the opinion pieces are also presented to give greater depth of understanding and analysis to the material covered in the earlier chapters of this book.

With a couple of exceptions, these pieces are not by academics. While it was stressed in Chapter 1 that this is not meant to be a 'traditional' academic book, it is worth reiterating the point here. This is because it would be unfair and inappropriate to look at and critique these opinion pieces through an academic lens. The contributors were asked to provide opinion pieces, not academic texts, and they have all risen to this challenge, with many producing pieces whose raw emotion comes through vividly. Consequently, these opinion pieces should be read for what they are: the opinions of people heavily invested in the world of animal welfare, coming at it from a variety of angles. Indeed, some of these angles can and do conflict with one another and this will become apparent upon reading the material in this section.

It is generally 'bad form' to repeat points in a piece of writing, but we will break with this convention here to repeat what has been said in the Acknowledgements section of the book. The people who have contributed to this section of the book are extremely busy, often out there in the world helping to drive forward animal welfare concerns. Their generosity of spirit in willingly contributing to this book is much appreciated. What is more, a debt of thanks is due to all of them for helping to evolve the thinking that has gone into the book as a result of the opinions they have expressed.

5 Public Aquariums in the 21st Century – What's Next, Before It's Too Late?

Christopher Andrews*

California Academy of Sciences, San Francisco, and Merlin Animal Welfare and Development, Tennessee

* Corresponding author: chris.andrews@merlinentertainments.biz

> The United Nations Strategic Plan for Biodiversity 2011–2020 is a key initiative ... to halt and eventually reverse the loss of biodiversity. The very first target of this plan states that 'by 2020, at the latest, people are aware of the values of biodiversity and the steps they can take to conserve and use it sustainably.' Zoos and aquariums worldwide, attracting more than 700 million visits every year, could potentially make a positive contribution to this target.
>
> Moss *et al.* (2015, p. 537)

Public Aquariums: Their First 150 Years

The Age of Enlightenment emerged from the centuries-long Age of Exploration and developed into the Industrial Revolution, and Charles Darwin's *Origin of Species* was published in 1859. The 18th and 19th centuries were a time of tremendous curiosity about science and nature, and major zoological institutions were established around the world, including the first public aquarium at the London Zoo in England in 1853. Over the next several decades, a tidal wave of, then novel, aquariums swept across Western Europe, North America and Japan, many displaying creatures that had never been seen before by the public. These aquariums were popular attractions, with an underlying assumption or practice of scientific research and public education. Significant facilities, even by today's standards, opened in large cities across Europe and North America. Then, around the middle of the 20th century, there was an escalating concern over the undeniable impact of humans on nature and wild places, which led to much needed environmental legislation in some countries, and the first 'Earth Day' in 1970. At the same time, there was the start of a new global wave of aquariums, arguably led by the New England Aquarium in Boston, Massachusetts in 1969, and driven by the increasing concerns for the environment and empirical data on aquatic animal care, new methods for large tank construction and glazing, high-quality synthetic sea water mixes, and improved closed life support and filtration systems. Suddenly, almost any aquatic species could be displayed, often far from the ocean. Public aquariums were also found to play a significant role in the economic development of derelict waterfront property and similar abandoned urban environments. Some aquariums, it appeared, could be funded through debt financing, although those that could successfully service a sizeable construction loan, and continue to operate financially effectively, proved to be few and far between. By the 1980s zoos had recognized that there was an urgent need for them to play a more active role in conservation and to safeguard the supply of animals for their displays, initially through managed breeding programmes of threatened species, as well as through partnerships with conservation organizations and by promoting behavioural change to their guests. Aquariums were a little slower to adopt a conservation focus, although by the end of the 20th century they too were promoting a triumvirate mission of overlapping roles: scientific research, public education and conservation. And the many faces of sustainability, from 'green' construction methods to sustainable operations, became a priority for all. But is this enough to justify the continued display of wild animals in human care, and, in some instances, to continue to remove them from their natural, if beleaguered and rapidly shrinking, natural habitats?

2000 and a New Millennium

The start of the 21st century has proved to be a challenging time for aquariums and zoos, certainly in North America and Europe. There was increasing evidence to show that a wide range of animal species, not just so-called 'higher' vertebrates, are, in fact, sentient creatures, able to suffer pain and feel emotions. They have lives beyond, and far more complex than, the hard-wired automatons that they were considered to be just a few years previously. With renewed vigour, proponents of animal rights and anti-captivity extremists questioned the need for aquariums and zoos, questioned their underlying motives, and questioned whether they were actually achieving all of the impacts that they claimed. The widely publicized film *Blackfish* captured the zeitgeist of the time, and aquariums and zoos were forced to reflect on their achievements, against a background of disturbing and increasing biodiversity loss, the Sixth Mass Extinction, and disappointing results from some of the vaunted captive breeding programmes of the previous 40 years or so. All of this at a time when aquarium displays had effectively stagnated, with no significant novel display ideas for many years (noting that bigger was no longer novel or even newsworthy). Indeed, some became jaded about aquarium offerings, well aware that they were now able to experience the world on a computer, a high-definition TV, a handheld device or a VR head set, all without leaving their home. The Age of Man had arrived.

A Future for Public Aquariums? Creating Relevance and Leading by Example to Maximize Conservation Impacts

Public aquariums can range from small coastal facilities of 1000 or 2000 square metres, which serve a predominantly local audience of a few tens of thousands each year, to major tourist attractions of tens of thousands of square metres with an annual attendance in the millions … and everything in between. Jellies to cetaceans, and octopus to sharks and living corals, can all be found thriving in public aquariums today. While most public aquariums are not-for-profit in their governance, recent years have seen a surge in for-profit aquariums, blurring the distinction between a solely mission focus and meeting the requirements of private owners and shareholders. Aquariums are as diverse as the animals they display and the people they attract. To be successful in the long term, however, it is vital that each aquarium has a strong sense of identity and is aware of how its scale and programmes fit into, serve and can be supported by the local community. One size or type does not suit all locations, and what works in London, England or Baltimore, Maryland may or may not work in Charleston, South Carolina or Orlando, Florida.

Public aquariums must put animal wellness first. Each animal must thrive, and must be seen to thrive, in their display, and aquariums must be seen to respect their animals. A 2015 survey by the Association of Zoos and Aquariums (AZA) in North America found that messages which promoted an aquarium's role in marine animal rescue, education of children, scientific research, and high-quality animal care resonated with the American people. The visiting public may perceive the animal's need differently, even inaccurately (e.g. size of display needed by some species), and aquariums must be prepared to be sensitive to these perceptions rather than fight them. The euthanasia of an animal at the end of its lifespan, when its quality of life has declined to a level deemed inappropriate by the attending veterinarian, is understood by most people. Euthanasia of surplus and otherwise healthy animals that result from, for example, overly successful breeding programmes is not appropriate, and management plans should prevent this whenever possible (see Chapter 2). The feeding of live vertebrate food items should be discontinued to the greatest extent possible, and never form any kind of public exhibition. Similarly, the necropsy of deceased animals can provide valuable scientific information, much like autopsy examinations of humans, and should only be carried out before an audience that understands the value and importance. Above all, aquariums must be completely transparent regarding their animal care programmes, and the welfare and conservation implications of how and from where they obtain their display animals. They must also have well-documented 'care for life' plans in place for all the species in their care, which include behavioural enrichment programmes, wherever relevant. Accreditation to respected professional organizations should be a requirement, and minimum governmental standards reviewed to ensure that they allow the animals to thrive in human care. In this regard, veterinarians will continue to play an increasing and vital role and must partner with the aquarium's curatorial team to ensure that the wellness needs of all the animals are met.

Aquarium visitors seek experiences that are fun, engaging and relevant to them, and that explain what they can do in their daily lives to help conserve wild places. Therefore, aquariums must *attract, intrigue, engage* and ultimately *involve* their guests in critical thinking and hands-on learning, and inspire conservation action with the ultimate goal of demonstrating positive behavioural change. However, information needs to be provided in the form of a hierarchical menu, so that each guest can pick their learning level and style, and this means that significant resources have to be devoted to formative and summative exhibit and education programme evaluations, far more than is commonplace in aquariums and zoos at the moment. In addition, rather than simply adding technology to the guest experience, which may be unavoidable at existing facilities, new facilities need to seamlessly blend live exhibits with digital technologies and mechanical interactivities while greatly increasing opportunities for animal–staff–guest interactions, the latter of which can be especially impactful. Significant new exhibit species may not be forthcoming, or needed, but innovative ways to tell stories that resonate with the guests can be found, perhaps learning from the renaissance of children's museums that is occurring, at least in North America.

Aquarium detractors, and even supporters, are becoming increasingly suspicious of unsubstantiated claims and institutional hyperbole. Credibility and consistency are both key and must be assured throughout all of the communication channels, including social media, and the *Ocean Literacy Framework* is a very useful tool for creating educational content. Education programming requires a broad, well-articulated education and engagement strategy, with close working relations between the education, marketing and curatorial teams, so as to establish learning goals and outcomes, and a balance between substance, style and the institution's brand. Content and information must be accurate and presented in a fun, engaging and meaningful way, and under the direction of staff qualified and experienced in all that informal science learning has to offer.

To be more impactful, communication programmes need to be less species-centric, less reliant on the easy option of unconnected, headline grabbing 'fun facts', and more focused on storytelling about human relationships with, and reliance on, the natural world. Why should they care? Focusing on habitats as special places, and the issues they face, will create relevance and solidify what the visitor can do to protect them. Losing a species is unforgivable; losing a habitat and all the animals that call it home is a tragedy. Exhibits on the Amazon rainforest, Indo-Pacific coral reefs, or great white sharks, for example, may be popular and even drive attendance, at least for a while, but they too must be presented in a fashion that demonstrates relevance to the visitor and develops support for local issues. Rachel Carson (1965, p. 56) captured the essence of the modern aquarium experience: 'If facts are the seeds that later produce knowledge and wisdom, then the emotions and the senses are the fertile soil in which the seeds must grow'. Since humans are a social and emotional species, and prone to nostalgia, all of which drives their learning and sometimes less-than-logical decision making, spending time in a natural setting that evokes memories has a special meaning for most.

Many aquariums display *hundreds* of species of animals, far more than are actually needed for each to fulfil their scientific research, education and conservation goals. Curators need to rigorously justify each species before its acquisition, highlight the essential benefits that each species brings to the display, and their ability to provide the care that enables the species to thrive in the aquarium. Biodiversity for the sake of biodiversity must be discouraged, and collection planning must be approached from the perspective of 'how much is really enough' to achieve the display's goals. The species count of most collections could be reduced by one-third without impacting their mission or attendance goals. That is the same-sized collection in terms of the number of individual animals (biomass), but just fewer species. Preference should be given to hardy, interesting species from captive-bred sources, managed fisheries and truly sustainable wild sources, especially if the sustainable harvest has local socio-economic benefits, effectively creating the 'sustainable aquarium'. Obtaining animals from the wild in a sustainable fashion, with those animals then thriving in human care, is a cause for celebration. Public aquariums should encourage the ornamental aquarium trade to move more proactively towards aquaculture and genuine sustainable use programmes in the wild, noting that the legal trade in exotic birds, reptiles and amphibians as pets is now sustained almost entirely from captive-bred sources.

Scientific research on novel display species must still occur, however, but with specific goals and desired outcomes: why *that* species? Is there a clear benefit to the species in the wild or its natural habitat? Even more research is needed on the methods to breed and rear important display species, and more partnerships and resources are required to rear display animals on a commercial scale, as is now happening, for example, in Florida and Hawaii. Public aquariums should critically review their role and results to date in the captive breeding of endangered fish species. Pragmatic decisions need to be made regarding the choice of species and the likely tangible *in situ* outcomes through long-term, institutional commitments and partnerships.

Aquariums must become much more aware of and reduce the energy footprint and environmental impact of their initial construction and subsequent operations, especially water usage and the energy needed for lighting and life support, and promote their corporate responsibility through their marketing and public relations activities. Leading by example is now a cost of doing business, which extends to the merchandise sold in the gift shop, the food and beverages sold in the café, the foods fed to the animals on display, and even applies to employee behaviours, such as how the aquarium staff commute to work each day.

Aquariums must become centres of excellence, not only for science education in general, but also to promote the role of females and especially minorities in science and conservation. Indeed, the aquarists and aquarium curators of today and tomorrow need to be far more than 'just' experts in animal care. They must also be able to interact with the public and media, speak passionately and with credibility on current aquatic conservation issues, and work and argue persuasively in a diverse, team-based environment. The now popular '70:20:10' approach to experiential, on-the-job learning and development (where 70% of workplace learning is informal, on the job; 20% is coach-/mentor-based; and 10% is via formal courses) is particularly pertinent to staff growth in the public aquarium industry, where collegial support and inter-facility sharing is commonplace. However, methods need to be developed to record this experiential learning, so that the staff may receive recognition, and so the learnings can be shared further afield. Since the spark that leads to engagement in science and the environment can occur at any age, aquariums also need to continue to focus on diverse audiences from early learning to lifelong learning, so as to fan the spark into a flame, whenever it may occur. There needs to be a pipeline, an attainable career path, for the middle school student, who is perhaps uninterested in science, to become an aquarist, a curator and more.

There are some well-documented successful aquarium and zoo conservation programmes, but the global impact of these efforts has not been enough. Aquariums must sharpen their focus on participating in and encouraging impactful conservation action. For some, acting individually or as a part of a larger consortium, advocating for policy presents an important opportunity. Some US aquariums worked with other conservation groups to ban shark-finning, and in 2016 a group of AZA member institutions enlisted their guests to lobby the US government to increase marine protect areas. Aquariums must continue to think globally, but do more by acting with local relevance, for example, engaging with schools, colleges, NGOs, and state and federal education and *in situ* conservation programmes. Since what has been done thus far is not working, or not working fast enough, non-traditional partnerships must be sought. Membership of NGO conservation organizations pales in comparison to the annual global aquarium- and zoo-going audience of nearly 1 billion, and, for example, the congregations of faith-based groups, many of whom provide spiritual guidance, education and health care in areas where biodiversity loss is at its greatest. Can common ground be found with non-traditional partners regarding stewardship of Planet Earth? After all, conservation is not about mourning what has been lost, but rather celebrating what can still be saved, and aquariums need to seek out any and all that will help them do more, faster. The stark reality is that the natural world and the biodiversity that safeguards the quality of life for humans are shrinking fast. Yet one in ten people on the planet visit an aquarium or zoo every year. If aquariums and zoos are conservation organizations, they must do more. What if that army of aquarium- and zoo-goers could be engaged and motivated to make a difference and to transform conservation within a generation, stabilizing conditions for the benefit of all?

Acknowledgement

Special thanks to Lori Walsh for improving this essay. The opinions expressed herein are those of the author, and do not necessarily reflect the opinions of any organization or company.

Supporting Bibliography

Carson, R. (1965) *The Sense of Wonder*. Harper & Row Publishers, New York.

Moss, A., Jensen, E. and Gusset, M. (2015) Evaluating the contribution of zoos and aquariums to Aichi Biodiversity Target 1. *Conservation Biology* 29, 537–544.

Supporting Websites

Association of Zoos and Aquariums: AZA, http://www.aza.org
Center for the Advancement of Informal Science Education CAISE: http://www.informalscience.org
Ocean Literacy Network: http://www.oceanliteracy.org
The Ocean Project: TOP, http://www.theoceanproject.org
Rising Tide: http://www.risingtideconservation.org
World Association of Zoos and Aquariums: WAZA, http://www.waza.org

6 A Tale of Two Zoos: Tourism and Zoos in the 21st Century

Lee Durrell*

Honorary Director, Durrell Wildlife Conservation Trust, Jersey, UK

* Corresponding author: Lee.Durrell@durrell.org

My zoo has had to cope with a dual personality in the last few years. For most of its existence, it believed in itself to be a 'zoo'. A decade ago it re-branded as a 'wildlife park', but now it is a 'zoo' again. This is Jersey Zoo, started by my late husband, Gerald Durrell nearly 60 years ago.

The somersault was caused by successive executive teams and their varying interpretations of the tourism they believe drives our success. Our single main source of income, as for most zoos, arises from our visitors – gate receipts and secondary spend – but we are located in a small catchment area. To make ends meet, we must be very attractive to visitors, local and non-local, perhaps more so than other zoos.

Before discussing zoos, tourism and animal welfare, some history is in order.

Gerald Durrell, British naturalist and author, established Jersey Zoo in 1959 with the idealistic vision that it would eventually be entirely devoted to the conservation of endangered species. It would contribute to this goal in ways he deemed zoos are suited for and capable of, although few, if any, zoos at that time followed them – or even believed in them. Gerry considered that a zoo's principal function was to aid species survival. It would achieve this by captive breeding of threatened species, research into their biology and behaviour that is not easily carried out in the wild, training conservation practitioners and catalysing actions to recover threatened species and habitats in the wild, all the while ensuring the well-being of the animals concerned. The front-facing role of such a zoo would be to raise awareness and support to induce pro-conservation and environment behavioural change in the visitors, be they locals or tourists.

These were all fairly novel approaches 60 years ago, but Gerry and his young team persevered. In 1963 we set up a member-based charitable trust, now called Durrell Wildlife Conservation Trust, to operate the Zoo and develop additional (non-commercial) support for the Trust's conservation objectives. By 1964 we had the laid the foundations for producing an in-house scientific journal; by 1968 we had begun to breed seriously threatened species and make observations on them in the wild; by 1972 we had hosted the first international conference on conservation breeding; by 1978 we had welcomed our first student for professional conservation training; by 1984 we had released captive-bred animals to boost declining wild populations; by 1987 we had begun to restore threatened habitats; by 1989 we had started grassroots community conservation programmes in threatened species' habitats; by 1995, the year Gerry died, the Trust embraced about 15,000 loyal members, each paying an annual subscription.

Jersey Zoo was self-sustaining in the early days, benefiting from enormous numbers of British tourists to Jersey, who flocked to the Zoo from the 1960s through the 1980s. Although income from the Trust's member subscriptions, donations and legacies (many from fans of Gerry's books) increased during this period, it was the Zoo's healthy commercial revenues that covered the core costs of the growth of overseas conservation programmes and professional training in Jersey. Of the latter, Gerry often said that he had always wanted to turn his zoo into a mini-university for conservation!

Come the 1990s, however, and with the rise of cheap airfares to exotic and/or sunny climes, Jersey became a bit of a backwater, and the tables were turned on Jersey Zoo. Revenues fell, subscriptions, donations and legacies could not cover the shortfalls, and we began dipping into our reserves to maintain our increasingly expensive activities, including Zoo operations.

Ecologically speaking, there are three options open to animals and plants facing severe resource shortages, especially on islands: adapt, migrate or die out. Jersey Zoo was determined to follow the first.

Adapting was not made easier by the anti-zoo movement that has emerged around the world over the last three decades, which seems to be particularly strong in the UK, our main source of visitors. The anti-zoo lobby claimed that zoos could not adequately provide for the welfare of their animals or contribute meaningfully to conservation. We began to hear comments at the airport from incoming tourists such as 'Jersey Zoo? Oh, I never go to zoos! I'm against them.' Many of our own staff, members and repeat visitors, clearly influenced by the negativity that had arisen over zoos, began to say that we were 'much more than a zoo' or 'a zoo that's not a zoo'. Visitor comment and self-opinion led to the change of name to 'Durrell Wildlife Park' in our marketing and media outlets in 2006.

Since the turn of the 20th century, many of the world's major zoos have upped their game, spending more and more on conservation, research, education and animal welfare, and some of the worst zoos of the world, in terms of animal welfare, have closed. Whether improvements and closures were forced by a more discerning public or were self-motivated is hard to say, but a good zoo these days believes it has a duty to make a genuine contribution to the protection and awareness of biodiversity and to attend to the needs of the animals in its care.

Nevertheless, the concept of 'zoo' continues to attract criticism. The popularity of the film *Blackfish* and the actions of pressure groups led Sea World in 2016 to announce the cessation of its breeding programmes for orca whales. A few months later, the incident at Cincinnati Zoo – a silverback gorilla, Harambe, was shot dead to protect a child – engendered widespread questioning of the role of zoos.

Back here in Jersey, however, recurring pressure from local residents and some staff, coupled with the arrival of a new CEO, led us in 2017 to drop the name Durrell Wildlife Park and revert to Jersey Zoo. It was a widely popular decision. The name that Gerry originally gave to his 'stationary ark' is one that clearly resonates more than 'wildlife park' for many of its stakeholders.

With this background in mind, I would like to pose some questions about zoos and offer my personal response to each of them, hoping they may add perspective to this book on animal welfare and tourism.

First, are zoos important in tourism? Do they attract economically significant numbers of people outside their own regions? Some of the big, famous zoos are certainly well-known tourist destinations, and this was the case for Jersey Zoo, when Jersey was in a tourist rich environment. But the majority of zoos attract more local people, those seeking 'a fun day out for the family', than non-locals. I believe, however, that this will change. Zoos will begin to attract visitors who will want to see animals for their own sakes. People will come to see them because they are rare, threatened and cannot easily be seen in places other than zoos. People will want to reconnect with the nature they realize is being lost.

A few people will think no further than the animal's rarity – the sensational aspect of 'Look here! This is one of the last of its kind!' But more and more of the concerned populace, the well-educated and environmentally aware, be they local or non-local, will visit zoos to seek knowledge of what is really happening to the natural world. Theirs will be a memorable and enlightening educational experience, much like visiting a modern museum with its innovative and interactive exhibits. People are already asking why animal numbers are dwindling, species vanishing and habitats being destroyed ... and what they can do about it. Moreover, they are the people more likely to expect zoos to address issues of animal welfare and well-being promptly and competently.

Thus zoos will gain in importance to tourism over the coming years, the greater proportion of visitors being those who expect reliable and thorough information and high standards in animal care. Note that most visitors will be more enthusiastic about large mammals, such as pandas, elephants and great apes, but there will always be some (and, let's hope, more in the future!) who will be eager to see small, humble creatures, like rare bats, songbirds and tortoises.

Second, do zoos differ from other tourism enterprises using captive animals? Elephant rides, tiger selfies and visits to crocodile and turtle farms are purely commercial endeavours, but most zoos are now governed by the moral imperative of biodiversity conservation. In future, the divergence will become greater, because so much more will be expected of zoos in terms of educating the public, reconnecting people with nature and meeting the needs of animals in zoos and in the wild.

Third, are zoos capable of ensuring the good welfare of their captive animals? The short answer is yes. The issue is the cost of safeguarding the 'five freedoms' (https://en.wikipedia.org/wiki/Five_freedoms), and that cost depends upon the species.

Fourth, are zoos capable of ensuring the well-being of their captive animals? The answer is not straightforward, because animal well-being is not clearly defined and perhaps is not definable. It is hard enough to define well-being in ourselves![†] But experienced, sensitive zoo practitioners and animal psychologists have a reasonably clear picture of an individual's mental state and its quality of life. Thus the answer to the question is a cautious yes, but with the caveat that much depends on the species, the individual and the person making the assessment. Again, a major issue is cost.

The most expensive species in terms of welfare and well-being include large-bodied animals, particularly mammals (i.e. the few mega-vertebrates that we humans have not killed off during our recent evolutionary history). Most of these are now seriously threatened in the wild – the pandas, elephants, great apes and others – but these are the species that visitors will flock to see.

Will zoos meet the costly challenge of ensuring their animals' welfare and well-being? If they are to remain viable, they will have to, as paying visitors want to see big animals, but only if their needs are taken care of and they are 'happy' in their captivity. And if zoos are to follow their moral imperative of aiding biodiversity conservation, they will have to, as so many big animals desperately need the help that good zoos can provide. Yes, there are good zoos holding only small-bodied endangered species, but their undoubted contribution to conservation is not the only one that zoos can and should make.

There is a mutualism between zoos and tourism – 'you help me and I help you' – which will surely grow. Good zoos attract people, and their municipalities often support events and developments that will make them more attractive, which in turn helps the municipalities.

I hope for more. I hope for a synergistic relationship between zoos and tourism, which would benefit the higher ideal of the protection of biodiversity, the greatest challenge to the planet today. The synergy will be that zoos proactively and enthusiastically stimulate tourism, and tourism proactively and energetically stimulates investment in zoos, with funding coming from the tourism, zoo and charitable sectors. 'Zoo tourists' will be people who are primed to help in the conservation of wild species and their habitats and who will want to do more as a result of their visits. They are already important to zoos now and will become vital in the future.

This tale of two zoos is inspired by one zoo, Jersey Zoo. According to the conventional definition, a zoo is 'a collection of animals on view to the public'. But in so many cases today this definition no longer applies, and in tomorrow's world I hope it applies to none. A zoo does and will do so much more than simply allow the public to view its animals, from conservation action to reconnecting people with nature to rewilding degraded habitats, all with great sensitivity to the animals in its care. Thus the long-ago vision of Gerald Durrell and the achievements of modern zoos are redefining the word. Zoos will one day be seen as valiant institutions, meriting respect, pride and support . . . and well worth visiting!

[†] Refer to Chapter 2 for a discussion of the scientific assessment of animal welfare.

7

A Comparison of Tourism and Food-provisioning Among Wild Bottlenose Dolphins at Monkey Mia and Bunbury, Australia

J. Mann[1]*, V. Senigaglia[2], A. Jacoby[1] and L. Bejder[2&3]
[1]Georgetown University, Washington, DC; [2]Murdoch University, Perth, Western Australia; [3]University of Hawaii, Honolulu

* Corresponding author: Mannj2@Georgetown.edu

Introduction

Tourism focused on viewing and interacting with cetaceans has grown exponentially in the last 20 years, becoming a multi-billion dollar industry worldwide (O'Connor *et al.*, 2009; Higham *et al.*, 2014). Although most tour and commercial operations are boat-based (i.e. whale- and dolphin-watching trips) or swim-with-dolphin operations, feeding wild dolphins from boats or the shore has become another popular means of gaining access to wildlife. To address some of the negative effects of food-provisioning wild marine mammals (e.g. Christiansen *et al.*, 2016), the practice is generally banned. For example, feeding marine mammals is illegal in the United States, as it constitutes harassment under the Marine Mammal Protection Act (NMFS, 1972). It is also prohibited in the commonwealth waters of Australia under the Environment Protection and Biodiversity Conservation Act 1999. However, Australian state governments regulate the conservation and protection of dolphins in coastal waters up to 3 nautical miles from shore, creating ambiguity that allows states to provision wild dolphins within coastal waters. There are currently four locations in Australia where tourists can legally feed wild dolphins: Monkey Mia and Bunbury in Western Australia and Tangalooma and Tin Can Bay in Queensland (see Fig. 7.1).

The focus of this comparison is to highlight the similarities and differences between Monkey Mia and Bunbury in terms of the costs and benefits of dolphin food-provisioning in relation to tourism, conservation education and research.

The oldest dolphin provisioning site is located at Monkey Mia where the practice of provisioning was initiated in the 1950s by fishers tossing their catch to Indo-Pacific bottlenose dolphins (*Tursiops aduncus*). The phenomenon attracted tourists and by the late 1980s, the

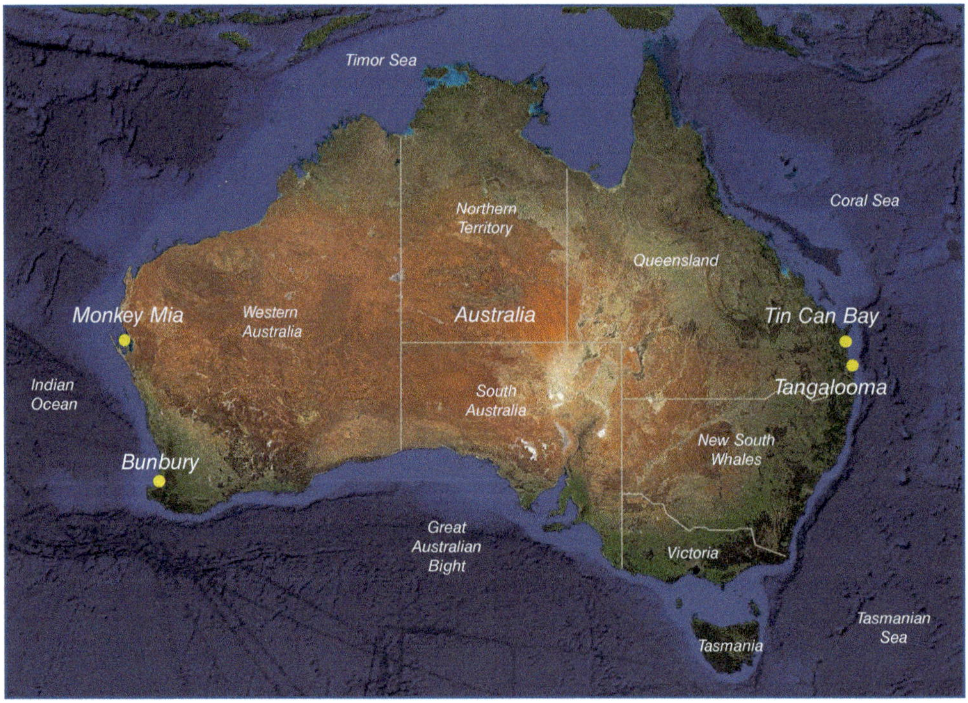

Fig. 7.1. Map of the four dolphin provisioning locations in Australia: Monkey Mia and Bunbury in Western Australia and Tin Can Bay and Tangalooma in Queensland

Western Australian government's Conservation and Land Management (CALM, currently called the Department of Parks and Wildlife, DPaW) stepped in to regulate and manage feeding. As a result, feeding free-ranging dolphins outside of DPaW supervision is now prohibited. Feeding dolphins at Bunbury was initiated in 1989 and is currently managed by the Bunbury Dolphin Discovery Centre (DDC), a non-profit organization that also offers dolphin-watching and swim-with tours. Although the DDC operates under a state permit issued by DPaW, the practice of feeding wild dolphins is not as strictly regulated as in Monkey Mia. At DDC, there are no clear limitations on the number and identity of the individuals that can be fed. Moreover, concerns have been raised following several reports of illegal feeding of free-ranging dolphins by recreational boaters (J. Symon, personal communication) and the increase in begging behaviour towards recreational boaters. At both sites, long-term research projects have been established (since 1984 at Monkey Mia, http://monkeymiadolphins.org, and since 2007 at Bunbury, http://mucru.org).

History and Management of Monkey Mia

From the 1950s to 1970s, Monkey Mia was a remote fishing camp with limited road access and very few tourists. The majority of interactions with dolphins involved tossing undersized fish and baitfish to them. Over time, a few dolphins began visiting the shoreline to beg for fish and interact with people, including Charlie (who was most likely a female). In 1974, Wilf and Hazel Mason bought the fishing campsite, and set up a shop for the growing number of visitors. Subsequently the Shire of Shark Bay and CALM built the Dolphin Interpretive Centre in 1986 and local rangers took over fish sales from the Masons and management of the dolphins. Around this time Monkey Mia was designated as a marine park. At this point, any dolphin that came close to shore could be fed and there were no limits on the amount of fish they were provided. By 1987 up to 35 kg of fish were sold to tourists for dolphin feeding daily. By the late 1980s, four females from two matrilines and three adult males, all members of an alliance, were regularly fed. Researchers had been established there since 1984 and began tracking individual life histories of provisioned and non-provisioned dolphins (Connor and Smolker, 1985). They helped the rangers set up data-collection sheets to determine when dolphins visited during the day and for how long. Meanwhile, transportation and local infrastructure improved, attracting even more tourists.

In February of 1989, seven dolphins died (including four offspring born to the provisioned adult females and all three adult males), which was linked to high levels *E. coli* bacteria in the water near the provisioning site. As a result, CALM took measures to avoid future harm by regular water testing and limiting the amount of fish fed to reduce the amount of time dolphins spent near Monkey Mia. Each dolphin was restricted to 60–62 kg per month (2 kg per day over the month). Instead of tourists buying their own fish, CALM rangers brought buckets of defrosted fish (one bucket per dolphin) three times per day, and fish were given to tourists individually so they could hand-feed the dolphins. Rangers spread the buckets (and dolphins) out, standing knee-deep in a 90 × 45 m 'Interaction Area' (see Fig. 7.2a,b) and selected individuals from the crowd. Rangers limited physical contact between humans and dolphins, but only when they were down at the beach. Outside of their view or work hours, tourists often touched, fed and swam with dolphins.

With the park renovated and accessible, over 100,000 tourists visited Monkey Mia annually by the 1990s. Since over 700 people might be in the water at the same time, rangers established additional protocols, which included keeping people knee-deep in line down the beach. The scientific team, which had been collecting data on the dolphins at the beach, in addition to those offshore, became more involved in management and recommended that no calves and

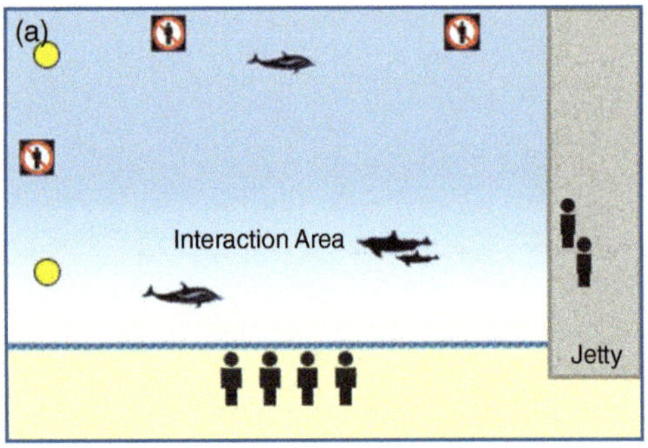

Fig. 7.2a. Diagram of the interaction area at Monkey Mia (not to scale). People can stand in the water up to their knees but are asked to step out of the water during the feeds and enter only when selected to feed a dolphin. The adjacent 45 m jetty is an excellent viewing platform for visitors. The yellow buoys mark the west boundary of the Interaction Area and are 90 m from the jetty. Swimming is not allowed in the Interaction Area.

Fig. 7.2b. Photograph of a feed at Monkey Mia. People stand along the shore of the interaction area, while a select few visitors are chosen to step into the water by DPaW volunteers and feed dolphins a fish.

males be fed and only daughters of currently provisioned females could be introduced (Mann and Kemps, 2003). This was one way to maintain the 'tradition' without disrupting family associations too much, since, as scientists learned, most foraging tactics were passed down from mother to daughter. Furthermore, males can become quite aggressive towards non-provisioned females brought into the Interaction Area for mating and people were often bitten and hit, whether or not they had provoked the attack.

In 1994, a confluence of events highlighting the problems with provisioning sparked a revision of the feeding practices at Monkey Mia. First, a calf that had been fed died immediately after weaning because he stopped hunting on his own. Second, one of the adult females became entangled in a net, most likely due to reduced wariness of human activity. Finally, calves of provisioned females were simply not surviving. This was attributable to the fact that the provisioned females show reduced care of their calves compared to non-provisioned females (Mann and Kemps, 2003; Foroughirad and Mann, 2013). Analysis of calf survival for the provisioned and non-provisioned females was strikingly different, which prompted intervention by CALM (Mann *et al.*, 2000). CALM instituted further restrictions and limited feeding times to the morning, between 8am and 12pm. Importantly, the length of time that the dolphins had to 'wait' for the feed was changed to 30 minutes, instead of an hour or more, so that the females would leave shore, engage in normal activities and care for their calves. The management changes worked because since those changes were implemented, calf survival markedly improved and dolphin visitation to the beach decreased – as intended. However, some behaviour patterns persisted and are described in more detail below.

History and Management at Bunbury

In the mid-1960s, Mrs Elevyn Smith commenced hand-feeding a small number of bottlenose dolphins from a jetty in the Leschenault Inlet in Bunbury. The practice became a popular attraction. Regular feeding stopped in the early 1970s after Mrs Smith's death, but occasional feeding of wild dolphins still occurred. By 1989 a non-profit community association called the Bunbury Dolphin Trust Inc. was established and initiated a more regular feeding programme (van Rooy, 2006) within a designated feeding area called the 'Interaction Zone' within Koombana Bay. The programme was interrupted in 1991 due to strong antagonism with local fishers who believed the practice encouraged dolphins to depredate crab pots. In fact, Wringe (1993a,b) reported an increase in depredation after provisioning became a regular practice. Fishers retaliated, even killing one dolphin in 1992. However, public attitudes towards the dolphins and wildlife conservation in general soon changed and food provisioning was reinstated at the time of the opening of the Dolphin Discovery Centre in 1994.

Currently, the provisioning programme is licensed and regulated by DPaW. The permit limits the daily amount of fish allowed per dolphin per day to 500 g, so that the animals still have to feed in the wild to obtain their required daily energetic intake (estimated to be up to 10 kg per day). Dolphins can enter the provisioning area, a 600 m^2 buoy delimited no-boat zone (see Fig. 7.3), multiple times during the day but can be provisioned only between 8am to 12pm and exclusively by the DDC volunteers. Within the provisioning area (also called 'Interaction Zone'), tourists are positioned in a straight line in knee-to-waist-deep water from the shoreline (see Fig. 7.4). Multiple volunteers space themselves evenly along this line among the tourists to control the interaction. At the same time a designated volunteer feeder enters the water at the end of the line when dolphins are to be fed. The volunteer supervisors are the senior volunteers in control of the interaction programme on the day and will often walk up and down the line in front of the guests to provide information about the dolphins and to answer questions that the guests may have. Unlike in Monkey Mia, Tangalooma and Tin Can Bay, there is a discretionary clause listed within the DDC licence conditions of operation to discourage feeding by the general public, such that all dolphin provisioning is carried out by trained volunteers.

Over the years, the DDC has developed a self-imposed protocol for provisioning. This includes detailed guidelines on how and when to feed dolphins. The DPaW permit does not specify the identity or the number of dolphins that can be fed; however, they are provided with quarterly reports outlining the results of the interaction programme. The DDC maintains a provisioning list that specifies which dolphin can be fed. This list, developed by the DDC marine biologist and long-term volunteer staff, can be modified at any time. The list only includes adult females with dependent calves of at least 6 months (with the exception of Osho, a male dolphin who started to regularly visit the interaction area with his provisioned mother). Currently, 12 dolphins appear on the provisioning list but only six are considered active (they have visited the provisioning area in the last 2 years). The permit does not require monitoring when a new dolphin is introduced into the provisioning programme. Detailed guidelines ensure the safety of dolphins and tourists. An educational component is not mandatory but during a dolphin's visit, tourists are opportunistically provided with information on dolphin biology and behaviour by the volunteers. These guidelines are based on the experience and scientific findings from other provisioning locations (e.g. Monkey Mia) and their efficacy in minimizing impacts of food provisioning on dolphins. Compliance with provisioning guidelines is dependent on the supervisor, who is in charge of the feeding procedures (V. Senigaglia, personal observation).

DDC volunteers made *ad libitum* observations on dolphin visitation from 1990 to 2001, when a systematic data collection began. Since then, data recorded include the identity of provisioned dolphins, amount and type of fish provisioned to each dolphin and the duration of each dolphin visit within the provisioning area (Fig. 7.3).

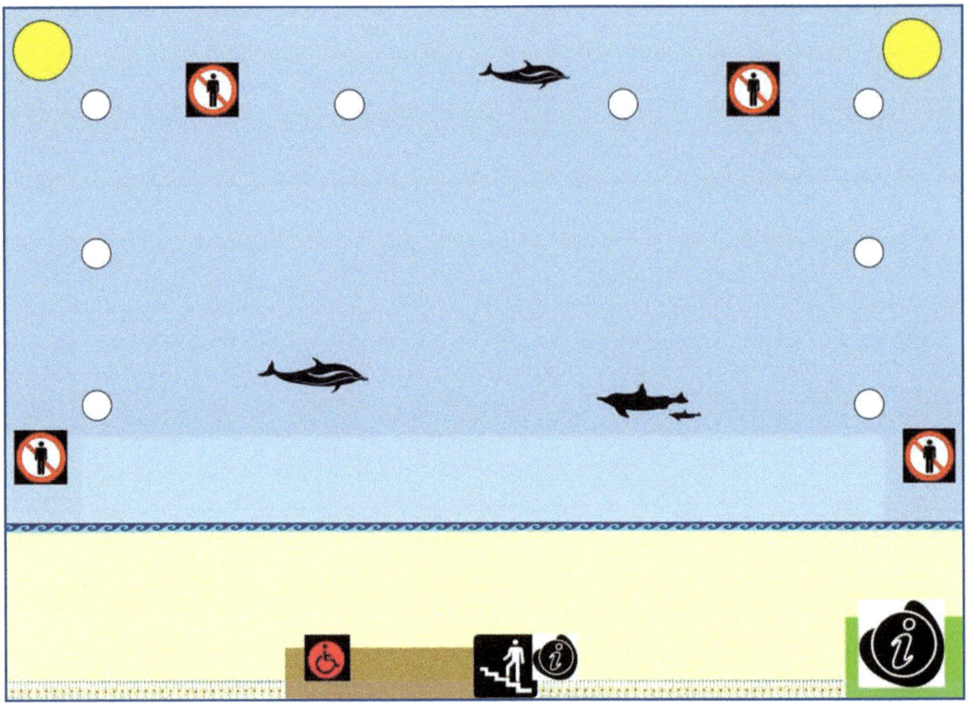

Fig. 7.3. Interaction Zone in Koombana Bay, Bunbury, Western Australia, in front of the Dolphin Discovery Center. The Interaction Zone is a no-boat area delimited by buoy. (Diagram courtesy of Dolphin Discovery Center.)

Tourism Experience at Monkey Mia

Many people who visited Monkey Mia before 1990 have fond memories of swimming and playing with dolphins. When there were fewer people and restrictions on interactions, the Monkey Mia dolphins did indeed allow people to stroke them and play games with them, such as passing seagrass blades back and forth. The dolphins even stroked people back with their pectoral fins. Not all interactions were so friendly, as visitors were regularly bitten or struck by one of the male dolphins. However, as tourism increased, the likelihood of harm to both humans and dolphins also increased. The rangers had the very difficult task of reigning in people's desire to pursue and touch the dolphins.

The research on the Shark Bay dolphins started to become well-known worldwide in the 1990s, as people learned that Shark Bay dolphins use marine sponges as foraging tools, males form multi-level complex alliances, and mothers nurse their calves for 3 to 8 years (Connor *et al.*, 2000; Mann *et al.*, 2000). As more scientific information about the dolphins became available, the rangers were able to transition the dolphin experience from close dolphin–human interactions to educational talks down at the beach that also explained the problems prior to more regulated feeding and interactions. The rangers continued to incorporate more information into their talks, allowing for the public to learn about wild dolphins and for them to observe the dolphins interacting with each other in their natural environment – Monkey Mia is one of the best places in the world to watch natural dolphin behaviour from shore as the calves and other dolphins hunt, play and socialize with each other. Furthermore, tourists get the unique opportunity to observe the dolphins hunting in very shallow water, sometimes so shallow that the rangers have to urge people to get out of the water so that they do not disrupt the chase. Non-provisioned dolphins also come close and interact with the provisioned dolphins.

Fig. 7.4. A mother and a calf within the Interaction Zone, parading in front of the line of tourists. Volunteers, wearing red shirts, stand within the line or slightly forward to better manage the interaction. (Photo courtesy of Dolphin Discovery Center.)

Even though only five adult females are fed, there are sometimes more than 20 dolphins just metres from shore, protected by the Interaction Area where no swimming and boating is allowed. Although the provisioning has brought dolphins to shore for close viewing, their close associates also visit the Interaction Area near shore to the delight of tourists (see Fig. 7.5).

Tourism Experience at Bunbury

Food provisioning, boat-based dolphin-watching and swim-with tours provide an important economic revenue for the DDC and the City of Bunbury that uses the local dolphin population as its tourism drawcard (Visit Bunbury, 2014). Dolphin food-provisioning is not advertised *per se*, but the DDC makes use of the dolphin 'beach visits' in advertising material, on the website and via social media and staff believe that provisioning plays a vital role in attracting the visitors. When visitors enquire about dolphin food provisioning times and procedures, the DDC specifies they are free-ranging animals and will not visit every day. They visit most often during the morning between 8 and 11am and they receive approximately 350–500 g if and when they choose to visit the Interaction Zone. When tourists enquire about feeding, staff from the DDC tend to refer to the fish handout as a 'token of appreciation' to dolphins as a reward for their visitation. Feeding, although not hidden, is conducted in a discreet manner as a condition of the DPAW licence.

In Bunbury, dedicated dolphin research was initiated in 2006 through the South West Marine Research Program (SWMRP) led by Murdoch University. The SWMRP was initially founded through a partnership between Murdoch University and the Bunbury Dolphin Discovery Centre, with support from the South West Development Commission, and is now composed of partners from industry, government, research and the community. The focus of the SWMRP is to conduct research into the dolphins occurring in Bunbury's coastal and estuarine waters to assess the long-term viability of the bottlenose dolphin population.

Since its inception, the SWMRP has monitored the dolphin population through year-round boat-based photo-identification transect surveys. Through the programme, we have a good understanding of the dolphin population abundance, habitat use, behavioural

Fig. 7.5. Two young girls get close to a dolphin female to feed her a fish, providing an up-close experience and photo opportunity. (Photo courtesy of Leighton de Barros, Sea Dog TV International.)

and foraging ecology, and genetic connectivity to other populations in south-western Australia (Sprogis *et al.*, 2016a,b; Manlik *et al.*, 2016). This information collected by the SWMRP has yet to be incorporated in the DDC exhibition displays, but is delivered to the visitors by volunteers and staff both during dolphin interactions at the beach and out on the boat tours.

Impact of Provisioning on Dolphin Welfare at Monkey Mia

With 30 years of systematic focal observations on females and calves in the Interaction Area and offshore, away from it, researchers have been able to document specific impacts of provisioning on maternal and calf behaviour, development and calf survival. Three comparisons were made: (i) the behaviour of provisioned mothers and their calves in the Interaction Area and offshore; (ii) the behaviour of non-provisioned females and provisioned females and their calves while offshore; and (iii) the survival of calves born to provisioned and non-provisioned females.

During focal observations, the research team collected detailed data on activity state, location (GPS and when near shore, locations near and far from human activity), mother–calf distance, associates and behavioural events. While provisioning impacts maternal and calf behaviour in numerous ways, the central finding is that provisioned adult females reduce care for their calves (nursing access, contact and proximity) (Mann and Kemps, 2003; Foroughirad and Mann, 2013). Offshore, provisioned females acted similarly to non-provisioned females, but their calves still received less care and had altered activity budgets. Provisioned females also occasionally begged at boats, whereas non-provisioned females have never been observed doing so.

Calves of provisioned females spend more time foraging and socializing and less time resting than their non-provisioned counterparts. They also had less contact with their mothers and

Fig. 7.6. A young calf tries to get into infant position to suckle but her mother is in very shallow water and rolls to her side away from the calf while the mother waits to be fed by tourists. (Photo courtesy of Megan Wallen, monkeymiadolphins.org.)

spent more time separated from them. At the Interaction Area, provisioned females spend considerable amounts of time in shallow water and, in doing so, do not allow their calves to gain 'infant position contact', a position under the mother's tail where the calf has nursing access – a critical form of maternal care. Calves stay further from people and consequently, further from their mothers. When calves do come close to their mothers near the beach, they whistle, rub on their mothers, and butt up against them, attempting to get into infant position (see Fig. 7.6). Occasionally these behaviours escalate to a full-fledged 'tantrum' with very loud whistling from the calf and constant circling of the mother. Such behaviours are virtually never seen offshore with the exception of two provisioned females (mother and daughter) who begged frequently at fishing boats anchored offshore. Their calves engaged in similar attempts at achieving infant position, which their mothers prevented during boat-begging by turning on their sides while close to the boat. Despite these behavioural changes, when the provisioning is controlled and minimized (e.g. restricted to morning hours and fewer fish provided), so that dolphins spend less time close to shore, the effect on maternal care is lessened.

Impact on the Dolphins in Bunbury

The resident population of Indo-Pacific bottlenose dolphins that inhabits the inner waters of Koombana Bay in Bunbury, is relatively small and exposed to a diverse array of human activities, including dedicated dolphin-focused tourism. Possible impacts of anthropogenic disturbance on the local dolphin population are under evaluation, but a pilot study conducted in 2009 documented an effect of recreational and commercial tourism on dolphins' activity (Arcangeli and Crosti, 2009). Population abundance, sociality, distribution and calving varies cyclically, with seasonal peaks during summer and autumn corresponding to the highest anthropogenic disturbance, due to a substantial increase of vessel presence during the summer months (Sprogis *et al.*, 2016). Females are usually encountered in sheltered waters, in particular, during the austral summer corresponding to the main calving season and are thus exposed to a greater anthropogenic pressure (Smith *et al.*, 2016)

A dedicated study of the ecological consequences of food provisioning has recently started. Maladaptive behaviour, such as dolphin begging behaviour towards recreational boats, which has been associated with food provisioning elsewhere (e.g. Donaldson *et al.*, 2012; Christiansen *et al.*, 2016) has been documented in Bunbury, along with several cases of propeller-related injuries. The potential impact of tourism and food provisioning on Bunbury's dolphin population is particularly concerning, given recent findings by Manlik *et al.* (2016) that forecasts a significant decline in dolphin abundance, which will jeopardize the population fitness unless reproduction rates are increased. This study compared the small and declining Bunbury dolphin population to the larger and more stable population in Shark Bay (where Monkey Mia is located).

The study shows that the Bunbury population is more sensitive to perturbations in reproduction and juvenile survival than the Monkey Mia population (Manlik *et al.*, 2016). Dolphin reproductive rate and success (calf survival) can be affected by human disturbance (Lusseau *et al.*, 2006). Anecdotal evidence suggests that provisioned female dolphins in Bunbury may have lower reproductive success than non-provisioned females. For example, a long-term provisioned individual, Shanty, has had a total of five stillbirths and another potentially dead one (J. Symons, personal communication). However, whether a direct causal link between reproductive success and food provisioning exists still needs to be investigated.

In 2016, the Western Australian state government allocated AUS$24.9 million for the redevelopment of the DDC and the revitalization of Koombana Bay foreshore. This is part of a bigger expansion plan of the Bunbury Waterfront and the Port of Bunbury, already the fourth largest in Western Australia (Landcorp, 2013). The project foresees the rebuilt Dolphin Discovery Center will include large interpretation displays, a restaurant and café, entertainment areas and a fourfold increase in the building footprint (South West Development Commission, 2016).

Comparison between Monkey Mia and Bunbury: Implications for Management

Monkey Mia has had a longer history of research than Bunbury, including quantitative observations of provisioned and non-provisioned dolphins using focal follow methods. This has enabled researchers to identify key behavioural differences that are linked to calf survival. Long-term demographic data have also been important for determining how provisioning affects life history parameters (such as weaning age, age at first offspring, and survival). In contrast, quantitative observations of Bunbury provisioned and non-provisioned individuals have not been collected. However, after 11 years of year-round boat-based photo-identification surveys along pre-determined transect lines throughout the study area, information on demographic parameters, (e.g. reproductive and survival rates), home ranges and habitat use, are now available to investigate potential negative consequences of food provisioning in Bunbury. If not properly managed, food provisioning clearly has negative impacts (Monkey Mia: Mann *et al.*, 2000; Sarasota, Florida: Christiansen *et al.*, 2016). The long-term SWMRP database and the findings from the ongoing study aimed to quantify possible impacts of food provisioning, will provide further localized information for the management of this activity in Bunbury.

As a consequence of the different management of food provisioning, the tourism experience also differs at the two sites. In Monkey Mia, the experience focuses on the provisioning itself, which is carried out by tourists supervised by DPAW staff. In contrast, the provisioning is not central to the experience in Bunbury, but rather it is a more discreet event in which tourists are passive spectators. At Bunbury, volunteers informally present some information on dolphin biology, ecology and conservation at their own discretion. At Monkey Mia there is considerable interaction between the rangers and scientists, so that information is updated regularly. There is a considerable potential to enhance visitor experience at both sites by providing much more comprehensive and engaging information.

Bunbury is an industrialized port characterized by heavy recreational traffic. This is in stark contrast to Monkey Mia, which is pristine and a World Heritage Site. Thus, the effect of dolphins becoming conditioned to food handouts in Bunbury most likely has more severe consequences. As dolphins' wariness towards people decreases, the chances for boat strikes and entanglements increases and there are more opportunities for the general public to illegally feed dolphins. In Bunbury, begging behaviour by dolphins away from the food-provisioning area is not uncommon. This maladaptive behaviour can be facilitated by provisioned animals via social learning and might spread through the dolphin population (Donaldson *et al.*, 2012) as an unwanted and unintended consequence of controlled food provisioning. Moreover, regulations to prevent disturbance (e.g. maximum distance, speed limits and the prohibition to feed and pet free-ranging dolphins) are breached on a daily basis by recreational boaters (V. Senigaglia, personal observation). These cumulative stressors, present in Bunbury, represent the main differences between the two sites and need to be considered in addressing management of food provisioning.

References

Arcangeli, A. and Crosti, R. (2009) The short-term impact of dolphin-watching on the behavior of bottlenose dolphins (*Tursiops truncatus*) in Western Australia. *Journal of Marine Animals and Their Ecology* 2, 1.

Christiansen, F., McHugh, K.A., Bejder, L., Siegal, E.M., Lusseau, D., McCabe, F.B., Lovewell, G. and Wells, R.S. (2016) Food provisioning increases the risk of injury and mortality in a long-lived marine top predator. *Royal Society of Open Science* 3, 160560.

Connor, R.C. and Smolker, R.S. (1985) Habituated dolphins (*Tursiops* sp.) in Western Australia. *Journal of Mammalogy* 66, 398–400.

Connor, R.C., Wells, R., Mann, J. and Read, A. (2000) The bottlenose dolphin, *Tursiops* sp.: social relationships in a fission–fusion society. In: Mann, J., Connor, R., Tyack, P. and Whitehead, H. (eds) *Cetacean Societies: Field Studies of Dolphins and Whales*. The University of Chicago Press, Chicago, pp. 91–126.

Donaldson, R., FinnH., Bejder, L., Lusseau, D. and Calver, M. (2012) The social side of human–wildlife interaction: wildlife can learn harmful behaviours from each other. *Animal Conservation* 15, 427–435.

Foroughirad, V. and Mann, J. (2013) Human fish provisioning has long-term impacts on the behaviour and survival of bottlenose dolphins. *Biological Conservation* 160, 242–249.

Higham, J., Bejder, L. and Williams, R. (eds) (2014) *Whaling-watching, Sustainable Tourism and Ecological Management*. Cambridge University Press, Cambridge, UK.

Landcorp (2013) The Western Australian Land Authority. Available at: http://www.landcorp.com.au/project/bunburywaterfront (accessed 21 January 2018).

Lusseau, D., Slooten, L. and Currey, R.J.C. (2006) Unsustainable dolphin-watching tourism in Fiordland, New Zealand. *Tourism in Marine Environment* 3, 173–178.

Manlik, O., McDonald, J.A., Mann, J., Raudino, H.C., Bejder, L., Krutzen, M., Connor, R.C., Heithaus, M.R., Lacy, R.C. and Sherwin, W.B. (2016) The relative importance of reproduction and survival for the conservation of two dolphin populations. *Ecology and Evolution* 6, 3496–3512.

Mann, J. and Kemps, C. (2003) The effects of provisioning on maternal care in wild bottlenose dolphins, Shark Bay, Australia. In: Gales, N., Hindell, M. and Kirkwood, R. (eds) *Marine Mammals. Fisheries, Tourism and Management Issues*. CSIRO Publishing, Collingwood, Victoria, Australia, pp. 304–320.

Mann, J., Connor, R.C., Barre, L.M. and Heithaus, M.R. (2000) Female reproductive success in bottlenose dolphins (*Tursiops* sp.): life history, habitat, provisioning, and group size effects. *Behavioral Ecology* 11, 210–219.

NMFS (1972) *Marine Mammal Protection Act*. Available at: http://www.nmfs.noaa.gov/pr/pdfs/laws/mmpa_regs_216.pdf (accessed 21 January 2018).

O'Connor, S., Campbell, R., Cortez, H. and Knowles, T. (2009) *Whale Watching Worldwide: Tourism Numbers, Expenditures and Expanding Economic Benefits*. International Fund for Animal Welfare, Yarmouth, MA.

Smith, H., Frère, C., Kobryn, H. and Bejder, L. (2016) Dolphin sociality, distribution and calving as important behavioural patterns informing management. *Animal Conservation* 19, 462–471. DOI: 10.1111/acv.12263.

South West Development Commission (2016) *Delivery: Annual Report 2015–2016*. Available at: http://www.swdc.wa.gov.au/media/annual-reports/2016/?page=1 (accessed 30 January 2018).

Sprogis, K., Smith, H., Rankin, R., MacLeod, C. and Bejder, L. (2016) Home range size of adult Indo-Pacific bottlenose dolphins (*Tursiops aduncus*) in a coastal and estuarine system is habitat and sex-specific. *Marine Mammal Science* 32, 287–308.

van Rooy, S. (2006) A review of the daily dolphin visits in Koombana Bay. Unpublished research conducted by Stephanie van Rooy at Van Hall Instituut.

Wringe, I. (1993a) Dolphin killed by blow: vet. *The West Australian*, 13 March, p. 3.

Wringe, I. (1993b) Dolphin magic a mystery. *The West Australian*, 20 September, p. 4.

8 The Tourism Industry and Shark Welfare

Wilfred Chivell*

Marine Dynamics Tours and Dyer Island Cruises, Gansbaai, South Africa

* Corresponding author: wilfred@sharkwatchsa.com

Does the Tourism Industry Have Obligations to Ensure Good Welfare of Sharks?

Absolutely, we have to protect the species that we rely on for a living as well as ensure that the fragile marine ecosystem remains healthy and at optimal function for the diversity of marine life to thrive in the future. It is a sad fact that the South African great white shark population is not showing the expected recovery since its decline prior to protection. They face many threats: along our own coastline we can lose around 25 or more annually in the Kwazulu Natal shark nets and drumlines. These nets are based on historic fatal attacks on swimmers in that area by sharks and there are now many more beach users in Kwazulu Natal because of the warmer waters. The great whites also migrate to unprotected waters such as those off Mozambique and the Western Indian Ocean, where they are targeted by local fishermen, their fins sent off to the Far East, their meat consumed by locals and the jaws and teeth sold as jewellery and trophies. The slow maturity and undocumented breeding of a great white shark is of great concern in light of these threats.

Like many other species, the sharks are in fact worth more alive than dead and the tourism around sharks in general contributes to knowledge and conservation of the species. The industry in South Africa ultimately helps protect and police this species by daily monitoring it as it frequents coastal aggregation sites. We know and recognize returning sharks, document new sightings, and we quantify and document those sharks that are not seen again. Should the shark cage-diving industry not be around, we feel certain that there would be high levels of shark poaching. Hunting for this animal was very prevalent in our Western Cape waters prior to the protective legislation and the introduction of cage-diving ecotourism in 1991. The employment and economic benefits generated by this successful industry contribute directly to helping ensure the survival of the species. One could liken great white sharks to the mountain gorilla, for, without tourism, this species would probably not have survived. There is significant research in South Africa to show that the activity has minimal impacts on the species (Johnson and Kock, 2006; Laroche *et al.*, 2007; Gallagher *et al.*, 2015).

The white shark population in Gansbaai is open, thus sharks do not live in the bay year-round; they are transient and usually spend between a few weeks to a maximum of a few months per visit (Towner *et al.*, 2013b). There seems to be a high degree of site fidelity where individuals return to the site intermittently between migrations. Our preliminary satellite tracking data shows that white sharks undertake extensive longshore migrations and will often remain away from Gansbaai for a year or more. The species spends time inshore while migrating, often patrolling sandy beach environments regardless of activities such as fishing or chumming taking place (chumming is scent-based attraction of the sharks, with no feeding). The importance of shark diving tourism has been discussed in detail in a scientific review paper by Gallagher *et al.* (2015).

Can the Shark Cage-Diving Industry Educate the General Public about the Need to Aid the Survival of Sharks?

Gansbaai in the Western Cape, South Africa, is known as the white shark capital of the world and attracts 85,000 visitors per annum to experience shark cage-diving. We have one of the most accessible shark populations with only a 20-minute boat ride to where the sharks aggregate. No scuba experience is required, so the activity has become popular with all ages, thus reaching a wider market. The opportunity to educate this number of people every year is very exciting, and there is no doubt that our industry as a whole has helped people find a new appreciation for the great white. This is evident from the swell of support towards the protection of the species and advocacy for it. Our team is involved in research including population studies, behavioural and movement ecology, the effect of environmental factors, and more. Our guiding marine biologist educates our clients onboard every trip. Clients of Marine Dynamics are able to financially support the research we do on great white sharks. Their support is a direct translation of understanding and experience to improve conservation and is a good measure of what we are achieving. This funding is used to support the operational costs and various research and animal rehabilitation projects of the Dyer Island Conservation Trust which I established in 2006. We have almost 20 scientific publications to date on the various species in our area with a focus on great white shark studies. This research has been possible because of the successful commercial businesses being able to support it (see Dyer Island Conservation Trust, n.d., 2016).

Research is essential to help drive conservation decisions around great white sharks. Some crucial studies from the area are listed below.

Great White Shark research from Marine Dynamics and the Dyer Island Conservation Trust to date (refer to Dyer Island Conservation Trust, n.d. for more details).

1) A humpback dolphin was bitten by a white shark and was photographed in Gansbaai in August 2006. This was the first documented interaction and potential predatory shark attack on any cetacean species in Gansbaai and is evidence that large great white sharks may opportunistically hunt humpback dolphins in this region of South Africa (Weisel *et al.*, 2010).
2) Dyer Island Conservation Trust biologists reviewed photographic data of white sharks previously smart position only (SPOT) tagged during an expedition in Gansbaai in 2004. Photos of re-sighted sharks indicated that bolted on satellite tags, known as SPOT tags, caused permanent damage if they remain on the shark for longer than 24 months (Jewell *et al.*, 2011).
3) In 2009 a white shark was traumatically injured by a boat in Gansbaai. The healing process was documented with photographs and video by Dyer Island Conservation Trust biologists and revealed extremely rapid healing in the species and no long-term effect on the behaviour of the shark (Towner *et al.*, 2012).
4) Jewell *et al.* (2012) used acoustic tagging data and explored white shark movements in Mossel Bay, South Africa. Tracking analysis revealed that larger white sharks are more selective and refined in the habitats they use than smaller sharks. Spatially restricted management strategies would aid enforcement of current protective legislation for the white shark in similar environments of limited resources and capacity.
5) Dyer Island Conservation Trust biologists performed population models on photographs taken over 5 years in Gansbaai of white shark fins. Their results found between 808 and 1008 white sharks may comprise the regional population, almost half the number previously reported (Towner *et al.*, 2013b).
6) Towner *et al.* (2013a) investigated the effects of environmental factors on the numbers and sexual composition of white sharks visiting Gansbaai over a 5-year period. This was a published chapter of Towner's (2012) MSc thesis through the University of Cape Town and the Dyer Island Conservation Trust. Warmer waters and other climatic changes have had significant effects on numbers of sharks, with females favouring warm and males cooler waters. The findings of this study could contribute to bather safety programmes because the incorporation of environmental parameters into predictive models may help to identify times and localities of higher risk to bathers and help mitigate human–white shark interactions.
7) Dyer Island Conservation Trust biologists collected and analysed manual tracking data sets from five sharks at Dyer Island, which Jewell (2012) used for his MSc with the University of Pretoria and the Dyer Island Conservation Trust. The results of the study were published and identified important core habitats used by white sharks at Dyer Island. It showed significantly different habitat use and movement patterns between white sharks in Mossel Bay and Dyer Island.
8) Chapple *et al.* (2015) and Dyer Island Conservation Trust biologists tested a new design of camera and tag that minimizes attachment damage and captures more data on swimming speed and behaviour than standard bio-loggers.

9) In 2012, Marine Dynamics and the Dyer Island Conservation Trust worked with OCEARCH and other South African scientists involved in satellite tagging of great white sharks. These data, available for 5 years, have revealed the incredible distances and areas travelled to by sharks and are supporting our local research.
10) Wcisel *et al.* (2015) looked at the role of refugia around the Dyer Island ecosystem in structuring the predator–prey relationship between white sharks and Cape fur seals.
11) Towner *et al.* (2016) documented sex-specific and individual preferences for hunting strategies in white sharks. White shark behaviour ultimately creates different pressures on other trophic levels, which is of particular concern in a complex and vulnerable marine system such as Dyer Island.
12) Dureuil *et al.* (2015) worked on a computer-aided framework for sub-surface identification of white shark pigment patterns. This assists in identification of individuals.

Creatively, infographics make crucial studies more accessible to a wider audience.

How does the Shark Cage-Diving Tourism Industry Balance the Needs of Sharks and Desires of Tourists?

The great white shark has been demonized for many years: at one time many believed that the only good shark was a dead shark. Thankfully, South Africa has been progressive in protecting this threatened apex predator since 1991. In the 1990s the shark's value changed, and as shark cage-diving tourism began, the shark was worth more alive. The industry of today is strictly regulated in South Africa by the Department of Environmental Affairs. Operators require the necessary permit, of which there are 13 in South Africa. Each operator must operate within the gazetted code of conduct (Nel and Peschak, 2006).

Tourists wish to dive with the great white and this is done with the safety of a cage. As the great white is a protected species, no touching is allowed. For most, this experience is about seeing the shark underwater and we have skilled crew on either side of the cage who know how to work safely with the sharks for the safety of sharks and clients.

To initially attract the sharks to visit our boat, we use an oily fish mix, known as a 'chum slick', which may attract some sharks to surface and circle the boat and cage hence allowing observation. Without this method, the sharks would not interact on the surface and diving would be almost impossible. The boats are based in the Dyer Island ecosystem, which great whites frequent naturally. Here the chum slick from the almost 60,000 Cape fur seals on Geyser Rock attracts one of the largest populations of sharks moving through the area. As noted earlier, these sharks are migratory, often travelling large distances before we may see them again. During the winter months (April to August) the sharks hunt around the island system as young seal pups take to the water for the first time. Shark boats will then work nearby. But in the summer months, it is immaterial how much fish oil an operator puts in the water: if the sharks have moved to the areas we call the shallows, then the boats must follow. In fact, for much of the time, this is the area where they are found. So the boats must go where the sharks are. Sharks are not fed through this interaction.

Tourists have also come to expect some education around the species and we meet this need through an onboard marine biologist, an educational briefing and a conservation talk.

What Influence Does the Film *Jaws* Continue to Have on Shark Cage-Diving and Public Education?

There is a percentage of people that arrive to see sharks in fear, but seeing the grace and calmness of great white sharks in their natural habitat quickly dispels that. Our guestbook comments confirm this with remarks such as 'Not what I expected' and 'They are beautiful not scary'.

Sensationalism and misleading headlines continue to perpetuate myths, and the role of the media here is crucial. In South Africa, our media have become more responsible in their reporting and we are often consulted by leading publications to provide fair and accurate comment so as not to demonize sharks. Unfortunately, this is not always the case across the world and so our task is to work on changing perceptions daily. The swell of support on social media to protect sharks has also made a huge difference for many who have found a new appreciation of the species.

References

Chapple, T., Gleiss, A., Jewell, J., Wileski, M. and Block, B. (2015) Tracking sharks without teeth: a non-invasive rigid tag attachment for large predatory sharks. *Animal Biotelemetry* 3(14).

Dureuil, M., Towner, A., Ciolfi, L. and Beck, L. (2015) A computer-aided framework for subsurface identification of white shark pigment patterns. *African Journal of Marine Science* 37, 363–371.

Dyer Island Conservation Trust (n.d.) Biologist and affiliates publication list. Available at: http://dict.org.za/pages/resource/science.php (accessed 1 October 2017).

Dyer Island Conservation Trust (2016) A decade of achievement 2006–2016. Available at: https://issuu.com/dyerislandconservationtrust/docs/dict_10_years_achievement_report (accessed 1 October 2017).

Gallagher, A.J., Vianna, G., Papastamatiou, Y., Macdonald. C., Guttridge, T. and Hammerschlag, N. (2015) Biological effects, conservation potential, and research priorities of shark diving tourism. *Biological Conservation* 184, 365–379.

Jewell, O.J.D. (2012) Foraging ecology of white sharks (*Carcharodon carcharias*), at Dyer Island, South Africa. Master's thesis, University of Pretoria, Pretoria, South Africa.

Jewell, O., Wcisel, M., Gennari, E., Towner, A., Bester, N., Johnson, R. and Singh, S. (2011) Effects of Smart Position Only (SPOT) tag deployment on white sharks in South Africa. *PLoS ONE* 6(11), e27242.

Jewell, O., Johnson, R., Gennari, E. and Bester, M. (2012) Fine scale movements and activity areas of white sharks (*Carcharodon carcharias*) in Mossel Bay, South Africa. *Environmental Biology of Fishes* 96, 881–894.

Johnson, R. and Kock, A. (2006) South Africa's White Shark cage-diving industry – is there cause for concern? In: Nel, D.C. and Peschak, T.P. (eds) *Finding a Balance: White Shark Conservation and Recreational Safety in the Inshore Waters of Cape Town, South Africa; Proceedings of a Specialist Workshop*. WWF South Africa Report Series – 2006/Marine/001. WWF South Africa. Die Boord, South Africa, pp. 1–19.

Laroche, R., Kock, A., Dill, L. and Oosthuizen, W. (2007) Effects of provisioning ecotourism activity on the behaviour of white sharks *Carcharodon carcharias*. *Marine Ecology Progress Series* 338, 199–209.

Nel, D. and Peschak, T. (eds) (2006) *Finding a Balance: White Shark Conservation and Recreational Safety in the Inshore Waters of Cape Town, South Africa*. WWF South Africa Report Series – 2006/Marine/001. WWF South Africa. Die Boord, South Africa.

Towner, A. (2012) Great white sharks (*Carcharodon carcharias*) in Gansbaai, South Africa: environmental influences and changes over time: 2007–2011. Master's thesis, University of Cape Town, Cape Town, South Africa.

Towner, A., Smale, M. and Jewell, O. (2012) Boat strike wound healing in the white shark (*Carcharodon carcharias*). In: Domeier, M. (ed.) *Global Perspectives on the Biology and Life History of the White Shark*. CRC Press, Boca Raton, pp. 77–82.

Towner, A., Underhill, L., Jewell, O. and Smale, M. (2013a) Environmental influences on the abundance and sexual composition of white sharks *Carcharodon carcharias* in Gansbaai, South Africa. *PLoS ONE* 8(8), e71197.

Towner, A., Wcisel, M., Edwards, D., Reisinger, R. and Jewell, O. (2013b) Gauging the threat: the first population estimate for white sharks in South Africa using photo identification and automated software. *PLoS ONE* 8(6), e66035.

Towner, A., Leos-Barajas, V., Langrock, R., Schick, R., Smale, M., Kaschke, T., Jewell, O. and Papastamatiou, Y. (2016) Sex-specific and individual preferences for hunting strategies in white sharks. *Functional Ecology* 30(8), 1397–1407.

Wcisel, M., Chivell, W. and Gottfried, M. (2010) A potential predation attempt by a great white shark on an Indo-Pacific humpback dolphin. *South African Journal of Wildlife Research* 40(2), 184–187.

Wcisel, M.A, O'Rian J, De Vos A, Chivell W. (2015) The role of refugia in reducing predation risk for Cape fur seals by white. *Behavioural Ecology and Sociobiology* 69(1), 127–138.

9 Tourism, Wildlife Conservation and Animal Welfare

Dr Jane Goodall, DBE*

Founder – the Jane Goodall Institute and UN Messenger of Peace (www.janegoodall.org)

* Corresponding author: mlewis@janegoodall.org

In many developing countries, tourism is a major source of foreign exchange, and this means that governments are more likely to approve legislation to protect existing national parks, reserves and so on and to approve additional areas for conservation of wildlife. This applies to the central government and also to local governments in regions where tourism has been developed. The tourist industry creates a large infrastructure that benefits businesses, ranging from airlines, hotels and taxis to shopping centres and traders in local arts and crafts. But conservation of wildlife can only be successful in the long run if local communities buy into it, which means they too must benefit from tourism.

Poverty, Habitat Destruction and Human/Animal Conflict

A major problem for conservation is that so many people in and around wildlife habitats are living in poverty, and this has a negative effect on the environment. Let me give an example from my own experience. I began my study of the chimpanzees of Gombe National Park in Tanzania in 1960. At that time, Gombe was part of the so-called 'equatorial forest belt' that stretched from the western areas of Tanzania and Uganda through central Africa and across to the West African coast. But when I flew over Gombe in 1991 in a small aircraft, I was shocked to see that the tiny national park, only some 35 km^2, was surrounded by completely bare hills. The local communities had survived, and to a large extent lived in harmony with their environment, through small-scale family farming and sustainable use of natural resources. But old traditional ways had been disrupted by colonialism, first German and then British, by missionaries and more recently by President Nyerere's attempts to relocate scattered farms into a centralized location to practise communal agriculture. Population size had increased and by 1991 there were more people living in the area around Gombe than the land could support. Overused soils had lost their fertility. Trees had been cut down by villagers desperate to grow more food or make charcoal in order to make some money. On the steep slopes, this had led to massive soil erosion and the many streams were becoming silted up. It was obvious that the people were struggling to survive.

This was when I realized there was no way we could conserve the chimpanzees unless we could improve the lives of the surrounding communities. Since 1994 the Jane Goodall Institute (JGI) has successfully worked to do so through our holistic TACARE programme, now operating in 77 communities throughout chimpanzee habitats in south-western Tanzania. We operate similar programmes in five other chimpanzee range countries.

In most of the chimpanzee habitats in Central and West Africa, people have relied on subsistence hunting. Humans were just one more carnivore species and man and animal lived in harmony. But here, too, human population growth and commercial activities such as logging and mining is disrupting traditional ways of life. Today the bushmeat trade, the *commercial* hunting of wild animals, along with the live animal trade, has decimated wildlife.

Everywhere poverty, habitat destruction and human population growth has led to increasing competition for land and natural resources between humans and wild animals. It is easy to understand that animals deprived of natural resources are driven to raid human crops and it is equally easy to understand the anger and despair of villagers when their meagre crops are destroyed by elephants, bushpigs, baboons or chimpanzees.

How Can Tourism Help?

Clearly, it is desperately important to provide some sort of assurance to local communities that conserving and protecting animals and their habitat is more important, for them, than destroying it. Programmes like our TACARE are one way of doing this. We have improved the lives of hundreds of people and they have become our partners in conservation. But this requires a huge commitment in time and constant fundraising.

Tourism is another way that communities can benefit from conserving their wildlife. It can provide jobs: hunters make excellent guides, local people can be trained to work in tourist camps and lodges, and there is a ready market for locally grown food. The new growth of ecotourism represents an effort to ensure that tourism benefits local communities. Visitors spend time in villages to witness traditional dancing, learn about local cultures and have the opportunity to buy local arts and crafts, which greatly benefits women. We have many examples of visitors who, after being introduced to the problems faced by so many people living around conservation areas, have gone home and raised money for health or education programmes and even given talented young people the funds to pursue higher education.

One other benefit of wildlife tourism that should be mentioned is the effect on the visitor of close contact with animals in their natural habitat. So many people have told me how experiencing chimpanzees or gorillas in the forest, or seeing an elephant or giraffe close up, was a life-changing experience. When they get home, they often become involved in conservation programmes, helping to raise money to pay for equipment for rangers, caring for orphans and reintroduction programmes and spreading awareness.

Negative Effects of Tourism on Wildlife

Tourism must be properly organized and controlled to avoid adverse effects on the wildlife and wild environments that we are trying to protect. There is an unfortunate tendency to allow too many visitors in order to increase the revenue. On the Serengeti, for example, a pride of lions on a kill may be surrounded by more than ten tourist vehicles. Someone told me they once counted 19. The famous Yellowstone National Park in America suffers from similarly large invasions of visitors. Unless the number of visitors per day is restricted, this problem can only get worse, as guides can now communicate by radio, informing other vehicles where to find the action. Even though vehicles are usually required to follow certain roads or trails, guides and drivers are tempted to disobey this rule to ensure that their group gets the best possible view. This can be very disruptive to the habitat. Tourist vehicles may interfere with the movements of an individual or a group of animals. I was told of one situation on the Serengeti when more than 15 tour buses rushed to give their groups a good view of wildebeest crossing a river. Faced by such a disruptive human presence, the animals turned back and panicked. Calves lost their mothers, and some drowned.

Of course, wild animals sometimes become habituated to the presence of tourists, but even so, this may still inhibit normal behaviour. At one time I spent hours, day after day, parked some distance away from the den of a family of bat-eared foxes in Ngorongoro Crater. After a few days I was able to watch as the cubs played and their parents hunted. But when another vehicle arrived and moved in too close, the foxes, although they did not seem afraid, ceased their activities, curled up and appeared to sleep. When the other car left, they at once began to play and hunt again. I have been told that the sleeping patterns of some dolphins were disrupted by tourists swimming among them.

The main chimpanzee community at Gombe is very well habituated to the presence of humans, as we have been studying their behaviour since 1960. But in chimpanzee society, many females transfer into neighbouring communities during adolescence, thus ensuring genetic diversity. When tourists encounter such a young still unhabituated female travelling with a habituated group of males, she will run off and as a result, no longer protected by the males, she may be subjected to aggression from community females who often resent these newcomers.

There is one problem specifically related to great ape tourism and that is the fact that these primates, genetically so close to humans, are at risk of contracting human respiratory diseases.

For this reason, and because we can contract diseases from other primates, tourists may be asked to wear masks.

In some areas, tourists go on walking safaris, which is good except that, too often, they deviate from designated trails. Mount Kilimanjaro in Tanzania, and many other such areas, are being harmed by people trampling over fragile habitats and endangering plant life. Dropping litter is often a major problem, as it may harm some animals.

And while tourists buying local crafts can be beneficial, there are also occasions when wildlife is adversely affected by such sales. The tourist markets in Dar-es-Salaam, for example, sell hundreds of tropical seashells all of which were, of course, taken from the ocean when their occupants were still alive.

Conclusions

It is clear that properly regulated tourism, when visitors are restricted in number, and required to obey strict codes of conduct, can be extremely beneficial to conservation efforts. Many areas around the world that are protected today are maintained only through tourist revenue. The mountain gorillas in Rwanda, made famous by the work of Dian Fossey, would almost certainly have become extinct without the booming tourist trade. But the danger of overexploitation looms large and we must be vigilant and do our best to ensure that governments and safari companies understand.

10

Managing Tourism's Animal Footprint

Daniel Turner*

Former Associate Director on Tourism and EU Compliance, Born Free Foundation (www.bornfree.org.uk), now Founder and Director of Animondial (www.animondial.com)

* Corresponding author: danielnicholasturner@gmail.com

> We believe the way tourists interact with captive whales and dolphins needs to change and we want to play an active role in supporting this transition ... We will not sign up any new attractions that feature captive whales and dolphins for theatrical shows, contact sessions (such as 'swim-with' programmes) or other entertainment purposes.
>
> Virgin Holidays (February 2017)

> ... if an animal attraction is found not to be fully compliant with the ABTA *Global Welfare Guidance for Animals in Tourism*, Thomas Cook won't sell it.
>
> Group Chief Executive, Thomas Cook (April 2017)

> Zoos are not appropriate in 2017. They are relics of the past, and the arguments to justify keeping animals in captivity no longer stand up. The sad reality is that the animals are held captive primarily for our entertainment not for reasons of conservation and it is time that this stopped.
>
> Chief Executive Officer, Responsible Travel (April 2017)

In 2016 and 2017, some of the best-established British travel companies made groundbreaking decisions to cease their association with certain captive animal attractions, end elephant riding or remove zoos from their holiday itineraries (Born Free Foundation 2016, 2017; Travel Weekly, 2017; STA Travel, 2017; TUI, 2017). Is this just a coincidence, or is this an indication that travel companies have decided to take a more compassionate approach towards animals in tourism? As former Associate Director on Tourism matters at the Born Free Foundation, and now an independent consultant to the travel industry, I consider here the reasons behind these welcomed announcements.

The recent wave of announcements by various travel companies that they are ceasing their promotion of certain commonplace animal attractions is no coincidence but rather the result of years of work by, among others, the Born Free Foundation. A recognized charity that since its inception has campaigned to end captive animal exploitation, Born Free had compromised this ideal for a constructive and pragmatic approach to influencing change, through working with the travel businesses, as opposed to campaigning against them.

While targeted campaigning, exposing animal exploitation and the 'naming and shaming' of specific companies have certainly helped to focus the travel sector, it is seemingly public opinion that drives change forwards. It is, however, important to consider what shapes public opinion, the significance of industry influencers, and how functional and permanent change may actually be achieved.

Industry Influencers

Since the 1980s, the global travel industry has struggled with the terms 'ecotourism', 'sustainable tourism' and 'responsible tourism'. While the industry has been driven to 'do the right thing' for people and the environment, it nevertheless remains focused on selling holidays and excursions at a profit. The relevance of these terms varies, but the overall concept of preventing irreversible and detrimental change to travel destinations remains the same. A more responsible approach towards travel is becoming increasingly accepted and is gradually influencing change. But how is this is being achieved?

The availability of reliable, evidence-based information is a vital component in achieving permanent change. Influencing commonplace practices is unlikely unless there is significant evidence that those practices have negative impacts that provoke disapproving public opinion. Demonstrating the damaging effects of exploitative tourism practices has helped shape strategies to improve resort hotel construction, reduce energy consumption and protect local communities. The same can be said for excursions and practices that involve animals.

Prior to 2004, the Born Free Foundation lobbied the travel industry to change its practices relating to captive animal attractions. This dogmatic approach, however, did little to change the industry's promotion of exploitative animal practices. In 2004, following engagement with the Federation of Tour Operators (FTO), Born Free agreed to share its knowledge and supporting evidence, and to assist in the production in 2008 of the *Travelife Animal Attractions Handbook* (Federation of Tour Operators, 2008), which helped to educate the industry on how certain practices, promoted through tourism, impact on animal welfare and influence change (TUI Travel plc, 2011). This publication was superseded by ABTA's *Global Welfare Guidance for Animals in Tourism* (ABTA, 2013), which establishes standards in animal protection on those attraction providers contracted by ABTA-member tour operators. ABTA, the British travel association, asked Born Free to develop the *Guidance* (Born Free Foundation, 2013), while a review panel of 200 species experts and stakeholders ensured that the *Guidance* and its intentions were both comprehensive and practically achievable.

To this day, ABTA's *Global Welfare Guidance* remains the only all-inclusive guidance for the travel industry on this complex topic. Through a set of seven separate documents, the *Global Welfare Guidance for Animals in Tourism* imposes minimum requirements, and best practice guidance, on animal attraction providers in global destinations. This includes wild animals kept in captivity, domestic animals and wildlife viewed in the wild. According to ABTA members, any contracted attraction that fails to comply with these minimum requirements, or exercise any of its identified 'unacceptable' practices, will cease to be contracted and promoted. For instance, ABTA's *Global Welfare Guidance* states that where people are permitted to be photographed with animals, these should be free from bad practices, identified as including premature mother and offspring separation, animal mutilation (removal of skin, tissue, teeth or bone structure to reduce risks in handling), sedation and other restrictions that prevent the animal's natural behaviour. Therefore, these standards seek to eradicate practices such as using wild cats, which often have their claws removed or are under sedation, primate species that can have their teeth removed or filed down, or reptiles, which can have teeth or venom glands removed, or in some observed cases, have their jaws taped or sown shut (Fig. 10.1).

According to Born Free's postbag, the use of wild animals in 'souvenir photographs' is commonplace in many zoos and popular tourist attractions. Causing the animals concerned significant distress and discomfort and, in some cases, placing people at risk of injury and disease, these practices have been classified as 'unacceptable' by ABTA's *Global Welfare Guidance*, and any attraction exercising these activities is recommended to be removed from sale.

The Blackfish Effect

Public opinion is certainly an influencer of travel industry practices, but it should not be considered the only influencer. The documentary film *Blackfish* exposed the negative impact of captivity on the mental state of orcas and has been revolutionary for the anti-captivity lobby, resulting in the reputations and profits of institutionalized animal attractions being seriously damaged. Why was the film more effective than decades of lobbying by anti-captivity NGOs? Could it be due to the film engaging the mainstream public and producing tangible information and evidence? Could the provision of information in an effective manner make targeted campaigning and public lobby obsolete?

Targeted Campaigning

Reputation is everything for a commercial enterprise and travel businesses are no exception. Competition between the multitude of mainstream and specialist tour operators is fierce and any advantages or actions that taint reputation are given full attention. The impact of tourism on animal welfare and protection has received significant media attention and failures to address the highlighted issues have challenged travel businesses. While often causing reactionary and

Fig. 10.1. A python, used in tourist souvenir photographs, whose jaws have been taped shut in order to reduce the risks of injury on the handler. ©Born Free Foundation

defensive responses, targeted campaigning that does not provide an alternative, or offer a viable solution, tends to fail in delivering the desired long-term change.

The Pragmatic Approach

Following successful engagement with the FTO, Born Free decided to invest its efforts in constructive collaboration with the travel industry. This included the drafting and development of bespoke guidance, an evaluation of existing animal excursions, the development of auditing documentation, staff training, and ad hoc advice on animal attractions and activities involving animals. The reaction to this pragmatic and constructive approach was highly encouraging. ABTA, representing the majority of UK tour operators, has established an industry working group focused on animal welfare matters; numerous travel businesses have created company policy on animal protection and reviewed their practices; while many businesses have made significant changes to how they engage with animal attraction providers, which ones to promote and what animal activities they continue to offer to their customers (Fig. 10.2). This represents a much needed change in an industry. While this change was influenced by targeted campaigning and public opinion, it has only been achieved through constructive engagement, effective education and the provision of practical solutions to address the entrenched issues.

This kind of pragmatic approach continues to encourage more travel businesses to review their animal practices and consequently helps to influence the animal activities offered by the excursion providers. Such attractions are commonly established in tourist resorts and popular destinations, usually operating within the law and offering popular activities with animals.

Fig. 10.2. Elephant-back riding was the topic of a targeted campaign in 2016, which caused numerous tour operators to remove these activities from itineraries; actions that have not eradicated the problem. However, improvements are likely through collaborative efforts between the elephant camps, NGOs and tour operators that seek to overhaul the elephant tourism industry and phase out bad practice. ©Born Free Foundation

Influencing their practices, such as addressing animal exploitation, improving animal welfare standards and ceasing detrimental practices, is more likely to be achieved with the support of the international travel industry.

Targeted campaigning in 2016 caused many UK, Dutch and German travel businesses to cease their inclusion of elephant riding in holiday itineraries. However, evidence suggests that change in how these animals will be used in the wider travel industry will only be realized through constructive engagement with tour operators and their suppliers.

While a combination of targeted campaigning, channelled public opinion and constructive engagement with travel businesses may well have helped to establish safeguards for animals in tourism practices, in 2017, this commitment is still largely confined to businesses based in Britain, the Netherlands and, increasingly, Germany. Greater emphasis must also be applied to public-facing initiatives elsewhere in the world to stem the demand for exploitative practices with animals. ABTA's *Global Welfare Guidance for Animals in Tourism,* and its supporting implementation documentation (ABTA, 2017), is a valuable component in this endeavour and, while it is tempting to address its inconsistencies through the creation of a second edition, or even establish additional, more robust welfare standards, stakeholder efforts must instead remain focused on encouraging its global recognition, adoption and implementation of its 'minimum requirements'. Only then will we truly address the extent of animal exploitation in tourism practices.

References

ABTA (2013) *Global Welfare Guidance for Animals in Tourism: A Best Practice Guidance Manual.* ABTA, London.

ABTA (2017) Animals in tourism. Available at: https://abta.com/working-with-the-industry/animal-welfare (accessed 22 April 2017).

Born Free Foundation (2013) Working with the travel industry. Available at: http://www.bornfree.org.uk/campaigns/zoo-check/travellers-animal-alert/travel-industry-information (accessed 22 April 2017).

Born Free Foundation (2016) Thomas Cook calls on the travel industry to better protect animals in tourism. 13 December. Available at: http://www.bornfree.org.uk/campaigns/zoo-check/zoo-news/article/?tx_ttnews%5Btt_news%5D=2381 (accessed 22 April 2017).

Born Free Foundation (2017) Responsible Travel's decision to remove zoos from its holidays applauded. 3 April. Available at: http://www.bornfree.org.uk/news/news-article/?no_cache=1&tx_ttnews%5Btt_news%5D=2486 (accessed 22 April 2017).

Federation of Tour Operators (2008) *Travelife Animal Attractions Handbook*, ABTA, London, UK.

Responsible Travel (2017) Responsible Travel drops all zoos worldwide. Available at: http://www.responsibletravel.com/copy/blog-post-five (accessed 1 April 2017).

STA Travel (2017) Our animal welfare policy. Available at: http://www.statravel.co.nz/animal-welfare.htm (accessed 22 April 2017).

Thomas Cook (2017) Demonstrating our commitment to animal welfare. Available at: https://www.thomascookgroup.com/demonstrating-our-commitment-to-animal-welfare (accessed 22 April 2017).

Travel Weekly (2017) Virgin Holidays makes captive whales and dolphins pledge. 20 February. Available at: http://www.travelweekly.co.uk/articles/273315/virgin-holidays-makes-captive-whales-and-dolphins-pledge (accessed 22 April 2017).

TUI Travel plc (2017) Animal welfare and biodiversity. Available at: https://www.tuigroup.com/en-en/sustainability/sus_business/destination/welfare-and-biodiversity (accessed 22 April 2017).

TUI Travel plc (2011) *Guidelines for Environmental Sustainability in Hotels*: Animal welfare, p. 72. Available at: http://www.tuitravelplc.com/system/files/susrep/TUITravelGuidelinesforEnvironmentalSustainabilityinHotels_0.pdf (accessed 22 April 2017).

Virgin Holidays (2017) Virgin Holidays position on holidays involving captive whales and dolphins. Available at: https://www.virginholidays.co.uk/cetaceans (accessed 22 April 2017).

11 Elephants and Tourism

Jan Schmidt-Burbach*
World Animal Protection

* Corresponding author: JanSchmidt-Burbach@worldanimalprotection.org

Revered, celebrated, exploited, feared: the relationship between people and elephants has been diverse throughout history. Once present in large numbers in the wild, relentless destruction and fragmentation of their habitat, hunting and capture has led to a steep decline of wild elephant numbers. The fate of the endangered Asian elephant is especially worrying: there are approximately one-tenth the number of animals remaining in the wild compared to their African relative. With the decline of the wild populations and the spread of industrialization throughout the elephant-range countries, the traditional uses for captive elephants have changed, too. As the largest land-based animal, elephants have always posed a special attraction to people. Elephants' awe-inspiring stature and unrivalled strength inspired the development of practices to capture elephants for spiritual, religious and practical applications. Used to transport goods, participate in ceremonies, as war animals, as diplomatic gifts or for logging timber, they have been used to serve people for approximately 3000 years, with the earliest hints for capturing elephants dating back 4000 years (Kurt, 1992), approximately the same time that horses were first domesticated by people. Yet, unlike horses, elephants never underwent a domestication process (Roots, 2007). Instead of adapting elephants better to captive purposes through selective breeding, a process that could have eventually led to a domesticated species, elephants throughout the millennia have almost exclusively been caught in the wild. These elephants have been subjected to intensely cruel practices in order to tame them.

Today, the practical need for elephants has largely disappeared. There is no use for elephants as war animals, logging of timber is strictly regulated in most countries and often done with the use of heavy machinery, and goods are more efficiently transported via roads, boats or air. Accordingly the numbers of captive Asian elephants has plummeted. An estimated 100,000 elephants were captured during the past century (Sukumar, 1992), while in 2003 approximately only 16,000 remained in captivity (Sukumar, 2003), and this is an outdated figure. While many of the existing captive elephants are kept for purposes such as ceremonial use, ranger patrols or as status symbols, the development of mass tourism in some of the Asian elephant-range countries has led to an increasing number of elephants being used as an exotic attraction for travellers. In 2015, approximately 3000–4000 elephants were used in tourism (World Animal Protection, 2017). This development has also led to ethical, animal welfare and conservation concerns in relation to the use of captive elephants for tourism entertainment.

Using an endangered animal species for any profit-making purpose raises important ethical questions, and using captive elephants for tourism poses particularly complicated ones about whether the purpose of entertaining or possibly educating people justifies their use. Elephants have always been kept by communities or individuals because they presented a value that outmatched the need for the resources to maintain the animals. Logging timber, transporting goods or participation in ceremonies led to benefits that sustained a demand for captive elephants. Tourism came into play in recent decades as an alternative that allowed owners to continue providing for the existing captive elephants and making a livelihood when other sources of income had disappeared. However, with the rise in tourism numbers, this has quickly developed into a purpose that sustains a demand for captive elephants. Is the purpose of providing tourists with a short experience of a captive, endangered elephant worth the continuation of elephant-keeping? Who pays the price for this practice?

Animal Abuse Behind the Front Stage of Tourism Experiences

Elephants are highly intelligent, socially complex and incredibly powerful animals. Weighing several thousand kilograms, they are a force to be reckoned with and, especially bull elephants, have earned a reputation for being very dangerous. To ride an elephant or to train it to perform tricks requires that these animals obey a human, a creature incomparably weaker than an elephant. Traditionally this obedience is achieved by training the elephants at a young age, when they are still easier to handle. This initial training, often referred to as 'breaking' or 'crushing', lays the foundation for any further use of an elephant and varies in methods from region to region. However, the common denominator of the various methods is the use of physical punishment (see Chapter 2) in combination with other techniques, such as withdrawal of food or limiting the freedom to move, in order to establish dominance over the elephant. Only such dominance, in combination with tools such as bull-hooks, sticks or spears, allows control of the elephant in stressful situations and in the vicinity of other people, such as tourists. Some experienced elephant trainers understand that punishing an elephant too much risks it becoming permanently aggressive, and they will take care not to cross that fine line. Yet some force is required to allow for control over such a powerful animal if it is to be used for tourist rides or show performances. A well-trained elephant is the life-insurance of its keeper, who bears the responsibility for the actions of his elephant. While this training has been practised for centuries by communities relying on elephants, recent research has linked the breaking of elephants with the development of post-traumatic stress disorder, similar to what people develop after experiencing traumatizing events (Rizzolo and Bradshaw, 2016).

In addition to the training, the life of an elephant in tourism could not contrast more to the life it would lead in the wild. Most elephants will be restrained on chains when not used for rides or shows, in order to prevent them from causing damage to property or injury to people. They have limited opportunities to interact with other elephants, and their diet is comparatively monotonous and basic. Also, expert veterinary care is often not accessible or limited.

Through my work with World Animal Protection, I have led a team of researchers that has been surveying and monitoring the animal welfare conditions across over 200 elephant tourism venues in Asia, at times repeatedly, over a timespan of 8 years (World Animal Protection, 2010, 2017; Schmidt-Burbach *et al.*, 2015). This research has highlighted the severe welfare concerns for elephants in the tourism industry and is urging changes that would lead to an improvement of the situation. One of the key challenges in achieving such change through a shift in consumer demand is that the suffering of elephants in many of the conventional tourism venues is largely invisible to the outsider. A regular visitor would climb into the saddle of a waiting elephant, let the mahout (the person caring for the elephant and controlling it) guide the elephant for a 15–30-minute ride along a designated path, feed a few treats to the elephant after the ride and then leave the venue again. Fig. 11.1 shows a typical, larger-scale elephant-riding venue in Thailand that claims to receive between 700 and 1000 visitors per day. This brief experience with an elephant does not allow tourists to recognize the monotony and inadequate conditions for the elephant, nor the training procedures the animal would have gone through a long time before the ride. Neither would a tourist realize the often common exploitation of the mahouts through low wages, high risk of injury and inadequate living standards at the venue. The often surprisingly positive feedback by tourists on experiences at venues that provide severely inadequate welfare conditions to the animals reflects this misinterpretation of the elephants' situations. Worryingly, mass tourism that supports such conventional elephant tourism is growing rapidly in countries such as Thailand, the country with the highest number of elephants in the tourism industry. From 2010 to 2016 the number of international visitors to Thailand has doubled from 15 million to 32 million tourists (World Tourism Organization, 2017) and going hand in hand with this is a massive demand increase for elephant rides and performances.

Fig. 11.1. Elephant camp in northern Thailand offering rides and elephant shows to hundreds of visitors per day.

However, the continuing exposure of the problems for elephants has led to some positive developments. Over the past 10 years, World Animal Protection has observed the development of progressive alternatives to the conventional elephant riding and show performance attractions, diversifying captive elephant tourism. These alternatives offer observational experiences where elephants are granted highest possible freedom by ranging freely in semi-wild habitats under supervision by mahouts as shown in Fig. 11.2. Other venues offer close encounters with elephants that do not include riding or performing, but still require constant control over the elephant. These developments are important steps towards recognizing the needs of captive elephants better, yet it must be clear that they still rely on trained elephants. Activities that offer close direct contact with visitors are potentially highly dangerous for the visitors, as elephants remain difficult to predict. Thus, while most of these alternatives may provide better or even the best possible conditions for the existing captive elephants, they may not offer a truly sustainable alternative for future captive elephants. Sanctuary models that rely entirely on elephants trained 100% humanely (e.g. through techniques that are based on cooperation rather than domination) are at present very scarce in Asia, as their approach differs from the present local understanding of captive elephant–human relationships, that is based on the millennia-old tradition of elephant-keeping. Such sanctuaries would only offer observational and educational activities for visitors, but they require significant resources to be established. Yet, the increasing recognition by responsible tourism and elephant stakeholders of the importance of good welfare for elephants is taking steps in the right direction that, if replicated and developed appropriately, may shift the situation.

Elephant Tourism as a Means of Preserving Wild Populations in the Face of Destruction of Natural Habitats

In the face of a decrease in wild elephant populations, some conservationists may regard captive breeding of elephants as an important tool for the survival of elephants as a species. Indeed, zoos

Fig. 11.2. Elephants at a sanctuary-type venue in Thailand that provides greatly improved welfare to captive elephants, while offering observational experiences for tourists.

and other wildlife institutions often engage in captive breeding programmes for various endangered animal species. These programmes are guided through international collaborations and detailed protocols for scientific monitoring exist, which aim to help these institutions preserve genetic diversity and eventually reintroduce captive bred animals back into the wild. While some of these programmes are perceived to be controversial, due to being costly, technically challenging or yielding a limited success rate due to environmental factors not being controlled, they have also led to a few great success stories over the years. However, when such captive breeding is carried out without proper scientific management and within a private, profit-driven industry that relies on trading of the captive-bred animals, as is mostly the case for elephants in tourism, then the impact of these breeding efforts needs to be carefully evaluated. The risks of actually opening up a market for wild elephants by incentivizing the poaching and laundering of wild elephants to supplement a profitable captive population are huge.

Parallels to the commercial farming of endangered animals come to mind. Wildlife farming often claims to contribute to conservation by meeting a demand for a product with the legal supply of animals from a captive-bred population. Theoretically, this aims to protect the remaining wild populations from poaching, yet studies have shown this assumption to be too simplistic (Bulte and Damania, 2005). All too often, the existence of a legal captive population that holds high value actually incentivizes poaching and enables the laundering of wild animals into the legal captive population (Brooks *et al.*, 2010). Sourcing animals from the wild is often cheaper and quicker than breeding them in captivity, thus opportunities to capture wild animals are readily taken. And since legal captive populations are often difficult to monitor in order to ensure that all animals are indeed captive-bred, this opens doors to launder sales of the wild caught animals into the captive population (Tensen, 2016). The elephant tourism industry meets many of the criteria that ring alarm bells for such mechanisms in wildlife farming, suggesting the need to carefully evaluate the often made conservation claims.

Often one comes across the opinion that wild Asian elephants are already doomed and that keeping them in captivity is the only hope of preserving them. This fatalistic thinking risks diverting efforts and attention away from the crucial need to increase the protection of wild elephants and their habitats at all costs. Without chances to live in the wild and to contribute to the complex ecosystems of forests, what conservation purpose would captive elephants serve – chained, trained in cruel ways and employed to entertain tourists?

Having said that, there are possible conservation benefits of captive elephant populations – if governed by science, rather than money, and with the ultimate aim of fortifying wild populations and protecting their habitat.

Can There Be Ethical Elephant Tourism Experiences?

With this understanding, it is clear that there are severe concerns around the impact of conventional elephant tourism. Yet tourism does not need to be the problem; in fact, it must be part of the solution. In order that this can happen, our expectations of such tourism activities need to change away from close contact towards observational and educational experiences.

It cannot be ignored that thousands of captive elephants rely for their survival on financial support. Preferably, such support would be provided by the responsible governments and institutions while adhering to best possible welfare standards, discouraging further illegal poaching of wild elephants through reducing the commercial value of elephants, and ensuring better protection of the animals in the wild. Yet in the absence of such initiatives, ethical tourism can play a crucial role in supporting the existing elephants if principles are being followed that will not lead to a continuation of the highly commercialized practice that leads to the above welfare and conservation concerns. Supporting such elephant-friendly projects is the key in order to incentivize shifting more and more of the existing captive elephants to such places. Places that genuinely provide best welfare to elephants, that do not sustain the need for cruel training and breeding of captive elephants, and that respect mahouts and provide opportunities for their education and professional development towards a future not dependent on captive elephants.

An important aspect of ethical tourism also needs to include the recognition of Asian cultures of keeping and living with elephants, which is truly unique. Cultures are always fluid and are continuously evolving according to changes in times, the environment, society and economy, among others. Our growing understanding of elephant welfare, the ongoing socio-economic development of local communities, the high risks for keepers in working with elephants, and the commercialization of elephant tourism all have impacts that lead to cultural changes in the long run. Care must be taken not to arrest the development of local communities for the sake of 'culture preservation', but instead recognize and respect traditions and cultures, while enabling opportunities that are in line with the needs of communities and of elephants according to current best knowledge. Ethical tourism, for example, can play an important role in exploring new ways of generating income for local communities that may have in the past depended on working elephants but which may find themselves struggling today or in the future. Valuing the knowledge and traditions in these communities, and supporting them through an ethical tourism that will not continue to rely on captive elephants, or that may even encourage communities to help in protecting elephants in the wild, would be an ideal scenario.

Ethical elephant tourism is also important in supporting the protection of wild elephants. Well-managed and strictly regulated visits to national parks or rehabilitation facilities to view elephants in their natural habitat would provide resources to institutions protecting wild populations directly. Such experiences also provide a vastly higher educational value to tourists that could actually be witnessing natural behaviour of elephants and learning about their role in the ecosystem. Such tourism could also help to mitigate human–elephant conflict situations by making the presence of wild elephants financially rewarding for communities.

In a nutshell, ethical tourism can play an essential role in protecting elephants better, but only if tourism attitudes change towards becoming a contributor rather than a consumer.

References

Brooks, E.G.E., Roberton, S.I. and Bell, D.J. (2010) The conservation impact of commercial wildlife farming of porcupines in Vietnam. *Biological Conservation* 143(11), November.

Bulte, E.H. and Damania, R. (2005) An economic assessment of wildlife farming and conservation. *Conservation Biology* 19(4), August.

Kurt, F. (1992) *Das Elefantenbuch – wie Asiens letzte Riesen leben*. Rasch und Roehring Verlag, Hamburg.

Rizzolo, J.B. and Bradshaw, G.A. (2016) *Prevalence and Patterns of Complex PTSD in Asian Elephants (Elephas maximus)*. Centre for Asian Studies, University of Kelaniya, Colombo, Sri Lanka, pp. 291–297.

Roots, C. (2007) *Domestication*. Greenwood Press, Westport, CT.

Schmidt-Burbach, J., Ronfot, D. and Srisangiam, R. (2015) Asian elephant (*Elephas maximus*), pig-tailed macaque (*Macaca nemestrina*) and tiger (*Panthera tigris*) populations at tourism venues in Thailand and aspects of their welfare. *PLoS ONE* 10(9), e0139092.

Sukumar, R. (1992) *The Asian Elephant: Ecology and Management*. Cambridge University Press, Cambridge, UK.

Sukumar, R. (2003) *The Living Elephants: Evolutionary Ecology, Behaviour, and Conservation*. Oxford University Press, New York.

Tensen, L. (2016) Under what circumstances can wildlife farming benefit species conservation? *Global Ecology and Conservation* 6 (April), 286–298.

World Animal Protection (2010) *Wildlife on a Tightrope: An Overview of Wild Animals in Entertainment in Thailand*. World Animal Protection, London.

World Animal Protection (2017) *Taken for a Ride – The Conditions for Elephants Used in Tourism in Asia*. to be published. World Animal Protection, London.

World Tourism Organization (2017) *UNWTO Tourism Highlights*. Available at: https://www.e-unwto.org/doi/pdf/10.18111/9789284419029 (accessed 29 January 2018).

12 Lessons from Winnie-the-Pooh: How Responsible Bear Tourism Can Teach Us Respect and Compassion, and Benefit Bears

Sara Dubois*
University of British Columbia and British Columbia SPCA Chief Scientific Officer, Canada

* Corresponding author: sara.dubois@ubc.ca

> Life is a journey to be experienced, not a problem to be solved.
>
> A.A. Milne, *Winnie-the-Pooh*

The most famous bear tourist attraction to date is perhaps Winnie at the London Zoo from 1915 to 1934, who inspired author A.A. Milne's collection of stories for his son Christopher Robin. Named for the Canadian city of Winnipeg, the pet orphaned bear cub was purchased by a Canadian veterinarian in Ontario while en route to England to volunteer for cavalry service during the First World War (Walker, 2015). Later donated to the zoo, Winnie was a star attraction at a time when zoological collections were the only way most people could see a bear from a foreign and distant land.

A century later, bear tourism is still a very popular activity, perhaps inspired by generations of childhood stories about Winnie-the-Pooh, who, while self-defined as a bear of very little brain, was really a wise and thoughtful bear. Thankfully, now in many countries the barren and cramped cages of many zoo enclosures have been left behind and the true bear experience is sought by tourists out in the forests, rivers and valleys of bears' natural habitat. Canada is often a destination for adventurous travellers seeking just that; it is home to black bears like Winnie across the country, while grizzly bears range in the west and polar bears roam in the north. Thrill seekers may even venture deep into the wilderness to get a glimpse of the elusive 'Spirit bear', a rare white-phased black bear on the north-west coast of British Columbia. This chapter will focus on the potential animal welfare concerns for wild bears promoted as attractions by the tourism industry, with examples from western Canada.

The province of British Columbia has its own 'Big Five', analogous to the promoters of African wildlife tourism: grizzly bears, black bears, wolves, moose and cougar. Given prominence not just for their size or mythology in First Nations culture, these species are often considered keystone species in their rich and diverse ecosystems. The health of these animal populations can be used as a measure of the health of other smaller and/or lesser-known species of animals and plants. Their physical influence through prey–predator relations, plant and seed distribution and nutrient cycling help to determine the overall functioning of local ecosystems. Balancing the excursions to and viewing of British Columbia's wildlife and natural landscapes with protection of the environment for the future is critical to the thriving tourism industry, given that it is the province's third-largest industry for employment. The proud tourism slogan of 'Super, Natural British Columbia', and images of expansive coastline, mountains and rainforests, helped to draw 4.6 million international guests to the province in 2014 (BC Government, 2016a), equivalent to its resident human population that year.

As an animal welfare scientist who also trained as a wildlife biologist, I have witnessed the rise of animal tourism with great interest. Almost 20 years ago, I worked in a national park as a student biologist and met guests who came specifically to see wild animals, particularly bears. While some were motivated to take in the alpine meadows, glaciers and rivers, those carrying long lenses and binoculars were generally eager to see a wild animal in its environment. Travelling is an incredible way to connect with our natural world. It can inspire, energize, enlighten and even create empathy for those who live and experience the world very differently to oneself. Done responsibly, it can provide opportunities for communities to showcase their natural beauty, unique culture or people-powered innovations in a sustainable and economically beneficial way. Travel experiences, whether local, regional, or international, have the potential to expand our knowledge, respect and compassion for the world, something that can be neglected in our busy lives. Travellers often select destinations that will allow them to experience interactions with both domestic and wild animals. However, this animal tourism has unique considerations above and beyond the enjoyment and benefit to the traveller, such as the welfare and safety of the individual animals.

Just as the global tourism industry has had to face questions regarding ecologically and socially responsible practices, the concept of animal welfare is being discussed in tourism scholarship (Fennell, 2013; Sneddon *et al.*, 2016) and at the dinner table, thanks to media headlines, powerful documentaries, and critical reflection of animals' lived experiences, informed by growing bodies of related sciences. Scrutiny of cruel captive situations and the forced use of wild animals for entertainment have reached a critical mass in a post-*Blackfish* era. The true meaning of 'sanctuary' is being questioned as photogenic tigers are removed from a world-famous temple, while the absence of respective standards and their enforcement is brought to the public's attention. The controversies of trophy and canned hunting have become scars on a specific sector of the tourism industry after the death of Cecil the lion and revelations documented in the documentary film *Blood Lions*. Although generally sought out by people who are motivated by their enjoyment of animals, animal tourism is not without harms to animals and requires serious reflection on the ethical considerations for both captive animals and those living in the wild. In addition, even those individuals who are motivated to have close and special encounters with wild animals may in fact be endangering their personal welfare and safety, as well as that of the animals, especially in the era of selfies and social media (e.g. National Post, 2015).

When I am planning a travel adventure, I often select my destination based on what wild and free animals I will be able to experience. I source local field guides to identify what I might be lucky enough to see; novel wildlife is always of great interest. Although I will personally avoid captive animal attractions designed for entertainment, it is still important to note that four zoos and one wildlife rehabilitation centre, with a zoo permit, in British Columbia currently have captive bears on public display and are actively promoted for tourism. These animals were placed in permanent captivity by government officials as they were deemed unsuitable candidates for rehabilitation and release at the time. Given the advances and experiences of bear rehabilitation over the past decades and the scientific recognition of rehabilitation as a legitimate wildlife management option (Beecham *et al.*, 2015), this form of bear captivity and display is destined to be phased out. However, the need for true bear sanctuaries, which prioritize bear welfare over public viewing and tourism, will remain in countries retiring bears from bile farms, circuses and dancing slavery, rescuing victims of the exotic animal trade, and rehoming bears from deplorable or closing zoos (Poulsen, 2014; Animals Asia, 2016; Detroit Zoo, 2016; Wildlife SOS, 2016).

While the numerous national and provincial parks are a popular destination for tourists to discover British Columbia's wildlife, bears are also frequently seen near human-occupied areas on popular hiking trails and campsites, and in towns and backyards that intersect bear habitat, which is much of the province. Government estimates suggest there are approximately 120,000–150,000 black bears and 15,000 grizzly bears in the province and about 3% are legally killed, or 'harvested', each year (BC Government, 2016b). However, there is considerable uncertainty in these population and mortality estimates, given that they are based on models of suitable habitat and not counting animals, and the estimates assume that females are generally not killed since hunters are discouraged from killing females (Artelle *et al.*, 2013). Further, deaths from non-hunting activities, such as road- or rail-related accidents, human–bear conflict, and poaching, are much higher than from hunting (Lamb *et al.*, 2016) and often go unaccounted for, adding to the uncertainty in predictive modelling of populations. Despite scientific opponents of killing being concerned that bear populations may be less than half of government figures, rendering harvest rates unsustainable (MacDonald, 2014), both species can be legally hunted in the province by residents and non-residents. It is of note that grizzly bears are listed as a threatened species in the adjacent province of Alberta and cannot be hunted there.

Although bear population estimates vary, there is no debate that there is a serious conflict between two tourism sectors in British Columbia: the guided viewing of bears and the guided hunting of bears. Both activities are sold as packages to international and Canadian tourists alike, with each sector defending the economic benefits it contributes, the jobs it creates and the service it provides to eager customers. A recent study by the Centre for Responsible Travel evaluated these claims in the Great Bear Rainforest where both viewing and hunting of black and grizzly bears take place (CREST, 2014). The study determined that bear viewing in this area greatly outweighs the economic value of bear hunting, generating more visitor spending and direct government revenue, providing more jobs, and attracting more visitors than hunting (CREST, 2014). Further, this trend must be mirrored throughout the province as the number of companies offering bear viewing tours, and participants therein, far outnumbers guide outfitters, companies and clients hunting bear.

For obvious reasons, the hunting of bears is incompatible with their welfare, given that death is not instantaneous and pain and suffering results from the multiple shots required to the body, or from a non-lethal arrow in bow hunting. Animals also have a biological self-interest in living and reproducing, so death is a welfare issue in and of itself. As bear meat is generally not the main motive of the bear hunt, and meat is not required to be removed from the carcass, most British Columbians not surprisingly oppose the activity (Insights West, 2015). Thus, it is important to question the ethics of the few, but active, companies that participate simultaneously in both bear viewing and bear hunting activities. Although it is not illegal to sell both experiences as a business, the actions of these companies that scout locations for the most accessible and biggest bears to capture photos for guests one week, and then return the following week with hunters, is deceptive and repugnant. Further, bear viewing is a multi-visit opportunity as non-consumptive tourism that is sustainable, whereas hunting bears is consumptive, offering only a one-time use per bear 'harvest'.

Evaluating the overall effect of tourism on bear welfare, it is important to note that tourism impacts can occur not only during scheduled viewing tours or unintentional encounters when in 'bear country', such as during a hike, but also as a result of tourism-related development in bear habitat. Welfare is assessed by how an animal's overall well-being is affected in terms of its physical health, emotional state, and any impediments to natural living (Fraser, 2009). So considerations for stress, injury, disruption of natural behaviours, limiting access to food resources, and separation of family members are a few possible negative welfare effects, the duration and severity of which should be minimized. Specifically in relation to viewing tours where there is greater control around visitor activity, encounters can range from approaching by boat, on foot or horse, by ATV or other motorized vehicle. The approach distance and duration, tour group size, season and location of tour should all be considered in relation to animal welfare to minimize any negative effects.

The activity of viewing bears is unlikely to provide direct welfare benefits to the viewed bears. However, bear tourism can provide indirect benefits to bears through local economic contributions that create incentives for policy makers (e.g. taxes, viewing fees, or local jobs) to preserve bear habitat and resources, ultimately allowing bears to thrive in their natural environments. As bears can provide ecosystem services to the forests they reside in (Reimchen, 2000), responsible bear tourism can also allow natural processes to continue relatively undisturbed. Greater appreciation and awareness of bears sparked by close interactions in nature may be an awe-inspiring experience for some tourists, which can lead to deeper respect and compassion for non-human animals. The indirect welfare benefits here can come from greater advocacy for bears and their habitats. This may filter down to other species living in these habitats that might not have the same draw for tourists, thus leading to additional protections.

It is important to recognize that the tourism industry can play a significant role in either encouraging or discouraging close encounters with wild bears. For example, in Finland, attracting bears by artificial feeding is legal and promoted as a way to encourage a profitable brown bear viewing industry (Kojola and Heikkinen, 2012). In Quebec, an experimental study feeding black bears for tourism purposes led to decreased bear movement and increased bear density that exceeded social carrying capacity (Massé *et al.*, 2014). The concern with attracting bears intentionally for close encounters is that they may become habituated or even food-conditioned, leading to significant behavioural changes towards humans. Although the Finnish study did not correlate nuisance bear activity with tourism feeding (Kojola and Heikkinen, 2012), and the Quebec study did not report on human–bear interactions (Massé *et al.*, 2014), neither study considered long-term animal welfare effects. In British Columbia it is illegal to feed bears, and even inadvertently leaving out attractants like pet food, unpicked fruit, compost or garbage can result in fines (BC Government, 1996). Although it may appear to be relatively harmless to feed bears natural foods to get a closer look, neither the effects on long-term animal welfare nor the effects on conservation justify artificial feeding of wildlife in tourism in most circumstances (Dubois and Fraser, 2013a).

Prohibiting wildlife feeding and regulating approach logistics is one way the tourism industry can help to ensure good bear welfare, while meeting tourist desires to view bears responsibly. Trading away access for animal welfare was supported by a majority of dolphin viewing tourists (Bach and Burton, 2016) and similar research on bear viewing would be informative. Regardless of such investigations, public education and enforcement on feeding and approaching bears are needed for both tourists and locals (Calgary Herald, 2015; Vancouver Sun, 2015; CTV Vancouver Island, 2016) to prevent 'problem bear' issues.

The labelling of a 'problem bear' occurs when the animal is involved in repeated human–bear conflicts, or when it causes property damage, obtains anthropogenic food, kills or attempts to kill livestock or pets, or is involved in vehicle collisions (Hopkins *et al.*, 2010). In British Columbia each year, between 50–100 grizzly bears and 500–1000 black 'problem bears' are killed by government officials or landowners (BC Government, 2016b). Although bear attacks on humans in the province are rare (Herrero and Higgins, 1999), the high number of bears killed by management actions is controversial given the uncertainty of bear population estimates. Responsible bear tourism should aim to prevent any 'problem bear' activity.

When human encounters with bears go wrong, assigning blame to humans or bears can vary based on the location and specifics of the encounter. Given that attitudes towards wildlife vary between wildlife viewers, hunters and other outdoor recreationalists (Daigle *et al.*, 2002), different individuals may experience the same encounter differently. Other factors to consider in assessing where fault lies, include the nature of the encounter (offensive vs. defensive), location of the incident (within a national or provincial park, hiking trail vs. town), habitat type and feeding source, bear age and family structure (e.g. mother with cubs), what the humans were doing at the time of the encounter, and availability and policy of wildlife management officials. For example, outside national parks, bear relocation options in British Columbia are limited due to potential territory conflicts and government policy for non-endangered wildlife populations. Further, rehabilitation efforts are aimed at bear cubs or young only, and thus adult bears correctly or wrongly blamed for bad behaviour can be quickly labelled 'problem bears'.

Attitudes toward bear encounters vary between individuals, but also between groups of people. For example, communities that have a lot of experience with bears may have higher bear-tolerance levels. It is also important to recognize that tourists eager to interact with bears may hold different attitudes from locals. For example, when bears learn bad habits from tourists and remain in those areas long after the tourists have gone, residents are left to deal with the consequences. Furthermore, tourists who are not intentionally participating in animal tourism may have less tolerance for close encounters with bears than local residents used to living in 'bear country' and may call for management action quicker (Dubois and Fraser, 2013b). Any group, whether resident or tourist, with a low tolerance for bears can influence bear-management decisions and the killing of 'problem bears'. Consequently, public education and awareness are key components to reducing human–wildlife conflicts. Bear tourism has a captive audience for promoting these messages and a platform for providing effective examples of coexistence.

The resort community of Whistler, British Columbia, with approximately 10,000 permanent human residents, is in prime black and grizzly bear habitat and has a long history of bear tourism. It is best known as a world-class tourist destination and host of the 2010 Winter Olympic and Paralympic Games. It is also the site of the infamous post-Olympic sled dog cull (Fennell and Sheppard, 2011) that galvanized the community further to be accountable for responsible animal tourism. For decades, the local charity Get Bear Smart Society (2016), has offered a successful model for communities in 'bear country' to provide education, research and advocacy programmes for tourists and locals alike. Working in partnership with local businesses, residents and wildlife officials, 'problem bear' killings are rare, despite the very frequent encounters between bears and people. The challenge with any charity providing such services, rather than a solidly funded government initiative, is that the programme relies on unpredictable funding and often the efforts of volunteers. This is an opportunity for the tourism industry to provide sustainable funding in communities where bear viewing is significant and to incorporate mandatory fees to help subsidize community bear-management services.

A final opportunity for the tourism industry to benefit bears is to hold wildlife management accountable for bear welfare and conservation and policies that still permit hunting of uncertain and controversial populations. British Columbia has experienced the ire of tourism protests and international environmental campaigns before, with the harvesting of old-growth forests. International pressure and threats of decreased tourism dollars for the provincial economy can send shock waves to policy makers. The tourism industry's messages about bear viewing opportunities can promote both bear conservation and welfare, as individual bears have not only inherent value but are also socially integral as members of their populations.

Thankfully, today the face of bear tourism has changed from barren cages to natural bear viewing, and responsible tourism that promotes bear welfare is possible. The lessons of respect and compassion told in the stories of Winnie-the-Pooh may have inspired many of us bear enthusiasts in our youth to explore the natural world a little more gently. As A.A. Milne suggests: 'Some people talk to animals. Not many listen though. That's the problem' – perhaps responsible bear tourism is our chance to listen.

References

Animals Asia (2016) *End Bear Bile Farming & Captive Animal Welfare*. Available at: https://www.animalsasia.org/us/our-work/end-bear-bile-farming/ (accessed 24 October 2016).

Artelle, K.A., Anderson, S.C., Cooper, A.B., Paquet, P.C., Reynolds, J.D. and Darimont, C.T. (2013) Confronting uncertainty in wildlife management: performance of grizzly bear management. *PLoS ONE* 8(11), e78041.

Bach, L. and Burton, M. (2016) Proximity and animal welfare in the context of tourist interactions with habituated dolphins. *Journal of Sustainable Tourism* 25(2), 181–197.

Beecham, J.J., De Gabriel Hernando, M., Karamanlidis, A.A., Beausoleil, R.A., Burguess, K., Jeong, D.H., Binks, M., Bereczky, L., Ashraf, N.V.K., Skripova, K. and Rhodin, L. (2015) Management implications for releasing orphaned, captive-reared bears back to the wild. *Journal of Wildlife Management* 79(8), 1327–1336.

BC (British Columbia) Government (1996) Wildlife Act. Available at: http://www.bclaws.ca/civix/document/id/complete/statreg/96488_01 (accessed 24 October 2016).

BC (British Columbia) Government (2016a) *BC Jobs Plan*. Available at: https://bcjobsplan.gov.bc.ca/app/uploads/sites/21/2017/03/3797_JobsPlan2016_Booklet_0303.pdf (accessed 24 October 2016), p. 31.

BC (British Columbia) Government (2016b) Predator conflicts & statistics 2011–2016 – grizzly bear and black bear. Available at: http://www2.gov.bc.ca/gov/content/environment/plants-animals-ecosystems/wildlife/human-wildlife-conflict (accessed 24 October 2016).

Calgary Herald (2015) Visitor fined $1,000 for feeding black bear in Banff National Park. Available at: http://calgaryherald.com/news/local-news/wardens-notice-increase-in-visitors-feeding-wildlife-in-national-parks (accessed 24 October 2016).

CREST (Centre for Responsible Travel) (2014) Economic impact of bear viewing and bear hunting in the great bear rainforest of British Columbia. Available at: http://www.responsibletravel.org/projects/documents/Economic_Impact_of_Bear_Viewing_and_Bear_Hunting_in_GBR_of_BC.pdf (accessed 24 October 2016).

CTV Vancouver Island (2016) 'Want another one?' Video of person feeding bear near Tofino sparks probe. Available at: http://vancouverisland.ctvnews.ca/want-another-one-video-of-person-feeding-bear-near-tofino-sparks-probe-1.2896145 (accessed October 2016).

Daigle, J.J., Hrubes, D. and Ajzen, I. (2002) A comparative study of beliefs, attitudes, and values among hunters, wildlife viewers, and other outdoor recreationists. *Human Dimensions of Wildlife* 7(1), 1–19.

Detroit Zoo (2016) Detroit Zoo to provide sanctuary to aging polar bear. Available at: https://detroitzoo.org/press-release/detroit-zoo-provide-sanctuary-aging-polar-bear (accessed 24 October 2016).

Dubois, S. and Fraser, D. (2013a) A framework to evaluate wildlife feeding in research, wildlife management, tourism and recreation. *Animals* 3(4), 978–994.

Dubois, S. and Fraser, D. (2013b) Local attitudes towards bear management after illegal feeding and problem bear activity. *Animals* 3(3), 935–950.

Fennell, D.A. (2013) Tourism and animal welfare. *Tourism Recreation Research* 38(3), 325–340.

Fennell, D.A. and Sheppard, V.A. (2011) Another legacy for Canada's 2010 Olympic and Paralympic Winter Games: applying an ethical lens to the post-games' sled dog cull. *Journal of Ecotourism* 10(3), 197–213.

Fraser, D. (2009) *Understanding Animal Welfare: The Science in Its Cultural Context*. Wiley-Blackwell, Chichester, UK.

Get Bear Smart Society (2016) Get Bear Smart Society home page. Available at: http://www.bearsmart.com (accessed 24 October 2016).

Herrero, S. and Higgins, A. (1999) Human injuries inflicted by bears in British Columbia: 1960–97. *Ursus* 11, 209–218.

Hopkins III, J.B., Herrero, S., Shideler, R.T., Gunther, K.A., Schwartz, C.C. and Kalinowski, S.T. (2010) A proposed lexicon of terms and concepts for human–bear management in North America. *Ursus* 21(2), 154–168.

Insights West (2015) British Columbians and Albertans condemn trophy hunting. Available at: http://www.insightswest.com/news/british-columbians-and-albertans-condemn-trophy-hunting (accessed 24 October 2016).

Kojola, I. and Heikkinen, S. (2012) Problem brown bears *Ursus arctos* in Finland in relation to bear feeding for tourism purposes and the density of bears and humans. *Wildlife Biology* 18, 258–263.

Lamb, C.T., Mowat, G., McLellan, B.N., Nielsen, S.E. and Boutin, S. (2016) Forbidden fruit: human settlement and abundant fruit create an ecological trap for an apex omnivore. *Journal of Animal Ecology* 86(1), 55–65. DOI: 10.1111/1365-2656.12589.

MacDonald, N. (2014) Grizzly toll: B.C.'s controversial trophy bear hunt. Macleans Magazine. Available at: http://www.macleans.ca/society/grizzly-toll-b-cs-controversial-trophy-bear-hunt (accessed 1 October 2016).

Massé, S., Dussault, C., Dussault, C. and Ibarzabal, J. (2014) How artificial feeding for tourism-watching modifies black bear space use and habitat selection. *Journal of Wildlife Management* 78(7), 1228–1238.

National Post (2015) Selfies with grizzlies: park visitors looking for photo ops are putting themselves – and wildlife – in danger. Available at: http://news.nationalpost.com/news/canada/selfies-with-grizzlies-park-visitors-looking-for-photo-ops-are-putting-themselves-and-wildlife-in-danger (accessed 24 October 2016).

Poulsen, E. (2014) *Bärle's Story: One Polar Bear's Amazing Recovery from Life as a Circus Act*. Greystone Books Ltd, Vancouver, Canada.

Reimchen, T.E. (2000) Some ecological and evolutionary aspects of bear–salmon interactions in coastal British Columbia. *Canadian Journal of Zoology* 78(3), 448–457.

Sneddon, J., Lee, J., Ballantyne, R. and Packer, J. (2016) Animal welfare values and tourist behaviour. *Annals of Tourism Research* 57, 234–236.

Vancouver Sun (2015) Tourists fined for feeding bear in Whistler. Available at: http://www.vancouversun.com/technology/tourists+fined+feeding+bear+whistler/11402872/story.html (accessed October 2016).

Walker, S. (2015) *Winnie: The True Story of the Bear Who Inspired Winnie-the-Pooh*. Henry Holt and Company, LLC, New York.

Wildlife SOS (2016) Wildlife rescue and rehabilitation. Available at: http://wildlifesos.org/wildlife-rescue-and-rehabilitation (accessed 24 October 2016).

13 Donkeys and Mules and Tourism

Stephen Blakeway[1*] and Glen Olivier Cousquer[2]

[1]*Self-employed One Welfare Specialist, Devon, UK;* [2]*Lecturer and Programme Coordinator in Conservation and One Health Medicine, University of Edinburgh, UK*

* Corresponding author: stephen.blakeway@outlook.com

Introduction

Tourists in the 21st century are diverse, multinational citizens of an increasingly interconnected world and are in a unique position to report injustice and to grow and spread humanity. Tourism can play and does play a significant role in tackling exploitation and safeguarding the welfare of non-human animals. Of the many animals who suffer exploitation in the name of tourism, mules and donkeys are attracting increasing attention.

Tourists may encounter donkeys and mules in a variety of situations. Both species are often found offering riding activities whether on beaches, in cities or in the countryside. Both species have earned a reputation as pack animals, ideally suited to mountainous terrain. They are also commonly found in sanctuaries where they serve as visitor attractions for tourists. Feral or semi-feral donkeys may be encountered living wild. They may figure on menus and, soon, we may notice them through 'novel' donkey products from donkey milk, meat and hide farms.

Tourist encounters with mules and donkeys raise challenging ethical and practical questions. Tourists and the tourism industry need to recognize and become more cognizant of these challenges. This will require a coordinated approach if answers are to be found to complex problems.

At an individual level, however, we are all able to contribute. We can, for example, choose to engage proactively with animal welfare when we travel. We can educate ourselves, we can exercise our curiosity, we can observe, we can question. We can set out to talk openly and respectfully to people about animals and animal welfare. We can use our money intelligently, making more of an effort to base our choices as consumers on animal welfare criteria. We can alert veterinary professionals and local authorities to an animal's plight. We can document and report back what we see, feeding this information to organizations and professions who are actively seeking to understand and address the underlying issues strategically and proactively. Perhaps most importantly, we can give praise and encouragement to those who are looking after their animals well.

This short piece assumes that the current status quo regarding animal welfare in tourism is unacceptably low; that people care about the welfare of other people and animals; that we all have a responsibility to make the world a more humane place; and that a movement for more ethical treatment of animals in tourism is growing.

Here, we seek to share four things. We present and discuss a handy practical framework for assessing welfare; we consider the role of the tourist and tourism industry in assessing mule and donkey welfare; we provide a set of questions to ask when visiting an animal collection or sanctuary; and we provide some ideas for thinking about the human communities of which the mules and donkeys are members. As part of this process, we provide the reader with some perspectives and insights into specific situations and emerging issues.

Assessing Welfare

Assessing the welfare of others is a challenge for all of us. The ideal would be that every non-human animal, like every human animal, lives a 'good life'. A good life implies a life that has positive experiences, not just an absence of negative ones. Each of us experiences the world differently, yet we can use common 'indicators' to assess quality of life. Absence of negatives for donkeys and mules would require bits and harness that do not wound. Evidence of positives includes alert, engaged behaviours and good, mutually beneficial relationships between animals and people in a working community. Various frameworks and detailed checklists have been developed to help in assessing welfare, some simple, others requiring expert training. These include the 'Five Freedoms', which have guided welfare thinking in production animals for over half a century. Each can be useful in specific situations.

Table 13.1. The Hand Welfare Assessment Framework.

The Hand Welfare Assessment Framework
Thumb: Behaviour/demeanour Quality of relationship between animal and handler
First finger: Body Condition Score: 1 to 5, where 1 is skeletally thin, 5 is obese
Second finger: Wounds and other surface lesions, including in the mouth from bits
Third finger: Movement and lameness
Little finger: Other signs of injury or disease – including the results of a veterinary clinical examination where this is possible
Palm: The whole life of the animal (e.g. how many owners it has had, what happens at the end of its working life)

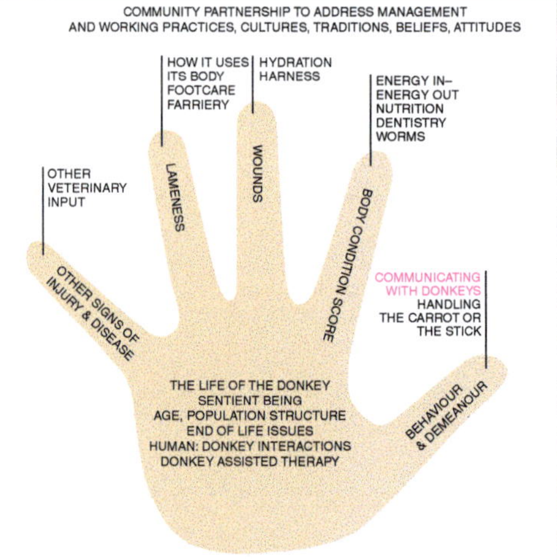

Illustration by Judy Whiteside

One simple handy 'tool' developed specifically within The Donkey Sanctuary for overseeing the welfare of donkeys around the world is exactly that – a hand – with the thumb and each finger pointing to a particular aspect of the animal, and the palm reminding us to look into the whole life of the animal (see Table 13.1).

The Hand provides the user with a readily available *aide-mémoire* (Blakeway, 2014). It is intended to be memorable, to make best use of what we see before us, and to help us look at the whole animal in a more systematic way, providing a more holistic view that does justice to the rich detail of the animal's biographical existence. The language can be kept simple to make it understandable by people of all ages, including children. If we want to record or report what we have seen, the Hand framework reminds us to record all aspects of the animal's appearance, to describe the whole animal, as well as encouraging a conversation with the handler about its life. Often with working animals we do not see where they live, so we cannot easily assess 'inputs' such as water, food, or shelter, but where we can find this information, it can enrich the welfare picture. Assessing the welfare of every animal we come across is a good exercise and helps us when we need to make specific decisions.

The Role of the Tourist and Tourism Industry

If, as a tourist, we are considering using an animal on our travels, we need to see ourselves as active members of a wider community who have to work together to ensure that animals are not exploited in the name of tourism. This requires us to take a proactive approach – we need to ask companies for their animal welfare policies and seek assurances that these are fully implemented. We should look to travel with companies and organizations that view the animal as part of the team, and care for its welfare as we would for our own or for that of our friends. On the ground, we need to check for ourselves that everything is as it should be. The tourist needs to be able to say 'No' and refuse a service. It is here that the Hand can serve us well. The thumb reminds us to look for animal owners and handlers who have trusting, loving relationships with their animals. The first and second fingers remind us to request that the animal be examined without any harness to check its body condition, and to see it is not wounded, particularly by its harness. The second finger also reminds us to pay attention to its mouth because bits, which are there to control the animal, often through discomfort and pain, can do great damage to the tongue, gums and teeth. We also need to see the animal in motion to check it can move freely and is not lame. Where someone with veterinary or para-veterinary training is on hand, a full clinical examination adds to the assessment.

Where animals are essential to the success of a trek or expedition, they need to be brought into the planning from the beginning. For example, there needs to be spare capacity in case an animal is injured or falls sick. The quality and quantity of food and water available to them is as important as it is for the human members of the expedition. There needs to be provision for shelter in extreme weather, and first aid care in case of accidents and injuries.

Overloading is an alarmingly common problem affecting mules and donkeys working in tourism. A travel company's animal welfare policy should ensure that no animal is overloaded. While many people lobby for specific rules regarding weight carried or distance covered, there are too many variables such as terrain and altitude to make this practically meaningful. The main rule, which is now at the heart of best endurance horse sporting practice, is that the animal finishes the event as healthy as it started. We can keep on top of this by regularly checking the Hand indicators to assess welfare. Certainly, we each need to remain mindful of our own weight and should take responsibility for deciding whether we are too large for a particular animal to carry.

Research undertaken on the exploitation of mules in mountain tourism has demonstrated how action inquiry-led research can transform the consciousness of the tourism industry (Cousquer and Allison, 2012; Cousquer and Alyakine, 2014a,b; Cousquer, 2015). This work with the trekking and expeditions industry has allowed the relationships and responsibilities towards pack mules across this service supply chain to be mapped out so that this global community now has a better appreciation and understanding of the consequences of their practices on mule welfare. This work has resulted in the development of welfare guidelines, industry standards, and policy development and implementation strategies. Companies now exist that have developed and are implementing dedicated policies to deliver better welfare. The emergence of such companies has transformed what was a desperate situation, where clients had little choice, to one in which clients can choose to travel with ethically minded companies that recognize the importance of mule welfare.

Accreditation schemes for working animals in tourism have been suggested and may one day become part of the picture. Accreditation schemes, as seen in the food and farming industry, face three main challenges: instead of being once-and-for-all standards, to be effective they need to raise the welfare bar year-on-year, with entry available at quite a low level to encourage buy-in even from poor people with limited resources; they need to be supported by institutions that between them offer training as well as policing; they need public understanding and trust, which is diluted if the number of schemes proliferate. Organizations that start to accredit run the risk of losing the trust of their existing supporters if they cannot achieve all of the above and thereby appear to be complicit in preserving poor welfare practices. For these reasons, the industry is starting off by developing, introducing and advertising animal welfare standards to their users.

Animal Collections and Sanctuaries

As a tourist, visiting an animal collection or sanctuary is a specific choice we make in order to engage with animals. The seven questions in Box 13.1 are proposed here to encourage deeper thinking when visiting animal collections or sanctuaries.

Box 13.1. Seven questions about animal collections or sanctuaries.

1) What is its purpose?
2) How does it ensure that its animals have and enjoy 'a good life', with good mental well-being?
3) How does it ensure that its animals are in good physical health?
4) How does it extend benefit to animals outside the Sanctuary?
5) How does it extend benefit to people?
6) How does it care for its natural environment?
7) How is it safeguarding the security of its animals' futures?

Of these questions, the first two are often the least considered. The second question is possibly the most important, yet often gets overshadowed by the third, with the physical health of the animals taking precedence over their mental well-being. The second question requires engagement with behaviour. Only through an animal's behaviour can we get clues to its mental health, if it is happier through changes to its situation, or if it is bored. And by communicating with the animal, we can help it modify its behavioural responses so that it is better able to cope with essential health management practices such as hoof trimming. Current best practice is to have structured longitudinal observational behavioural studies and some sanctuaries are looking at how the public can contribute actively to these in some way.

One way of extending benefit to people is by encouraging volunteer helpers and visitors on the principle that mutually beneficial interactions between animals and people help protect the mental health of both. Some sanctuaries report informal benefits noted by parents of children who have had the opportunity to spend time during their holidays with donkeys. And some sanctuaries have developed this further into more structured forms of animal-assisted therapy.

The Global Federation of Animal Sanctuaries (GFAS) is a body that aims to raise standards across the sanctuary world by developing standards and offering accreditation. Tourists can help this process by acquainting themselves with the standards, and asking sanctuaries they visit whether they are members and how they feel they compare to the GFAS standards.

Animals as Part of Human Communities

Apart from possibly a few genuinely wild animals living in the remotest corners of our planet, animal welfare cannot be considered in isolation from the human communities in which they are embedded. Recognizing and engaging with the people who have power over the animals is essential if our observations and concerns about working animal welfare are ever to be properly addressed. Human communities are rarely homogeneous. Where there are working animals, some will be looked after well, some badly. Some owners will be richer, some poorer. In places where tourism has grown, such as in some cities, at some famous archaeological sites, and in some of the more accessible mountain areas, the numbers of animals are now far greater than in pre-mass-tourism times. This makes human and animal livelihoods vulnerable to the vagaries of tourism demand. In the Middle East, fear of terrorism is making life harder for humans and animals together. What happens to the animals that were working and are no longer in demand? Those still working directly with animals are often the poorest and least powerful in their communities. They have limited buffers for their own welfare. Where people cannot afford decent food or housing for themselves, they will not be able to afford good food or stables for their animals. More humane handling, dispensing with vicious bits, is possible, but requires training that is not readily available. Better welfare in tourism is possible but will almost certainly cost more and if we, the tourists, want it, we should be prepared to pay for it. Trickle-down economic theories are just that, a trickle.

However, the roughness of these social surfaces also provides opportunity in the way that the roughness of a rock face allows it to be scaled. Heterogeneity gives rise to choice. This provides opportunities for tourists to reward those who value welfare. The better, more committed owners or handlers are the people who take training when offered it, and potentially become members of local welfare associations that can lead a way forwards.

Some local practices are unacceptable and need to be highlighted, as do the actions of local businesses who suppress improvements for short-term financial gain. Equally, some business practices within the international tourist industry are unacceptable. Exploitation needs to be made visible and, where appropriate, denounced. In these cases, we can petition for better practice.

Conclusion

We, the tourists, have great responsibility. We are the ones with the spare cash to go on holiday. We have a responsibility to inform ourselves. We must not use animals badly just for our recreation. We must refuse to use animals with poor welfare, but neither should we turn our backs on them. We have a responsibility to suspend our judgement on local people less fortunate than ourselves, and instead talk to them, understand their circumstances and economic pressures, and be prepared to help where we can. We need to engage with tourist companies, let them know that we expect, and indeed demand, good welfare and will pay for it.

In summary, we tourists are responsible for the welfare of animals involved in tourism. We can and have to make a difference, and we will be most effective if we work together. When we get home, we can use opportunities to encourage wider societal engagement. We can encourage the veterinary profession in its global responsibility to extend its reach to get affordable animal health care and welfare into every poor and otherwise marginalized community worldwide. You can feed your observations and experiences back to the animal welfare charities so that they can improve their effectiveness. You should talk to fellow tourists. Engaging strangers politely in difficult conversations is an art, and one that we will never get right every time. Nevertheless, the occasional difficult conversation is a small price to pay for the rewards of building a movement for more ethical treatment of animals in tourism.

Acknowledgement

The authors acknowledge the work of The Donkey Sanctuary in developing and spreading the use of the Hand through its international work, and in supporting the work of Glen Cousquer.

References

Blakeway, S. (2014) The multi-dimensional donkey in landscapes of donkey–human interaction. *Relations. Beyond Anthropocentrism* 2(1), 59–77. Available at: http://www.ledonline.it/index.php/Relations/article/view/657 (accessed 28 January 2018).

Cousquer, G.O. (2015) Promoting pack mule welfare on expedition. *The Professional Mountaineer* 9, 14–17.

Cousquer, G.O. and Allison, P. (2012) The mountain guide's and expedition leader's ethical responsibilities to pack animals on expedition. *Annals of Tourism Research* 39(4), 1839–1858.

Cousquer, G.O. and Alyakine, H. (2014a) Knowing the expedition mule: animal welfare and the growth of the Moroccan mountain tourism industry. In: *Proceedings of the 7th International Colloquium on Working Equids*. 1–3 July 2014, Royal Holloway, London.

Cousquer, G.O. and Alyakine, H. (2014b) The impact of a holistic approach to animal welfare within Moroccan mountain tourism. In: *Proceedings of the 7th International Colloquium on Working Equids*. 1–3 July 2014, Royal Holloway, London.

14 Cats and Dogs International

Darci Galati*
President/CEO of CANDi

* Corresponding author: dgalati08@gmail.com

The idea for CANDi – Cats and Dogs International – was born when my three young daughters and I were on a family vacation in Mexico in 2006. We were literally astounded by the staggering number of stray cats and dogs in the vicinity. There did not seem to be any animal welfare laws in place to protect them, let alone humane shelters or even veterinary care. Most of the animals were emaciated and in desperate need of medical attention. This had a profound effect on my children, who were distraught at the notion that they would soon be flying back home and leaving behind the cats and dogs they had fed and helped to fend for themselves. I knew I had to do something and I promised my daughters that I would make a difference. That was the impetus behind the creation of CANDi, a non-profit global organization with a mission to save the lives of stray animals at tourist destinations.

I later learned that most of the stray animals, like the ones we helped feed, are killed prior to peak tourist season. The feral cats are poisoned en masse as they are considered to be vermin, while the stray dogs are rounded up and executed. This involves a horrendous electrocution at the pound. During one of my visits, I spotted a small Jack Russell terrier and his brother who were going to be electrocuted the next day. I ended up rescuing him and he has been my constant companion ever since. He is now living the life of luxury with me and three other dogs I rescued and brought back to Canada.

Like most tourists, I thought I could not bring home a dog I rescued on vacation due to quarantine restrictions. I found out that this is thankfully not true in most places in the Caribbean, Mexico and other parts of the world. Bringing home a rescue dog is simpler than people think. All that needs to be done is to take the dog to a local vet and have him tested and vaccinated within 10 days of travel time. Choosing a pet-friendly airline is also key to bringing back a rescued dog.

I experienced this same situation when I rescued a 3-week-old puppy I found near death and lying unconscious on the beach in Mexico, during a trip for the WSPA (World Society for the Protection of Animals, now World Animal Protection). I took the puppy to the vet and went through the protocol required for travel. However, once I got to the airline counter, I was told by the agent that their Agricultural Department was closed so I would not be allowed to fly back with her. I made a great fuss, as I had all of her documentation and they had no one certified to check us in. Finally, they relented and called a local vet who stamped us through, after I paid a small fee. These types of incident can be expected where staff are not experienced in handling animal travel. It is important to know that although it is an uphill battle, it is worth fighting for, as the alternative – leaving the dog behind alone to die – is not a viable solution.

With all the lessons I learned under my belt, I was finally ready to launch CANDi. CANDi's army of volunteers included people from all walks of life, from Canadian Football League players to a country singer, and we were soon on our way to activating our first spay-neuter clinic in Mexico in 2006.

Since that time, we have partnered with local animal rescue groups in Mexico and orchestrated biannual clinics in Cancun, spaying and neutering over 10,000 cats and dogs. CANDi's spay-neuter clinics alone have prevented millions of stray animals being born into a life of suffering, starvation and disease. One unsterilized female dog and her offspring, if all of them survived, could produce 67,000 puppies in just 6 years; and one unsterilized female cat and her offspring could produce as many as 425,000 kittens in 7 years.

In addition to our no-cost sterilization campaigns, CANDi provides other programmes that can easily be replicated in any part of the world as humane and sustainable alternatives in helping to combat the stray animal population. These programmes can easily be implemented by the travel industry at no cost to the tourist destination. One example is the Cat Café programme, which RIU Hotels and Resorts implemented on their resort properties. Globally, RIU has been a leader in corporate social responsibility and they are once again paving the way as pioneers in their field by advocating animal welfare under the umbrella of corporate social justice. The issue of stray animals is a global one, as it is estimated that there are more than 600 million strays worldwide, and CANDi's partnership with RIU is projected to continue this collaboration in other tourist destinations such as Jamaica, the Dominican Republic and Cuba.

Another story which resonates for me personally is the story of Hule. We received a report at one of our last Cancun clinics that a dog in the neighbourhood had been attacked with a machete. Unfortunately, this horrifying type of abuse is not uncommon for stray dogs. One of our volunteers went and found the dog, a female cocker spaniel that was severely injured, and our volunteer vets were able to save her life after 4 hours of surgery. She was named Hule, which means 'rubber', because she was so resilient and bounced back from her near-fatal attack against all the odds. Her story gained international media attention which led to her adoption, and she is now living a healthy, happy life in Toronto, Canada.

There are a thousand similar stories in Mexico, Puerto Rico, the Caribbean and other parts of the world where stray animals still roam the streets. Without volunteers, funding and donations from the public, organizations such as CANDi cannot continue their work. CANDi is a 100% volunteer-driven non-profit organization and all our programmes, including the Cat Café and the free sterilization clinics in poor communities within tourist destinations, are completely replicable in any part of the globe. Humane spay-neuter programmes are the only safe and ethical solution to help reduce suffering for millions of stray animals who have very little hope of survival due to starvation, disease, neglect and abuse.

CANDi's goal is to partner with the travel companies, who want to include humane treatment of animals at tourist destinations within their corporate social responsibility programmes, to raise awareness about the ethical treatment of animals and implement animal welfare standards. We look forward to the day when this will be the practice across all levels of the travel and tourism industry. CANDi, partnering with travel companies and compassionate travellers together, can help to make this happen.

15 Animal Welfare – Driving Improvements in Tourism Attractions

Clare Jenkinson* and Hugh Felton
Association of British Travel Agents, London, UK

* Corresponding author: cjenkinson@abta.co.uk

Viewing and interacting with animals can be a popular and rewarding part of a holiday. ABTA consumer research found that one in four people had some kind of interaction with animals as part of their trip and it was recognized that the travel industry can play an important part in enabling the experience to be a positive one for customers, local people and, most importantly, the animals themselves.

Travel provider members of ABTA's Animal Welfare Working Group analysed the rapid growth of animal attractions and animal interactions experiences within the supply chain. Strong links have developed between tourism destinations and animal attractions, and for customers good animal welfare standards were becoming increasingly important. Our members were noticing an increase in customer feedback relating to poor welfare standards.

Safaris are perhaps the most obvious example where animals are central to the itinerary, but interaction with animals on holiday is more common than one may think. Examples of animal interactions in a holiday setting may include mules carrying bags on a trekking holiday, a parrot show as a hotel entertainment programme, watching performing dolphins in a marine park or volunteering on a conservation project. Given the breadth and array of potential animal interactions, the potential for contributing to abuse is very real. A recent high-profile example was the tiger 'sanctuary' in Thailand, known as Tiger Temple, which was accused of breeding tigers to sell body parts. Tourists were seen as an intrinsic part of this abuse by paying to visit and pet tigers.

The Federation for Tour Operators (FTO), which is now part of ABTA, began the process of developing guidance for animals in tourism in 2006. In 2008, the FTO published the animal attraction handbook, which was endorsed at the time by the British and Irish Association of Zoos and Aquariums (BIAZA), the international wildlife charity Born Free Foundation, as well as a number of leading experts in animal welfare.

Animal welfare continues to be a critical part of our sustainable tourism agenda, and with increasing use of social media for animal welfare issues our members requested a common solution. ABTA collaborated with the Born Free Foundation to develop comprehensive guidance and industry standards, which resulted in the ABTA *Global Welfare Guidance for Animals in Tourism* (2013). This guidance underwent a multi-stakeholder consultation process involving experts from around the world as well as tour operators and travel agents from the ABTA Animal Welfare Working Group. ABTA continues to consult and work with the Born Free Foundation on its animal welfare strategy.

The guidelines comprise seven separate documents. The central booklet is called the *Global Welfare Guidance for Animals in Tourism* and covers important issues such as the acquisition of animals, animal sanctuaries, wildlife souvenirs, volunteer tourism, and the role animal welfare has to play in relation to the protection of livelihoods. The *Global Welfare Guidance* is supported by six specific guidance manuals on animals in captive environments: namely, dolphins in captive environments; elephants in captive environments; wildlife viewing; working animals; and unacceptable and discouraged practices.

ABTA supports its members to improve animal welfare in their supply chain and works with them to create awareness of the criteria set out in the ABTA *Guidance* and take proactive steps to improve standards in animal welfare. There are now third-party audit companies that are able to audit attractions against the requirements set out in the ABTA *Guidance*.

Some of the largest ABTA members have taken a leading role in implementing the ABTA *Guidance*. TUI Group and Thomas Cook have asked excursion suppliers that feature animals to comply with, and be audited in some cases against, the *Global Welfare Guidelines*. For example, Thomas Cook launched a new animal welfare policy in 2017 that required all animal attractions and outings sold to evidence full compliance with the ABTA *Guidance*. They stated that if an attraction was found not to be fully compliant with the *Global Welfare Guidance for Animals in Tourism*, they would not sell it. Thomas Cook have reported that early results from their audits were disappointing, citing a lack of engagement from a number of suppliers and the findings of the audits themselves. Subsequently the company made the decision to remove 16 excursions from their offering in reaction to these results.

Since 2013, suppliers of TUI Group excursions featuring animals have been asked to comply with, and be audited against, the ABTA *Guidance*. TUI have openly communicated the value of working with their long-term suppliers to help drive continuous improvement and most recently have committed to a rolling programme of audits, with over 100 audits planned over the 2016–17 seasons. These have been planned in destinations where TUI have a presence and they believe that through auditing and a close working relationship with suppliers, they can meet customer expectation on the animal welfare standards in excursions.

There are further examples of where ABTA members have taken a proactive approach to animal welfare and have used the ABTA *Guidance* to underpin their work. For instance, in 2014, Virgin Holidays convened a multi-stakeholder process which brought together experts from around the world to focus on the issue of captive whales, dolphins and porpoises (collectively known as Cetacea). As an outcome of this engagement, they committed to better understand the complexity of the issues associated with animal welfare and tourism and to secure a pledge from the companies with which they worked to no longer take whales and dolphins from the ocean and explore a long-term vision for captive cetaceans in tourism. In addition, Virgin have most recently committed to not contracting any new attractions that feature captive whales and dolphins for theatrical shows, contact sessions (such as 'swim-with' programmes) or other entertainment purposes.

To stay in the animal welfare debate and actively encourage change, rather than merely replace their own customers with less-discerning ones, Virgin have said that they will work with their existing suppliers of captive cetacean attractions to encourage evolution of their product offerings and ensure compliance with the ABTA *Guidance*.

Other leading examples include Buffalo Tours, an organization with a strong presence in Asian destinations. They have successfully collaborated with the Travelife for Tour Operators initiative to develop an elephant camp certification, based on the ABTA *Guidance*. Buffalo Tours continue to work collaboratively to improve the welfare of elephants, as well as provide responsible travellers with the best possible elephant experience. Their ultimate aim is to improve overall industry standards for elephant tourism in Asia.

Alongside the work with our members, ABTA plays a role in raising awareness of animal welfare issues with destinations stakeholders and encourages governments and authorities to use the ABTA *Guidance* as a tool to support policy and enforcement. Ultimately, tour operators will have greatest traction with their suppliers if they present consistent messaging, based on evidence rather than opinion, and this is why industry collaboration, both within the UK and internationally, is so important, and why ABTA feels it has a pivotal role to play in this area.

Reference

ABTA (2013) *Global Welfare Guidance for Animals in Tourism: A Best Practice Guidance Manual*. ABTA, London.

16 Animal Welfare and Tourism: The Threat to Endangered Species

John M. Sellar*
Retired, formerly of CITES, Switzerland

* Corresponding author: john.m.sellar@globalinitiative.net

Introduction

The Convention on International Trade in Endangered Species of Wild Fauna and Flora (CITES) was established in 1973 and, for over four decades, has sought to ensure that trade in the animals and plants listed in its Appendices is legal and sustainable (see CITES, n.d.a). This piece of international law only addresses aspects of welfare in relation to the transportation of live animals across borders and at no other time.

Its existence does, however, provide a legal basis for national authorities in one part of the world to investigate the circumstances following the discovery of, for example, non-indigenous specimens in their territory. Regrettably, the need to do so has been demonstrated on several occasions in recent years.

Appendix I of the Convention lists those species regarded as being at most risk of extinction. One will find there, for instance, elephants, rhinoceroses, tigers and great apes. It is important to acknowledge that those species are included, not because of reasons such as loss of habitat, but because their populations have been adversely impacted by unsustainable trade or their populations are so small that trade cannot take place sustainably. Appendix I-listed species may not be traded internationally for commercial purposes.

However, it is essential to take note of some relevant specific provisions of CITES. For instance, this prohibition on trade relates purely to the reason for the import and it is this aspect that unscrupulous traders exploit from time to time. Movements of Appendix I specimens may be conducted if the CITES authority in the State of import is satisfied that they will not be used for a 'primarily commercial purpose' (Article III, 3c; see CITES, n.d.b). The phrase 'primarily commercial' is not defined in the text of the Convention itself but guidance on its meaning is provided in a Resolution (see CITES, n.d.c), first adopted in 1985 and revised several times in the years since. The effect of this is that importation for 'zoological' purposes has generally been treated as being non-commercial. Since what is being regulated is the import, the impact of this is that it is permitted for the exporter to demand payment, and for the importer to make such a payment, as long as the importer does not intend, thereafter, to use the specimen for profit.

A practical example of this would be when a zoo decides to pay, for example, a government or agency in Africa, in order to acquire an elephant to add to its range of species. If the country of export has a sufficiently large population of elephants to authorize such a movement, this can comply with the requirements of CITES.

Unfortunately, dishonest traders or criminals seek to misuse what was intended to cater for a legitimate wish to contribute to zoological collections of live animals. Experience has also shown that the operators or management of some zoos have knowingly participated in such unprincipled and criminal behaviour.

Before describing some examples of this from the past, it is worth taking time at this stage to reflect upon what is meant by the word 'zoo'. CITES has never defined, or provided guidance with regard to, the words 'zoo' or 'zoological'. It is left to national authorities to determine what form of facility or activity warrants such a description, just as it is for them to conclude whether an import is, or is not, primarily non-commercial.

Today, in most countries that might regard themselves as being part of the developed world, a zoo tends to be defined as an institute where live animals are kept and displayed for educational purposes; often intended to enable members of the public to come close to species that they would otherwise never encounter or be able to see in their natural habitats. It is not uncommon for such places to also engage in a range of scientific research, perhaps to understand animal behaviour, undertake captive-breeding with a view to supplementing endangered wild populations, or carry out other conservation-related work. Many such zoos are affiliated to bodies such as the World Association of Zoos and Aquariums, which expects members to conduct their activities in an ethical and humane manner and contribute to education and conservation. A common principle of this type of zoological institute is that they will be non-profit-making or that any profits generated will be ploughed back into education, research and conservation or used to enrich the lives of specimens in the collection. One example of this is the manner in which, today, most zoos in Europe and North America house specimens in appropriately sized enclosures, often mimicking their natural environments, as opposed to them being almost imprisoned in concrete boxes fronted by metal bars.

To a significant extent, European and American civil society has driven the move to higher standards of animal welfare, combined with a desire on the part of visitors that touring a zoo should be an enriching and educating experience, rather than simply an opportunity to gawp at imprisoned exotic creatures. While there are undoubtedly zoos and other facilities displaying animals in parts of the world which do not meet these benchmarks, one can usually rely upon relevant authorities and agencies to monitor facilities and take action where and when appropriate.

Regrettably, this is not what one can, all too commonly, find in the developing world. In many countries in Asia or parts of continental Africa, visitors will see animals kept in sometimes appalling conditions, with large mammals often pacing back and forth across the limited length of their cage-like compounds in a classic stress-induced display. Additionally, information boards or educational material may be in short supply, or utterly absent, and the primary aim is to simply attract the paying public to do nothing other than observe exotic species for entertainment. Worst of all, at some facilities, animals may be trained to perform for visitors (see Fig. 16.1) or to interact with them in inappropriate, and at times highly dangerous, ways.

Experience has shown that the management in zoos like those described immediately above may be motivated almost wholly by profit and a simple desire to attract as many visitors as possible. One of the ways to reach that goal will be to have in their collection examples of the rarest, most exotic, and consequently most endangered, species. It is this motivation that may lead to unethical behaviour, which, in turn, offers opportunities that may be exploited by criminals, as the following cases illustrate.

Fig. 16.1. Performing bear in a Chinese zoo that also operates a circus on its premises. ©John Sellar

Gorillas

In 2002, the CITES Secretariat, a group of Geneva-based UN officials who support and monitor implementation of the Convention, received information about a movement of four juvenile gorillas from Nigeria to Malaysia. The circumstances seemed suspicious and the Secretariat looked into the matter.

It was learned that an export permit had been issued by the Nigerian authorities authorizing trade between a zoo linked to a university in that country and the Taiping Zoo of Malaysia. The four young gorillas had all been declared as captive-bred. However, enquiries uncovered that the facility in Nigeria housed one adult female gorilla, which was too old to be sexually active. The only other gorilla on the premises, a male, had been stuffed by a taxidermist some years previously and was housed in a glass case; not much room for reproduction there.

It emerged that the CITES export permit had been issued corruptly and the Secretariat subsequently gave evidence to a commission of inquiry established by the government of Nigeria. Unfortunately, none of the individuals principally responsible for what happened in that country were ever brought to justice. The gorillas were seized from the Taiping Zoo and returned to Africa. However, no one in Malaysia was prosecuted either, despite strong intelligence alleging that at least one person from the zoo had visited Nigeria to arrange the acquisition and ought, therefore, to have known that what was taking place was fraudulent. While DNA profiling was unable to pinpoint the exact geographical origin of the gorillas, it suggested that they probably had been captured from the wild in Cameroon and subsequently smuggled into Nigeria.

Had this matter not come to light, there seems little doubt that the presence of four young gorillas would have acted as a considerable crowd-puller for Taiping Zoo and that it would have inevitably profited, perhaps substantially. This case attracted considerable attention in the media and among the conservation community, with the gorillas being nicknamed 'The Taiping Four' (see Animal Welfare Institute, n.d.). It demonstrated poor oversight on the part of CITES national authorities, since even the slightest amount of research would have shown a total absence of gorilla captive-breeding in Nigeria and four juveniles being traded together should also have immediately prompted suspicion. It will probably never be known whether corruption, as opposed to incompetence, played the most significant role.

Orangutans

In 2004, the CITES Secretariat was alerted to the presence in Thailand of large numbers of orangutans that were in facilities, some registered as zoos, where the animals were engaged in public performances (see Fig. 16.2); many juveniles having been trained to engage in mock 'Thai boxing' matches. Subsequent investigations led to 57 orangutans being taken into government care from just one facility alone. The manager of the company which operated that facility received a suspended prison sentence. During police investigations, over 100 orangutans were seized across the country.

In 2007, a Secretariat official visited a 'zoo' in north-west Cambodia that was attached to a large resort and casino complex. The resort's owner and managers maintained this facility as a way of entertaining visitors who were not interested in gambling. Some of these animals had been trained to perform and it was learned that at least two had allegedly died during this process, as a result of the overuse of electric cattle prods. It appeared that all the animals had been smuggled into Cambodia, probably via Thailand.

The orangutans, mainly juveniles and adolescents, spent most of their day in a concrete-walled area, which resembled a prison exercise yard. Aside from two small trees, there were no stimuli for the animals and the area was completely unsuitable for an arboreal species.

Fig. 16.2. Orangutan show in a Bangkok zoological park. ©John Sellar

Although a fine was imposed for this illegal possession, a provincial court declined to order confiscation and the animals are presumably still there today (see CITES, n.d.d). The fine, equivalent to over US$50,000, was paid within 2 days, indicating the financial strength of the resort.

Orangutans are not naturally present in the wild in either Thailand or Cambodia. DNA profiling of some of the animals in these cases indicated their country of origin as Indonesia.

Regrettably, confiscations of illegally traded juvenile orangutans continue to occur from time to time, albeit in smaller numbers, up to the present day.

Chimpanzees

In 2010, The CITES Secretariat became aware of significant trade in chimpanzees from Guinea, with China being the primary destination. The animals were apparently being imported to locations that had been registered by the authorities as zoos. It seemed, however, that several of these facilities were not operated in a manner that was truly zoological or primarily for scientific, education or conservation purposes.

Around 70 chimpanzees, perhaps even more, had been imported to China that year. In each instance, the animals had been accompanied by CITES documents declaring them as having been bred in captivity. Intelligence suggested that some of the chimpanzees were being trained to perform for the entertainment of fee-paying visitors.

Having visited Guinea in 2011, the Secretariat confirmed that no captive breeding whatsoever was taking place in the country and that all this trade was wholly fraudulent, criminal and appeared to involve substantial levels of corruption. The authorities in Guinea have yet to implement significant recommendations subsequently made by CITES and, at the time of writing (January 2018), the nation remains subject to sanctions prohibiting any trade in wildlife (see CITES Secretariat, 2014).

In 2015, a CITES official in Guinea was arrested in connection with the illegal trade in chimpanzees (CITES, n.d.e). It does not seem, however, that anyone in China has been prosecuted in relation to what occurred and no confiscations of chimpanzees appear to have been made there.

Regrettably, an investigation by BBC reporters (Shukman and Piranty, 2017) disclosed, in early 2017, that illegal trade in chimpanzees continues in West Africa. Follow-up enquiries indicate that individuals based in Guinea still play an important role in such crime.

Great Ape Considerations

There can be no doubt that the individual gorillas, orangutans and chimpanzees must each have suffered during their capture from the wild and the transportation or smuggling to their final destinations. Thereafter, many were kept, and some may even still be kept, in unsuitable conditions and were forced to engage in unnatural behaviour for the amusement and entertainment of human onlookers. Some died while being trained for such activity. It seems highly probable that others died while being taken from the wild or being smuggled, often thousands of miles across multiple borders.

What is perhaps less well appreciated are the large numbers of animals that will have been deliberately killed when those individuals were removed from their natural habitat. Mothers, but also other members of ape family groups, will inevitably defend their young and resist their removal. Experience has shown that whole communities and troops of chimpanzees and gorillas have been slaughtered in order to capture their juvenile members. Such highly endangered species simply cannot survive such illegal offtake.

What is equally depressing and frustrating is the regular way in which illegally obtained animals have subsequently been blatantly on open display in nations where their mere presence ought to have rung alarm bells for authorities, but where no action or investigation occurred for years, and not until prompted by United Nations officials. Just as despicable is the fact that persons and companies, claiming to be operating for zoological purposes, colluded fraudulently and corruptly with criminals and government officials in order to acquire these animals. Shamefully, veterinary surgeons must also have regularly interacted with, examined and treated, gorillas, orangutans and chimpanzees, knowing that their presence in those countries must have been suspicious; yet not one such professional ever contacted the authorities.

Other Endangered Species

In the course of his work, the author has personally witnessed:

- Members of the public being given the opportunity, for a fee, to be photographed while cuddling an exotic primate. This was on the platform of an underground station in Moscow.
- A Sun bear chained to a tree in the baking sun outside a restaurant in Asia, to help attract customers but also to advertise sales of wild animal meat.
- Tiger cubs suckling on a pig sow in a 'tiger zoo' in Thailand. At the same location, visitors being allowed to stroke adult tigers, not realizing that some of their teeth and claws had been extracted and that staff, armed with electric cattle prods, were nearby and ready to intervene should the tigers react 'negatively'.
- Visitors to a 'tiger farm' in China being offered, for a fee, the chance to throw live chickens into a tiger enclosure and watch them being torn apart.

In Conclusion

While the above examples illustrate the criminality that can lie behind what might be viewed, by the general public, as innocent displays or interactions with animals, they must also surely demonstrate a worrying ignorance or lack of concern on the part of sections of society.

In the early days of its existence, the CITES Convention saw not insignificant levels of illegal trade in live animals where circuses were the intended final destination. As more and more countries have either heavily regulated, or utterly prohibited, live animal performances, such criminal behaviour is now much less frequent. But it is not unknown. Intelligence received in the early 2010s indicated that live snow leopards were being smuggled from Asia to circuses operating in eastern Europe and ex-Soviet Union nations.

It is very apparent that cultural and ethnic policies towards animals differ markedly across the world. What is morally and ethically acceptable to one community may prompt howls of outrage in another. It is one reason why the drafters of the CITES Convention chose not to enter into the realms of animal welfare and, to a significant extent, stay clear of considerations relating to how specimens will be used, treated or consumed after import.

Unless moves emerge to amend CITES, or seek the establishment of a specific international animal welfare convention, it seems unlikely that significant changes will take place in the near future. For the moment, perhaps awareness-raising and education offer the most potential to ensure animal welfare. It is surely ironic, however, that this is exactly what one hoped for from the 'zoos' described earlier.

References

Animal Welfare Institute (n.d.) The Taiping Four gorilla scandal. Available at: https://awionline.org/awi-quarterly/2004-winter/taiping-four-gorilla-scandal (accessed 10 March 2017).

CITES (n.d.a) What is CITES? Available at: https://cites.org/eng/disc/what.php (accessed 10 March 2017).

CITES (n.d.b) Regulation of Trade in Specimens of Species Included in Appendix I. Available at: https://cites.org/eng/disc/text.php#III (accessed 10 March 2017).

CITES (n.d.c) Definition of 'primarily commercial purposes'. Available at: https://www.cites.org/sites/default/files/document/E-Res-05-10-R15.pdf (accessed 10 March 2017).

CITES (n.d.d) Great apes. Available at: https://www.cites.org/eng/prog/ape.php (accessed 10 March 2017).

CITES (n.d.e) CITES Secretariat confirms the arrest of former wildlife director in Guinea and applauds national authorities' work. Available at: https://www.cites.org/eng/guinea_arrest_20150903 (accessed 10 March 2017).

CITES Secretariat (2014) Great apes exported from Guinea to China from 2009 to 2011. Available at: https://www.cites.org/sites/default/files/common/docs/CITES-Guinea-China-great-apes.pdf (accessed 10 March 2017).

Shukman, D. and Piranty, S. (2017) The secret trade in baby chimps. Available at: http://www.bbc.co.uk/news/resources/idt-5e8c4bac-c236-4cd9-bacc-db96d733f6cf (accessed 10 March 2017).

17 Sport Hunting Tourism

Dr Jane Goodall, DBE*

Founder – the Jane Goodall Institute and UN Messenger of Peace (www.janegoodall.org)

* Corresponding author: mlewis@janegoodall.org

There is a section of tourism that is devoted to 'sport' hunters. Recently this became an international news item when a Minnesota dentist, Walter Palmer, killed Cecil the lion with a crossbow. Cecil was not killed outright but spent 40 hours wounded and in pain before he was found and finished off. Subsequently a rival male killed one of Cecil's cubs who were abandoned by Cecil's brother, Jericho. Almost certainly the other cubs have been killed as well. This is what lions do when they take over a pride, thus eliminating the genes of their rivals.

Palmer's behaviour was despicable on many counts. But the reason that his behaviour became the subject of anger and hatred around the world was because Cecil was a known individual. With a radio collar, although this was almost certainly invisible in his beautiful thick mane, he was part of a scientific study.

The question we should ask is this: Just because he was named, and loved and part of a scientific study, does that make him any different, in the world of the lion, than the other lions killed by 'sport' hunters? All those splendid individuals whose decapitated heads disfigure the walls of countless wealthy homes?

At least 600 trophy hunters kill lions each year. Each lion has its own personality and place in lion society, even if this is not known to us. Of course, lions are not the only animals targeted by 'sports' hunters. Palmer himself has killed all manner of creatures in Africa and North America. These hunters absolutely believe that what they are doing is not wrong. Even after Palmer had gone into hiding as a result of the hate mail he generated from around the world, another hunter, Sabrina Corgatelli, began boastfully posting pictures of herself grinning gleefully as she poses with the various animals she has been killing on her hunting safaris. The photo that was most shocking shows her gloating over the dead body of a big male giraffe. And she writes:

'Such an amazing animal!! I couldn't be any happier!! My emotion after getting him was a feeling I will never forget!!!'

Initially she seemed to excuse her action, commenting that after all, giraffes are very dangerous, and could hurt you very seriously, very quickly. But as the hate mail poured in, she became defiant, she and her boyfriend promising there will be plenty more such pictures for her internet 'haters'. We have already seen her with the corpses of various antelope, a lion, a leopard and a warthog with the most glorious tusks. And throughout these postings, Sabrina angrily defends her right to pursue her 'sport' hunting hobby.

On the internet, bow hunter 'Hero' Rebecca Francis was shown, with the same sort of delighted smile on her face, actually lying down by the body of the giraffe she had shot. Francis, we learn, is a mother of eight children, who has killed countless animals in North America and Africa with her crossbow. There are hundreds of other people doing this. Some even shoot animals that have been bred in game farms simply to be hunted.

Many of these tourist hunters defend their actions by claiming the money they pay for the pleasure of killing is what enables impoverished countries to pay for conservation of wildlife. It is a strange kind of argument with many flaws. For one thing, the money does not always end up in any conservation programme. Moreover, trophy hunting is probably having a damaging effect on the future of the species because the hunter will go after the lions with the biggest manes, antelopes with the biggest horns, warthogs with the biggest tusks. In other words, males in their prime – those that carry the genes likely to result in the perpetuation of strength and magnificence. We can never know what role Cecil's cubs might have played. He was killed and this led to their deaths.

18 Ethical Hunting

Brent Lovelock*
University of Otago, New Zealand

* Corresponding author: Brent.lovelock@otago.ac.nz

Hunting is indefensible. That is, unless, for example, you are a Maasai youth hunting a lion as part of a centuries-old cultural rite of passage; or a Papuan highlander hunting boar to support the meagre protein diet that you and your clan manage to survive upon. Few of us, even those most adamantly opposed to hunting, would go so far as to criticize such hunting practices, undertaken for subsistence and cultural reasons. While these are not examples of touristic hunting, they do, however, have some similarities with it.

I was in my local hunting store the other day, as the 'roar', our hunting season, is soon upon us, that joyous time of year when we find excuses to linger for hours over hunting magazines, and buy new gear, a new rifle, perhaps a new scope, a knife, ammo, new boots. All in anticipation of a trip into the hills after the elusive red deer stag. The store was humming with enthusiastic, mainly white males, all in their happy place, gently fingering the gleaming rifle stocks or squeezing into new camouflage gear. There were women there too, and children, all celebrating, in this shrine of hunting consumption, the arrival of that time of year when age-old cultural practices are played out. The question is whether or not this white working-class cultural practice of hunting is as defensible as that of the Maasai warrior or his Papuan counterpart?

Well, I hear you ask, we used to stone witches and keep slaves, but, happily, we have managed to relinquish those quaint cultural practices. So, really, what justification is there for anyone from the Western world to want to wander out into the hills and forests to kill Bambi? After all, we can all become accepted and functioning units of our communities without any need for a ritual killing of a wild animal, and there is generally plenty of protein on offer in the meat aisle of our neighbourhood supermarket. So, really, let's leave Bambi alone, shall we?

This question is slightly complicated by the fact that our motivations for engaging in hunting are often multiple and overlapping. Our cultural tradition of the 'roar' is certainly important here in New Zealand, with its opportunity to score a trophy animal, its associated social bonding, its seasonal dose of nature and healthy outdoor exercise, and what some claim to be the closest relationship with nature that is on offer. But increasingly in the West, we hunt for meat for our freezers. A recent survey in the US has found that the main motivation for hunters is now, strongly, to obtain meat for family and friends (Responsive Management, 2017). Hard economic times along with the growing locavore movement, focusing on local, naturally sourced food sources, have increased the importance of this motive. Even Facebook founder Mark Zuckerberg has recently taken up hunting, saying that 'food tastes doubly better when you have hunted the animal yourself' (Malloy, 2016), thus not only promoting self-provisioning through hunting, but helping to create a new 'acceptable' face of hunting.

So, perhaps, this more localized form of hunting tourism (inter- and intra-regional travel for hunting is by far the most common form of hunting tourism practised in the Western world) is as defensible as that of the Maasai and the Papuan? The 'perhaps' in this case does, however, cover some important issues, that include the ecological status of the game species, its population, and of course the manner of the killing. Even then, there are still ethical quandaries pertaining to motivation and outcome. Is it acceptable to place the head of the red deer stag that you shot, on the wall of your den, but only if you have his hind-quarters in your freezer?

Not many of those whom we would call international hunting tourists (i.e. those who travel for exotic safari hunts or commercialized expedition hunting) would take meat back home to their family and friends. Largely, this is because the species they hunt may not be edible (lion stew anyone?) or at least accepted as edible in Western diets. It may also be because, often, this type of hunting tourist is a long way from home, and to self-provision from the Kalahari to New York is impracticable, if not illegal.

The motivation of the international safari hunting tourist is likely to be a little different from those we have described above and, to generalize, will be mainly focused on the quality of the trophy and/or on obtaining a trophy from a new or exotic species. It is this focus that brings the practice into question. This apparently single-minded focus on killing a trophy animal is done for no other reason than to say that we have done so, and to put the photo on Facebook and the head on the wall. This type of activity may not involve the same level of interaction with nature, when the hunter tourist is cocooned to a certain extent by a gaggle of guides and trackers and bearers and drivers. It may be presented as a fair chase, but is it fair? What are the decisive factors determining whether a hunt is ethical? Is it some combination of the local/not local, self-provided/commercialized/guided, trophy/meat continua?

Or is it the manner in which the kill is celebrated? I recently took my teenage son hunting. I am an occasional hunter, and this was an opportunity to spend some quality time with my son and to get 'up close and personal' with nature. We tramped for 6 hours carrying our packs to our hunting spot, where we set up our wee two-person tent beside a mountain tarn. After a fitful night's sleep (aching legs and a puncture in my sleeping mat) we awoke to paradise, dawn sun and our mountain tarn a mirror for the golden tussock. We spent an hour glassing the hills, spying some Himalayan thar about a kilometre away, and carefully stalked up to within shooting range. I took the shot while my son 'spotted' for me with binoculars, and was happy to see the bull thar slump, instantly dead with a kill shot through the neck. We climbed up to his carcass to do the butchering, and to take as much meat as we could carry back with us. On arriving at this beautiful specimen, my son said, 'So how does it feel to take the life of a sentient creature?' He was winding me up, as teenagers are wont to do, but at that moment, as happens every time I shoot an animal, and possibly even more so as I get older, if not wiser, my emotions were a mix of something primal, that 'I had provided', that I had done what I was meant to do, that my programming had functioned, but sadness that this beautiful animal was no longer free to roam the hills. I rationalized that this was an introduced 'pest' animal that was harming this ecosystem, and also that we were taking the meat home.

I am not recounting this because I believe that a moment's sadness or self-reflection by a hunter will transform any hunt into an ethical hunt, but because I feel that the manner in which we engage with the animal and its environment, is somehow important. How we engage with others about the hunt is also important, especially in this age of connectivity. Effort and engagement seem central to ethical hunting.

The 'hunters' that Jane Goodall describes in her piece in this volume have perhaps been ignorant of these rules of engagement. Cecil the lion, the most charismatic, perhaps ironically more so in death, of the charismatic megafauna, has become a poster child for everything that is wrong about hunting. So sad, not just for the impacts so well described by Dr Goodall, but for the fact that such activities are probably occurring frequently, and that this single action has heaped suspicion and disrepute upon the entire hunting tourism sector. Unfortunately, that includes those hunts that *are* ecologically sustainable (e.g. in culling game populations that are unsustainably high, even if this may be genetically dubious, as Dr Goodall suggests), and that *do* contribute to the well-being of local communities. Hunting tourism is effective, arguably more so than ecotourism, in bringing in cash, and where well managed, hunting concession holders are required to invest substantially in community infrastructure, in poaching patrols, and can provide local employment and good supplies of bush meat. In this way, the 'ethics' of touristic hunting is essentially linked to good research supporting the ecological status of the game population, strong regulations and effective management, and efficient local capture of the economic benefits. Where this is not the case, we will see more Cecils and more pressure on jurisdictions to outlaw hunting (as in Botswana). The latter may be a case of throwing the baby out with the bath water.

References

Malloy, M. (2016) Mark Zuckerberg: animals taste better when you hunt them yourself. *The Telegraph*, 12 October. Available at: http://www.telegraph.co.uk/technology/2016/10/12/mark-zuckerberg-animals-taste-better-when-you-hunt-them-yourself (accessed 29 March 2017).

Responsive Management (2017) Research: proportion of American hunters who say they hunt mostly for the meat continues to grow. Press release, 30 March, Harrisonburg, VA.

Part III

19 The Future and Moving Forward Together

Introduction

In a traditional book, this would be the place to have a 'conclusion'. However, 'conclusion' suggests an end. Instead of wishing to see this as the point to conclude the discussion, this part is constructed as the position from which to move forwards, in research, industry and activist senses, in how we look at the relation between tourism and animal welfare and how we encourage the tourism industry and tourists towards preventing poor welfare of animals. We hope that the book, in addition to being a source of information and opinion, can help to drive improvements in animal welfare. Consequently, the chapter provides a brief look at the potential future of tourism and animal-related tourism, and animal welfare debates. What is the likely future of animal welfare in tourism? Finally, what should be the research agenda to improve welfare?

What is the Future of Tourism and Animal-related Tourism?

The UNWTO has predicted the continued growth of international tourism at the global level until at least 2030. By this time, the UNWTO estimates the world will see 1.8 billion international tourist arrivals per year. While it is much more difficult to estimate the scale of domestic tourism, it is safe to assume that it is, like international tourism, going to be a growing phenomenon for the foreseeable future. This growth is fuelled by a number of factors, all of which have been explored in detail in the tourism literature (see Lickorish and Jenkins, 1997; Hall, 2003; Cooper, 2016). One of the main drivers is the continued increase in the amount of disposable income available to people to spend on luxury goods and services such as holidays. In addition, an increasing tendency to utilize credit and loans to purchase such luxury goods and services is playing a role in the growth of tourist numbers. Continued decreases in the relative cost of travel and the enduring allure of an escape from the banal to the exotic promised by the tourism experience also drive increasing tourist numbers.

Linked to the continued growth of domestic and international tourist numbers is a recognition that the industry that supports them is likely to continue to increase. We expect to see the industry offering more facilities and attractions to tourists, creating more jobs, and generating more income, as a result of growing demand from tourists and investors keen to cash in on a growth industry. This will in itself aid future growth in the tourist population.

The tourism industry has long been a dominant economic driver in nations and regions that are today synonymous with tourism, for example, the Costa del Sol on the Spanish coastline and many of the Caribbean islands. This is an expanding issue: New Zealand's agricultural industry, traditionally the economic powerhouse of the nation, was eclipsed in 2016 by the tourism industry. This picture should not be seen as depicting a scene of uniform growth in the tourism industry and tourist visitations across the globe. Instead, it must be recognized that some destinations will continue to be more popular than others. Furthermore, some destinations are likely, as has been the case in the past, to suffer from declining visitor numbers and associated lack of investment in tourism infrastructure, while others will continue to grow and new destinations will emerge. Such trends are related to the socio-political stability of destinations, and their ability to continue to appeal to changing visitor markets and compete with other potential destinations. Growth, stagnation, and decline of destinations and attractions all have potential implications for animal welfare. In some instances they will offer chances for the improvement of animal welfare, while in others they will have negative effects. For example, developing tourism may provide economic growth within a destination that in turn helps to facilitate better animal welfare. Alternatively, development of tourism infrastructure may place pressure on natural environments and endanger both individual animals and entire species. Declining destinations, when faced with declining tourism-generated income may struggle to uphold their welfare obligations, to animals housed in zoos, for example. Yet at the same time, declining visitor numbers may ease pressure on natural environments, inadvertently improving animal welfare.

Set against the continued growth in domestic and international visitor numbers around the world, it is safe to suggest that demand for animal-related tourism is likely to continue to increase in the future. Furthermore, the reasons given earlier in this book to explain the rising popularity of animal-related tourism are only likely to become stronger in the future, which in turn is likely to further drive demand for this type of tourism. In particular, a continually urbanizing population that becomes ever more alienated from the natural world and the animals that inhabit it is likely, while on holiday, to wish to see and make contact with animals even more than it currently does. In addition, the increasing tendency of humans to view pets as part of the human family is only likely to continue to drive an increase in demand for what are perceived to be pet-friendly holiday experiences.

One implication of increasing numbers of tourists, destinations and attractions designed to cater to them, alongside a global population increasingly alienated from animals, may be that while the animals we love become increasingly desirable, both to see and as consumers, those that we hate or simply ignore at the moment may be pushed ever further to the fringes. Witness the mania for the annihilation of the mosquito, for example. This is likely to strengthen if climate change or increased tourism make mosquitoes more likely to spread diseases such as malaria in the tourist destinations of the European Mediterranean coastline.

Finally, the role of particular types of animals as employees in the tourism industry may well continue to grow in the future. This growth of non-human animals as employees, as distinct from tools (see Chapter 3) is at least partially linked to the increasing desire of people to have experiences with particular animals in the tourism experience. Witness the spread of meet-and-greet dogs, for example. It is the increasing recognition of the sentience of animals that leads to the need to identify them as employees rather than animated tools of the tourism industry. Hence, it is the issue of animal sentience and the related concepts of animal welfare and conservation to which this chapter now turns.

Where is the Animal Welfare Debate Heading?

Jane Goodall (2007, p. xii) has stated that there is 'increasingly compelling evidence that we are not alone in the universe, not the only creatures with minds capable of solving problems, capable of love and hate, joy and sorrow, fear and despair.' While scientific evidence may yet demonstrate that more animals can be classified as sentient, the weight of the currently available evidence for sentience in mammals, birds, reptiles, amphibians, fish, octopus, squid, crabs and prawns is substantial. This is not to say that all these animals have equal abilities, they clearly have not, but rather that they are above the threshold level that defines sentience. Whether or not an animal is sentient, all animals are living beings with some degree of nervous system, rather than automated objects so their welfare can be evaluated and must be considered. The obligation to consider the welfare of all animals is the same whatever the human view of the animal. We should consider the welfare of farm animals and pest animals in the same way that we consider the welfare of our pets and the iconic species of the animal conservation movement. There is certainly a groundswell of public opinion to shift the social conscience and scientific thought in this direction and to recognize the implications of such a shift for animal welfare debates. It is in this context that we see people increasingly concerning themselves with the welfare of animals and with addressing their needs. However, careful consideration must be given to the extent to which these people are imposing human-centric conceptualizations of animal welfare and needs on animals, as discussed earlier in the book. Such a human-centric position arguably does more to assuage human guilt and discomfort than actually meet the needs of animals as sentient beings.

Despite questioning whether concerns about animals have an animal-centric or human-centric focus, what is undeniable is the rise of such concerns. We are seeing this in relation to everything from the food we eat, to the clothes we wear, the leisure and tourism experiences we engage in, and the way we treat the animals with which we live our lives. Such a trend is likely to continue as the messages about animal sentience, welfare and needs continue to spread, driven partly by highly organized and dedicated animal protection groups, but increasingly by a general social conscience.

The ongoing discussions in society about animal welfare will continue to relate to and interact productively, and in other instances antagonistically, with the animal rights debate and the emergent issue of 'obligations'. As discussed earlier in the book, the focus is moving from ensuring that humans, as those in the position of power, recognize and give animals rights, to making sure that we recognize and act on our obligations to all animals and especially to those that are sentient beings. These obligations concern animal welfare but are animal-centric in every sense. If the rise of animal welfare debates is the dominant issue of today, the challenge for tomorrow is to drive an animal obligations agenda forward that champions an animal-centric position that is situated within the reality of a world in which humans hold the power. Such a call is immensely challenging as it requires the setting aside of the human-centric emotive positions that have driven animal welfare debates in the public sphere up to the current time. It is arguable that while this driver, and the debates it has been associated with, have been highly successful in shining light on the plight of innumerable animals and consequently raising concerns about animals in the social conscience, it is insufficient by itself to meet the needs of animals in the context of recognizing sentient beings that are capable of determining their own needs. Whether such a shift will come to fruition is impossible to tell at the current stage.

Shifts in thinking about conservation and sustainability, noted earlier in the book, hint at a future that sees animal welfare and conservation coming together under a unified sustainability umbrella that recognizes the dynamism of ecosystems and consequently focuses on resilience to change rather than maintenance of a status quo. Such a shift has yet to fully occur and is arguably meeting resistance from welfare and conservation groups whose foundations are built on one or other of these concepts and not both. To some, linking these concepts may appear a threat to the core values of these organizations. Yet if they are to fully achieve their stated goals, conservation and animal protection organizations are likely to benefit from recognizing the increasingly strong conceptual, practical and ethical linking of welfare, conservation and other concerns as part of sustainability.

What is an Animal?

We considered this surprisingly complex question, which spreads outside of the context of tourism and the boundaries of this book, in Chapter 2. However, it is important to reflect, even briefly, on how tourism has and continues to shape how we perceive animals. Animal-related experiences clearly have the potential to draw us closer to animals, in the process questioning and potentially helping to bring down the artificial human–animal distinction. Yet in doing so, animals also run the risk of losing their identity as what they truly are. Those most in danger are the pets we live in increasingly close proximity with, and the tourism industry, as noted elsewhere in this book, is playing a role in facilitating and increasing the central position these animals in general, and dogs in particular, play in the human family. The risk here is that the dog, or other non-human animal, becomes perceived as a furry human. This places unfair pressures and expectations on the dog, expecting it to conform to human rules and act like a human when it is not a human. It is an example of human-centric thinking that may appear to be driven by a desire to improve animal welfare, but is actually driven by human desires for human benefits.

Another issue raised here is that animals called 'pests' are still animals, and all sentient animals have the capacity to feel pain and fear. People sanction very different treatment of rabbits according to whether they are family pets, laboratory animals, kept for meat production, or wild 'pests' eating crops. This is not scientifically sound, as we should consider the welfare of each rabbit in exactly the same way. A rabbit is a rabbit and each one feels pain and has cognitive function (Broom, 2014). However, this shows how culture, which is place-specific, influences perceptions of animals. This reinforces the point made earlier in the book that while animal welfare is an objective concept, it is situated within a subjective setting. Other animals viewed as pests, but which are animals, and therefore deserving of our concern and compassion, include wasps, mosquitoes, house flies, slugs, house mice, rats, seals that take fish from a salmon farm, wood pigeons that eat cabbages and brush-tailed possums in New Zealand that prey on native birds and may carry bovine tuberculosis. While the tourism industry may not drive definitions of animals as pests, it certainly has the potential to reinforce or help to redefine such definitions.

In addition to potentially helping to change the nature of pets and their position in the world, the tourism industry is arguably influencing change in the perceived nature of domesticated animals. This is driven by attractions such as the petting zoos exemplified in Fig. 3.3 but also those farms that now offer themselves as tourist attractions for urban dwellers to discover where milk comes from. As the term 'petting zoo' indicates, the animals housed in them, which would often be more traditionally defined as farm animals than as zoo animals or pets, are presented as pets, to be touched and cuddled. Nowhere in these entities does the visitor learn about the more bloody realities of farming; the process of turning the cute baby sheep into roast lamb with mint sauce and roast potatoes on the side. Instead, these animals are for touching, stroking and holding, irrespective of whether they have actually been bred, like dogs and cats, over generations to not just tolerate, but actively seek in many cases, such interactions with humans. So while petting zoos and farm animal tourism experiences may educate visitors, to a limited extent, about the animals that food products come from, they may also be shifting the view of these animals from farm animal to pet and placing pressures on the individual animals to act in new ways.

The question must also be asked whether animal-related tourism has contributed to the domestication, to a small degree literally but especially in the minds of people, of the wild. Scientifically, domestication is 'the process, occurring over generations, by which a population of animals becomes adapted to man and to the captive environment by some combination of genetic changes and environmentally induced developmental events' (Broom and Fraser, 2015, p. 66). However, the social view of it can be traced back to the creation of zoos and circuses and the dominance of 'man' over beast or nature that this represented. By caging the wild animal and demanding through this incarceration that these animals conform to human-imposed rules (when to eat, sleep, mate), humans began a process of perceived domestication of wild animals. Recognition of this process can be seen in the admittance that animals in zoos that have been conditioned to the presence of humans will be unable to be released into the wild. This is a significant problem for the ability of zoos to act as vehicles for the re-populating of wild animals in their natural environment. Does this domestication end at the boundaries of the zoo or does it extend further into the animal tourism experiences? Another way to approach this question is to wonder what defines a zoo. Is it merely the walls that enclose an area containing animals and the cages in which the animals within this area are kept? Or is it the aims of the zoo, including entertainment, education, potentially a profit, and conservation? Or is the zoo defined by the aims and desires of the visitors? The answer is probably a mixture of all three. However, if we take the latter two, and especially the last one, we can see how these extend well beyond the physical boundaries of the zoo to encapsulate all types of wildlife tourism experience. In this way, while there may be differences between zoos, sanctuaries, national parks and the wilderness, there are also similarities. One of these is that they are all infiltrated by tourists to a greater or lesser extent. Another is that all of these tourists wish to see and potentially interact, in direct and non-direct ways, with the animals within these spaces. In this way, all wildlife tourism experiences have the potential to erode the 'wild' in wild animals, modifying them and increasing the perception that they are domesticated to varying extents.

An Animal Agenda in Tourism: Giving Animals a Voice and Stepping Outside the Human-centric Reality

Building on the previous sections of this chapter and the material and issues that have been discussed earlier in the book, attention now turns to discussing a potential future agenda for animals in tourism. This clearly must be situated within the broader human social context in which tourism and animal welfare both separately exist.

Animals are under pressure as never before from humans. We are squeezing the natural habitats of wild animals, we are consuming domesticated animals and their products in ever-greater quantities, and the pressures being placed on pets as they become more closely identified as a member of the human family are increasing. Alongside this is a rising social concern for the conservation of species and the welfare of individual animals. Some of this is driven from an animal-centric position, but arguably much is more aligned with human perspectives of animal survival and welfare and associated feelings of guilt and disgust.

Recognizing many animals as sentient beings means that we not only have a moral obligation to ensure good welfare of individuals and species survival, but that we must consider this from an animal-centric perspective. At the same time, this must be set within the reality of our own human perspective and the realization that it is humans who hold the power in the relationship and that this is situated within a neo liberal capitalist system across most of the world. It is within this complex setting that tourism must set an animal agenda for the future. By 'tourism' we mean not just the industry, but all the actors involved, directly and indirectly, in the tourism experience. As shown earlier in the book, there are many actors involved in and influenced by the tourism industry and they all need to be involved if tourism is to improve its animal welfare record and, in the process, spread the message of the good work being done in some parts of the tourism experience to all the other parts. The message here is that it is only through partnerships of all the tourism stakeholders that a sustainable approach to animal welfare in tourism can be achieved.

Arguably the biggest challenge facing tourism, and society in general, regarding animal welfare is the need to shift from a human-centric view of this to an animal-centric one. This speaks of the concept of obligations, raised earlier in the book, and also of a need to put aside human emotions related to how we perceive the treatment of animals. This is likely to be difficult for both the tourism industry and animal welfare organizations that have utilized human guilt and discomfort over the treatment of animals to push a welfarist agenda. However, the danger with this is that such an agenda becomes nothing more than a gilded cage that is actually fundamentally little different from the iron-barred and concrete-floored cages that zoo animals have traditionally been imprisoned in as exotic objects of human entertainment. A gilded cage constructed out of human guilt and associated perceptions of welfare is still a cage, as it gives primacy to human feelings over animals' wants and needs as displayed and constructed by animals. In other words, the welfarist agenda of the future, inside and outside tourism, should involve listening to the animals.

Such a call is, of course, easy to make, yet more difficult to undertake. There is the difficulty of cross-species communication and understanding. While not wishing to belittle this difficulty it is increasingly clear that, if we as humans are willing to try, then it is possible to listen to and understand animals as sentient beings (see Bekoff, 2007 and Horowitz, 2009 for a detailed discussion of this issue). There is also, of course, the difficulty of weaning animal welfare protagonists and their associated agendas off a human-centric, guilt-driven foundation. Does such a shift potentially endanger the very public support that has done so much to improve animal welfare in general over the last couple of decades? Education is the key here; we need re-education of a public that is now far more ready to accept animals as sentient beings and therefore more in need of an animal-centric welfare agenda than in the past. Feeding back into the potential of the tourism environment to offer productive learning experiences, it may be argued that tourism can play a role in helping in this transition that will, we hope, eventually lead to a more sustainable animal welfare agenda and a more sustainable position for animals within the tourism experience.

A pathway for tourism that raises animal welfare standards can be exemplified by focusing on zoos. The 'good' zoos and other animal tourism enterprises that have a serious interest in enhancing the welfare of not just the animals under their care but of entire species in general have, at heart, the same desire as animal welfare organizations and all the informed members of the public. As part of this, they seek to educate the public about the importance of welfare and conservation and to work in natural environments with local people to protect ecosystems and the wild animals that are a part of them.

Tourism attractions and welfare groups working together, as hinted at in Chapter 10, in the name of animal welfare and conservation has so much potential to offer where working against one another seems counter-productive. It is undeniable that there are 'bad' tourism operators and 'bad' tourists who just see animals as exotic objects of pleasure or economic gain. Carr (2018) presents a discussion of the continued desire of people to get up close to and interact with animals in inappropriate ways, despite all advice and pleading to the contrary. However, these should not be used as excuses to close down all animal-oriented tourism attractions and bar all tourists from seeing or interacting with any animals. Such an action, prompted by the 'bad' operators and tourists, may appeal to the most extreme animal rights protagonists, but is arguably both a human-centric approach and one that ignores the reality that animals exist in a human-dominated world. A sustainable place must be found for the animals where our obligations to them can be met.

It is not beholden on the individual good zoos to carry the fight alone to improve those zoos whose engagement with animal welfare is not at the same level. Rather, it is a role that industry bodies like the World Association of Zoos and Aquaria (WAZA) need to actively engage in. That said, individual zoos do have a role to play as 'role models' for others. It is in this context that it is heartening to see Jersey Zoo rebranding itself as a zoo after having abandoned the 'zoo' label for several years. It is not argued that everything is done perfectly at Jersey Zoo, but it may be suggested that it does a lot well in relation to animal welfare and that, in that sense, it can be, and should be, seen as a good role model for other zoos around the world to follow. There are, of course, other zoos that could equally be utilized as role models.

Apart from zoos, it is good to see organizations such as the WWF and World Animal Protection reaching out to and engaging with the tourism industry to improve animal welfare. More of this engagement is clearly necessary to drive the animal welfare agenda forwards effectively and permanently. What must be guarded against, though, is what has already occurred in relation to the issue of environmental sustainability. Here we have seen a process of green-washing, where some companies have sought to display their environmentally friendly credentials, not because they are necessarily 'green' but because being seen to be green is economically advantageous. The same advantage is to be had in an era of social concerns around animal welfare for those companies able to label themselves appropriately. Teaming up, and being seen to team up, with an animal welfare organization is one way to achieve this. Consequently, everyone must be on guard to ensure that the underlying reason for any such partnerships is to improve animal welfare rather than profit maximization alone. This does not mean that a company should not profit from such a partnership, but that part of the realistic aim should be to improve animal welfare. Thankfully, the animal welfare and conservation bodies house a healthy amount of cynicism about the motives of any industry operator and this will doubtless aid in ensuring that any partnerships are driven primarily by animal welfare concerns.

Does all of this mean that animal rights groups that sit on the extreme edge have no future relevance to animal welfare debates inside, or outside, tourism? The answer is very clearly and emphatically no. Such groups and individuals have a major role as the conscience of society; they are the ones who keep pushing for a better future and as such their existence and their practices and policies, which may irk many, continue to be important. Animal rights groups such as Sea Shepherd Conservation Society may not be ideal partners for tourism operators but their role is to keep pushing and demanding that we all do better and we up our game concerning animal welfare and conservation. This is a crucial role for they are, in a way, the moral guardians of society, always forcing us to confront uncomfortable truths and in that confrontation demanding we deal with them rather than continue to hide them.

It may be suggested that by adopting an animal-centric focus we must put to one side human preferences for particular animals over others and instead recognize the importance of all animals. In this way, while the notion that we may love, hate and eat some animals is still true, it does not assume the dominant position when discussing animal welfare. Instead, it is recognized as one of the factors influencing, and in some ways inhibiting improvements in animal welfare and detracting from the animal perspective.

Finally, it is clear that constant vigilance is required to ensure the good welfare of animals inside and outside tourism and to increase it in the future. Such vigilance requires us not to look simply at the surface of the tourism activity or operator, or tourist behaviour, but to dig deeper to examine the underlying rationale. Is this driven primarily by animal welfare concerns or by human-centric concerns governed by pleasure fulfilment or economic profit? Wherever it is driven by the latter, we must work to change it.

A Research Agenda

As stated in Chapter 1, this book was never meant to be a place for researchers to only talk among themselves. Rather, the intent was that researchers might reach out to those practically involved as tourists, tour operators, NGOs or animal welfare organizations. Constructing this book entailed engaging with the many people who have contributed opinion pieces to it, who are involved directly with practical issues. The issues raised and discussed are much more than topics for academic discussion or the material required to pass a course. This is not to belittle either of these things; they are, of course, important. However, this book is intended as a recognition that if we are to practise what we preach and help to raise animal welfare within tourism, there is no point writing only for other academics. As has been said throughout the book, this target requires all the actors to be informed and to work together and that includes far more people than a small group of academics and students. In parallel with (we hope) helping to change the world, the book raises some ideas for a future research agenda linked to animal welfare in tourism. There should be recognition that academics are on the list of actors who have a role to play in driving animal welfare concerns in tourism. Research can have the purpose of social affirmative action. As tertiary education providers increasingly say, and governments demand, research should be relevant to current and future world issues. In this way, we and all other students, researchers and teachers in the field are equal partners with the tourists, tourism industry, welfare organizations and other actors in having a role to play in advancing animal welfare in and through tourism.

So what is the research agenda we propose? As noted in Chapter 1, wildlife tourism is, to date, the most studied type of animal-related tourism. In comparison, there is a fairly limited, but emerging body of research looking at domesticated animals and pets. Yet among the animals studied, the focus has been firmly on those we like and are attracted to. For instance, within the context of domestic animals, horses and dogs have dominated researcher attention. This leaves the field of animal-related studies in tourism extremely biased and clearly indicates the need for future studies not to just focus on these animals but to begin to examine the position and experiences of all the other animals; including those that some of the public hate, eat, perceive to be boring or mundane, or know little about. There is also a need in future to ensure that studies of animals in the tourism field are actually grounded in an animal welfare perspective, something that has not always been the case to date.

The work in tourism on animal-related issues also needs to adopt a more animal-focused perspective that sees the animals as sentient beings rather than objects of tourist satisfaction. This calls for a refocusing of the conceptual foundation of tourism research dealing, directly or indirectly, with animals to orientate it towards idea of sentient animals and the importance of this sentience. Within this context, tourism studies have an important role to play in helping to determine how humans, tourists in this case, perceive animal sentience and what, if any, influence it has on any animal experiences they seek while on holiday and how they view the potential implications of tourism development for animal welfare. Such research will aid the development of plans and policies to increase tourist awareness of animal sentience and the importance and value of their welfare.

Tourism is not a discipline, but a multidisciplinary field of enquiry. As such, it has traditionally borrowed from and been of interest to a variety of disciplines to understand tourism as both an industry and social phenomenon. However, the emphasis has generally been on a human-centric focus that has not necessitated an interest in those disciplines traditionally focused on animals, such as zoology and veterinary studies. This must change if an animal-related focus in tourism studies is to be developed. This means that those working in the field of tourism studies must be open to the idea of expanding their disciplinary base. It also requires that those disciplines with a focus on animals broaden their horizons to incorporate tourism studies. Such a move speaks of the broader need for those interested in understanding animals to focus not just on the animals but also on the human social constructions of them. The latter is invaluable given the reality that animals, whether wild or domesticated, exist in a human manipulated and influenced world. Embracing animal studies and concepts from zoology and other biological sciences is important for social scientists as it provides a way of stepping back from human-centric, emotive-laden social constructs of animals and their needs. However, this must be done alongside social science perspectives and methods of analysis rather than in place of them. This meeting of disciplinary approaches allows for the strengths of both to be utilized. The expansion of cross-disciplinary links demands the recognition of the studying of tourism, and indeed of animal welfare, as serious academic endeavours.

Finally, we call for a holistic approach to the study of animal welfare in tourism that recognizes the need for all actors in the tourism sphere, including the animals themselves, to be taken into account and therefore for all their voices to be heard. It is only by this means that a thorough understanding of the nature of animal experiences in tourism can be developed and that researchers can actively help in ensuring good welfare of animals within tourism in a sustainable and, consequently, mutually inclusive manner.

References

Bekoff, M. (2007) *Animals Matter*. Shambhala, Boston, MA.

Broom, D.M. (2014) *Sentience and Animal Welfare*. CAB International, Wallingford, Oxfordshire, UK.

Broom, D.M. and Fraser, A.F. (2015) *Domestic Animal Behaviour and Welfare*, 5th edn. CAB International, Wallingford, Oxfordshire, UK.

Carr, N. (2018) Zoos and animal encounters: to touch or not to touch, that is the question. In: N. Carr and J. Young (eds) *Wild Animals and Leisure: Rights and Welfare*. Routledge, Abingdon, Oxfordshire, UK.

Cooper, C. (2016) *Essentials of Tourism*, 2nd edn. Pearson Education Limited, Harlow, Essex, UK.

Goodall, J. (2007) Foreword. In: Bekoff, M. *The Emotional Lives of Animals*. New World Library, Novato, CA, pp. xi–xv.

Hall, C.M. (2003) *Introduction to Tourism: Dimensions and Issues*, 4th edn. Pearson Education, South Melbourne, Australia.

Horowitz, A. (2009) *Inside of a Dog: What Dogs See, Smell, and Know*. Scribner, New York.

Lickorish, L. and Jenkins, C. (1997) *Introduction to Tourism*. Butterworth-Heinemann, Oxford, UK.

Bibliography

Ardoin, N.M. and Heimlich, J.E. (2013) Views from the field: conservation educators' and practitioners' perceptions of education as a strategy for achieving conservation outcomes. *Journal of Environmental Education* 44, 97–115.

Balcombe, J. (2016) *What a Fish Knows: The Inner Lives of Our Underwater Cousins*. Scientific American, New York.

Ballantyne, R., Packer, J., Hughes, K. and Dierking, L. (2007) Conservation learning in wildlife tourism settings: lessons from research in zoos and aquariums. *Environmental Education Research* 13(3), 367–383.

Bertella, G. (2014) The co-creation of animal based tourism experience. *Tourism Recreation Research* 39(1), 115–125.

Bostock, S. (1993) *Zoos and Animal Rights: The Ethics of Keeping Animals*. Routledge, London.

Brambell, F.W.R. (1965) *Report of the Technical Committee to Enquire into the Welfare of Animals Kept under Intensive Husbandry Conditions*. HMSO, London.

Brando, S., Broom, D.M. Acasuso-Rivero, C. and Clark, F. (2017) Optimal marine mammal welfare under human care: current efforts and future directions. *Behavioural Processes*. DOI: 10.1016/j.bcproc.2017.09.011.

Broom D.M. (2000) Welfare assessment and problem areas during handling and transport. In: Grandin T. (ed.) *Livestock Handling and Transport*, 2nd edn. CAB International, Wallingford, Oxfordshire, pp. 43–61.

Broom, D.M. (2002) Welfare in wildlife management and zoos. *Proceedings of the 4th International Congress on the Physiology and Behaviour of Wild and Zoo Animals. Advances in Ethology* 37, 4–6.

Brown, C. (2015) Fish intelligence, sentience and ethics. *Animal Cognition* 18, 1–17.

Brunner, B. (2005) *The Ocean at Home: An Illustrated History of the Aquarium*. Princeton Architectural Press. New York.

Buckley, R., Morrison, C. and Castley, J. (2016) Net effects of ecotourism on threatened species survival. *PLoS ONE* 11(2), e0147988. DOI: 10.1371/journal.pone.0147988.

Bulbeck, C. (2005) *Facing the Wild: Ecotourism, Conservation and Animal Encounters*. Earthscan, London.

Burgin, S. and Hardiman, N. (2015) Effects of non-consumptive wildlife-oriented tourism on marine species and prospects for their sustainable management. *Journal of Environmental Management* 151, 210–220.

Carder, G., Proctor, H., Schmidt-Burbach, J. and D'Cruze, N. (2016) The animal welfare implications of civet coffee tourism in Bali. *Animal Welfare* 25, 199–205.

Carr, N. and Cohen, S. (2015) Public face of zoos: images of entertainment, education and conservation. *Anthrozoos* 24, 175–189.

Catibog-Sinha, C. (2008) Zoo tourism: biodiversity conservation through tourism. *Journal of Ecotourism* 7(2–3), 160–178.

Cisneros-Montemayor, A.M., Sumaila, U.R., Kashner, K. and Pauly, D. (2010) The global potential for whale-watching. *Marine Policy* 34, 1275–1278.

Clayton, S., Fraser, J. and Saunders, C. (2009) Zoo experiences: conversations, connections, and concern for animals. *Zoo Biology* 28, 377–397.

Clubb, R. and Mason, G.J. (2007) Natural behavioural biology as a risk factor in carnivore welfare: how analysing species differences could help zoos improve enclosures. *Applied Animal Behaviour Science* 102, 303–328.

Cohen, E. (2013) 'Buddhist compassion' and 'animal abuse' in Thailand's Tiger Temple. *Society & Animals* 21, 266–283.

Cohen, E. and Fennell, D. (2016) The elimination of Marius, the giraffe: humanitarian act or callous management decision? *Tourism Recreation Research* 41(2), 168–176.

Conway, W.G. (1973) How to exhibit bullfrog: a bedtime story for zoo men. *International Zoo Yearbook* 13, 221–226.

Curtin, S. (2010) What makes for memorable wildlife encounters? Revelations from 'serious' wildlife tourists. *Journal of Ecotourism* 9(2), 149–168.

Dick, G. and Gusset, M. (eds) (2010) 'Building a future for wildlife'? Evaluating the contribution of the world zoo and aquarium community to in situ conservation. *International Zoo Yearbook* 44, 183–191. DOI: 10.1111/j.1748-1090.2009.00101.

Draper, C. and Harris, S. (2012) The assessment of animal welfare in British zoos by government-appointed inspectors. *Animals* 2, 507–528.

Dubois, S. and Fraser, D. (2013) A framework to evaluate wildlife feeding in research, wildlife management, tourism and recreation. *Animals* 3, 978–994.

Duffy, R. (2014) Interactive elephants: nature, tourism and neoliberalism. *Annals of Leisure Research* 44, 88–101.

Duffy, R. and Moore, L. (2011) Global regulations and local practices: the politics and governance of animal welfare in elephant tourism. *Journal of Sustainable Tourism* 19(4–5), 589–604.

Duncan, I. (2006) The changing concept of animal sentience. *Applied Animal Behaviour Science* 100, 11–19.

Fa, J.E., Flesness, N., Gusset, M. and Conde, D.A. (2014) Zoos have yet to unveil their full conservation potential. *Animal Conservation* 17, 97–100.

Falk, J. and Dierking, L. (2010) The 95 percent solution. *American Scientist* 98, 486–493.

Fennell, D. (2012) *Tourism and Animal Ethics.* Routledge, Abingdon, Oxfordshire, UK.

Fennell, D. (2012) Tourism, animals and utilitarianism. *Tourism Recreation Research* 37(3), 239–249.

Fennell, D.A. (2013) Contesting the zoo as a setting for ecotourism, and the design of the first principle. *Journal of Ecotourism* 12, 1–14.

Fennell, D. (2013) Ecotourism, animals and ecocentrism: a re-examination of the billfish debate. *Tourism Recreation Research* 38(2), 189–202.

Fennell, D. (2014) Exploring the boundaries of a new moral order for tourism's global code of ethics: an opinion piece on the position of animals in the tourism industry. *Journal of Sustainable Tourism* 22(7), 983–996.

Fennell, D. and Sheppard, V. (2011) Another legacy for Canada's 2010 Olympic and Paralympic Winter Games: applying an ethical lens to the post-games' sled dog cull. *Journal of Ecotourism* 10(3), 197–213.

Francione, G.L. (2004) Animals – property or persons? In: Sunstein, C. and Nussbaum, M. (eds) *Animal Rights: Current Debates and New Directions.* Oxford University Press, Oxford, UK, pp. 108–134.

Fraser, J. and Sickler, J. (2008) *Why Zoos & Aquariums Matter.* Available at: http://www.informalscience.org/sites/default/files/Why_Zoos%26Aquariums_Matter_Handbook.pdf (accessed 25 January 2018).

Frost, W. (ed.) (2011) *Zoos and Tourism: Conservation, Education, Entertainment?* Channel View Publications, Bristol, UK.

Frynta, D., Simkova, O., Liskova, S. and Landova, E. (2013) Mammalian collection on Noah's ark: the effects of beauty, brain and body size. *PLoS ONE* 8(5), 1–12.

Fuller, S. (2011) *The Economic Impact of Spending for Operations and Construction in 2013 by AZA-Accredited Zoos and Aquariums.* Available at: https://www.aza.org/assets/2332/aza_economic_impact_report_2013.pdf (accessed 25 January 2018).

Gusset, M. and Dick, G. (2011) The global reach of zoos and aquariums in visitor numbers and conservation expenditures. *Zoo Biology* 30, 566–569.

Heenehan, H., Basurto, X., Bejder, L., Tyne, J., Higham, J.E. and Johnston, D.W. (2015) Using Ostrom's common-pool resource theory to build toward an integrated ecosystem-based sustainable cetacean tourism system in Hawaii. *Journal of Sustainable Tourism* 23, 536–556.

Held, S. and Spinka, M. (2011) Animal play and animal welfare. *Animal Behaviour* 81, 891–899.

Higginbottom, K. (ed.) (2004) *Wildlife Tourism: Impacts, Management and Planning.* Common Ground Publishing Pty Ltd, Altona, Australia.

Higham, J. and Neves, K. (2015) Whales, tourism and manifold capitalist fixes: new relationships with the driving force of capitalism. In: Markwell, K. (ed.) *Tourism and Animals: Understanding Diverse Relationships.* Channel View Publications, Clevedon, UK, pp. 109–126.

Hughes, B.O. (1982) The historical and ethical background of animal welfare. In: Uglow, J. (ed.) *How Well Do Our Animals Fare? Proceedings of the 15th Annual Conference of the Reading University Agricultural Club,* pp. 1–9.

International Union of Directors of Zoological Gardens (1993) *The World Zoo Conservation Strategy: The Role of the Zoos and Aquaria of the World in Global Conservation.* Chicago Zoological Society, Brookfield, IL.

Kajewski, K. and Mardsen, V. (2013) *Demystifying 70:20:10.* DeakinPrime, Melbourne.

Knight, J. (2010) The ready-to-view wild monkey: the convenience principle in Japanese wildlife tourism. *Annals of Tourism Research* 37(3), 744–762.

Lees, C.M. and Wilcken, J. (2009) Sustaining the Ark: the challenges faced by zoos in maintaining viable populations. *International Zoo Yearbook* 43, 6–18.

Lemelin, H. (ed.) (2013) *The Management of Insects in Recreation and Tourism*. Cambridge University Press, Cambridge, UK.

Lindsey, P., Alexander, R., Balme, G., Midlane, N. and Craig, J. (2012) Possible relationships between the South African captive-bred lion hunting industry and the hunting and conservation of lions elsewhere in Africa. *South African Journal of Wildlife Research* 42(1), 11–22.

Lopez, G. and Pearson, H. (2017) Can whale watching be a conduit for spreading educational and conservation messages? A case study in Juneau, Alaska. *Tourism in Marine Environments* 12(2), 95–104.

Louv, R. (2005) *Last Child in the Woods: Saving our Children from Nature-Deficit Disorder*. Algonquin Books, Chapel Hill, NC.

Lovelock, B. (ed.) (2008) *Tourism and the Consumption of Wildlife: Hunting, Shooting and Sport Fishing*. Routledge, Abingdon, Oxfordshire, UK.

Lusseau, D. and Higham, J. (2004) Managing the impacts of dolphin-based tourism through the definition of critical habitats: the case of bottlenose dolphins (*Tursiops* spp.) in Doubtful Sound, New Zealand. *Tourism Management* 25, 657–667.

Maple, T. and Perdue, B. (2013) *Zoo Animal Welfare*. Springer, Berlin.

Maréchal, L., Semple, S., Majolo, B. and MacLarnon, A. (2016) Assessing the effects of tourist provisioning on the health of wild barbary macaques in Morocco. *PLoS ONE* 11(5), e0155920. DOI: 10.1371/journal.pone.0155920.

Marino, L., Lilienfeld, S.O., Malamud, R., Nobis, N. and Brogliod, R. (2010) Do zoos and aquariums promote attitude change in visitors? A critical evaluation of the American Zoo and Aquarium study. *Society and Animals* 18, 126–138.

Markwell, K. (ed.) (2015) *Animals and Tourism: Understanding Diverse Relationships*. Channel View Publications, Bristol, UK.

Mellor, D. (2016) Updating animal welfare thinking: moving beyond the 'five freedoms' towards 'a life worth living'. *Animals* 6(3), 21. DOI: 10.3390/ani6030021.

Miller, B., Conway, W., Reading, R.P., Wemmer, C., Wildt, D. *et al.* (2004) Evaluating the conservation mission of zoos, aquariums, botanical gardens and natural history museums. *Conservation Biology* 18, 1–8.

Mitchell, G., Tromborg, C.T., Kaufman, J., Bargabus, S., Simoni, R. and Geissler, V. (1992) More on the 'influence' of zoo visitors on the behaviour of captive primates. *Applied Animal Behaviour Science* 35, 189–198.

Moorhouse, T., Dahlsjö, C., Baker, S., D'Cruze, N. and Macdonald, D. (2015) The customer isn't always right – conservation and animal welfare implications of the increasing demand for wildlife tourism. *PLoS ONE* 10(10), e0138939. DOI: 10.1371/journal.pone.0138939.

Moorhouse, T., D'Cruze, N. and Macdonald, D. (2016) Unethical use of wildlife in tourism: what's the problem, who is responsible, and what can be done? *Journal of Sustainable Tourism* 25(4), 505–516.

Morrison, C., Simpkins, C., Castley, G. and Buckley, R. (2012) Tourism and the conservation of critically endangered frogs. *PLoS ONE* 7(9), e43757. DOI: 10.1371/journal.pone.0043757.

Moss, A., Jensen, E. and Gusset, M. (2015) Evaluating the contribution of zoos and aquariums to Aichi Biodiversity Target 1. *Conservation Biology* 29, 537–544.

Newsome, D., Dowling, R. and Moore, S. (2005) *Wildlife Tourism*. Channel View Publications, Clevedon, UK.

O'Connor, S., Campbell, R., Cortez, H. and Knowles, T. (2009) *Whale Watching Worldwide: Tourism Numbers, Expenditures and Expanding Economic Benefits*. International Fund for Animal Welfare, Yarmouth Port, MA.

Palmer, J. (1983) *Working Dogs*. Patrick Stephens Ltd, Cambridge, UK.

Powell, D. and Watters, J. (2017) The evolution of the animal welfare movement in U.S. zoos and aquariums. *Der Zoologishe Garten*. DOI: 10.1016/j.zoolgart.2017.04.007.

Rabb, G. (2004) The evolution of zoos from menageries to centers of conservation and caring. *Curator* 47(3), 237–246.

Rabb, G.B. and Saunders, C.D. (2005) The future of zoos and aquariums: conservation and caring. *International Zoo Yearbook* 39, 1–26.

Safina, C. (2016) *Beyond Words: What Animals Think and Feel*. Henry Holt, New York.

Schubel, J.R., Monroe, C., Schubel, K.A. and Bronnenkant, K. (2009) Environmental literacy through the lens of aquarium ocean literacy efforts. In: Falk, J.H., Heimlich, J.E. and Foutz, S. (eds) *Free-choice Learning and the Environment*, pp. 123–137. Altamira, Lanham, MD.

Shani, A. and Pizam, A. (2008) Towards an ethical framework for animal-based attractions. *International Journal of Contemporary Hospitality Management* 20(6), 679–693.

Singer, P. (ed.) (1985) *In Defence of Animals*. Basil Blackwell, Oxford, UK.

Smith, L. and Broad, S. (2007) Do zoo visitors attend to conservation messages? A case study of an elephant exhibit. *Tourism Review International* 11(3), 225–235.

Smith, L., Broad, S. and Weiler, B. (2008) A closer examination of the impact of zoo visits on visitor behavior. *Journal of Sustainable Tourism* 16, 544–562.

Sneddon, J., Lee, J., Ballantyne, R. and Packer, J. (2016) Animal welfare values and tourist behaviour. *Annals of Tourism Research* 57, 234–278.

Spedding, C. (2000) *Animal Welfare*. Earthscan, London.

Stearns, R. (2010) *The Hole in Our Gospel*. Thomas Nelson, Nashville, TN.

Taylor, L. (1995) *Aquariums: Windows to Nature*. Prentice Hall, New York.

Tlusty, M.F., Rhyne, A.L., Kaufman, L., Hutchins, M., Reid, G.M. *et al.* (2013) Opportunities for public aquariums to increase the sustainability of the aquatic animal trade. *Zoo Biology* 32, 1–12.

TUI Travel plc (2011) *Guidelines for Environmental Sustainability in Hotels*: Animal welfare, p. 37. Available at: http://www.tuitravelplc.com/system/files/susrep/TUITravelGuidelinesforEnvironmentalSustainabilityinHotels_0.pdf (accessed 22 April 2017).

Valentine, P.S., Birtles, A., Curnock, M., Arnold, P. and Dunstan, A. (2004) Getting closer to whales – passenger expectations and experiences, and the management of swim with dwarf minke whale interactions in the Great Barrier Reef. *Tourism Management* 25, 647–655.

Wilson, E.O. (2016) *Half-Earth*. Norton, New York.

Wulf, A. (2015) *The Invention of Nature: Alexander von Humboldt's New World*. John Murray, London.

Subject and *Author* Index